A NOBLE TREASON

Other books by Richard Hanser

PUTSCH! How Hitler Made Revolution
JESUS: "What Manner of Man Is This?"
THE GLORIOUS HOUR OF LT. MONROE
VICTORY AT SEA (in collaboration)

A NOBLE TREASON

The Revolt of the Munich Students
Against Hitler

by

Richard Hanser

G. P. PUTNAM'S SONS
NEW YORK

Library of Congress Cataloging in Publication Data

Hanser, Richard.
  A noble treason.

  Includes index.
  1. Munich. Universität—riot Feb. 18, 1943.   2. Anti-Nazi movement.
  3. Scholl, Hans, 1918–1943.   4. Scholl, Sophie, 1921–1943,   I. Title.
  DD256.3.H35   1979   943'.36   78-20832

ISBN 0-399-12041-6

Printed in the United States of America

Acknowledgments

Since the story of the White Rose has never been told on this scale before, the author needed the assistance of many people in gathering and forming the material of this book. None of the episodes and incidents here narrated is invented and none of the dialogue manufactured. Much searching and researching among many sources, both human and documentary, were required to validate the various phases of the story. In this undertaking, chief thanks must go to Frau Inge Aicher-Scholl, the sister of Hans and Sophie. Her short book *Die Weisse Rose* (it is in no sense a "little" book) tells the story of the White Rose vividly and movingly from the viewpoint of one in a position to know it best. The book, published in 1952 by the Fischer Bücherei of Frankfurt/Main, is an admirably sensitive, intelligent, and restrained narrative, something of a classic of its kind. Out of a natural, and fully justified, pride in the character and courage of her brother and sister, Frau Aicher-Scholl has made a study of the whole White Rose story and of its significance in the Germany of Adolf Hitler. She has been unstinting in supplying the author with information beyond the scope of her book and answering questions which arose in the writing of *A Noble Treason*.

The author also gratefully acknowledges the help and cooperation of others, without whose assistance the book could not have been completed. Helmuth Auerbach's collection of documents on the White Rose was indispensable, including as it does interviews, reminiscences, letters, statements, observations, and comments of many of the people who were directly involved. Herr Auerbach magnanimously put his papers at the disposal of the author who here thanks him again. Thanks are also due to Dr. Hermann Weiss of Munich's *Institut für Zeitgeschichte* for his good offices and to the staff of the *Institut* without whose cooperation no serious book on the Age of Hitler can be completed.

The author also wishes to acknowledge the help extended him at the National Archives and Record Services in Washington (Robert Wolfe, Chief, Modern Military Branch); the Berlin Documentary Center (Daniel P. Simon, Director); the Koblenz *Bundesarchiv* (Dr. Ritter); and the Hoover Institution on War, Revolution, and Peace (Agnes F. Peterson). The Reference Department of the New York Public Library was, as always, unfailingly helpful.

Frau Clara Huber was extremely helpful with facts and observations on the part that her late husband, Professor Kurt Huber, played in the events of the White Rose. Her daughter Birgit (Frau Wolfgang Weiss) generously contributed further facts and color relating to her father's life and death. Of great value was the documentation on Willi Graf assembled by his sister Annaliese Knoop-Graf and others under the title *Gewalt und Gewissen*. The author also expresses his appreciation for the useful details and illuminating comments contributed by Dr. Katharina Schüddekopf, a member of the group around Hans Scholl. I have drawn heavily on the letters, diaries, daybooks, journals, and recorded statements of the people involved, all of whom were literate and articulate and aware of their roles in the events in which they participated.

Acknowledgments are also due the authors of previous writings about the White Rose which were included in the research for this book. Notable among these were: James Donohoe, Klaus Drobisch, Ricarda Huch, Karl-Heinz Jahnke, Egon Larsen, Annedora Leber,

Christian Petry, Terence Prittie, and J. P. Stern. Research in Munich, the scene of the story, was greatly facilitated by the efficient assistance of Frau Karola Gillich. The author also wishes to thank his wife Anne for help and patience beyond the call of duty in making the manuscript presentable.

R.H.

This book is for David

"Somebody, after all, had to make a start."

—Sophie Scholl before the People's Court
in Munich, February 22, 1943

A NOBLE TREASON

One

A young Munich barrister named Leo Samberger opened his mail one morning in February of 1943, and, as he said afterwards, he couldn't believe his eyes. That was a time when every new day seemed to bring some new event to unsettle the nerves or stun the senses. The war, in its fourth year, had made the unexpected routine and the startling commonplace.

Even so, Leo Samberger was shaken when he opened what he thought was a letter but turned out to be a leaflet. It was neatly typed, single-spaced with no illustration or typographical flourish of any kind. It was a solid block of type that made no more concession to the reader than a page from a textbook. But Leo Samberger caught his breath as he ran his eye down the page.

> . . . *The day of reckoning has come, the reckoning of German youth with the most detestable tyranny that our people has ever endured* . . .

Leo Samberger's first thrill of excitement was laced with little stabs of suspicion and fear. It was disturbing, a shock, to read such a statement plainly printed in black and white, however much he himself might privately approve of it. In the Germany of Adolf Hitler such sentiments had the same impact as open blasphemy would have had in Rome at the time of the Inquisition.

Leo Samberger turned the leaflet over, examined it intently. Could it be a plant, a trap? The Secret State Police, the Gestapo, was not above circulating such material as this to see whether or not the recipient would report it to the authorities. Not reporting it would be almost as grave a crime as originating it. Not reporting it would be taken to mean that the recipient approved of it, thus exposing himself as an enemy of the state. Arrest and prosecution would follow, promptly and inevitably.

But Samberger, who had a degree in law from the University of Munich, sensed immediately that this was not the product of a security agent trying his hand at literary entrapment. This had a cogency that could come only from someone who was at home in the use of language, and it had a passion that only conviction could inspire.

> . . . we demand from Adolf Hitler's state the return of our most precious possession, the personal freedom of which he has basely and treacherously deprived us . . .

With an intensity that broke through every phrase, the leaflet denounced the "corporal of World War I" whose amateur strategy had just cost the German people 300,000 of their sons in the bloodbath at Stalingrad. Here the leaflet, in its bitterness, used sardonically the saying that the Ministry of Propaganda had popularized to hail the achievements of Adolf Hitler: *"Führer, wir danken Dir!"* — "Leader, we thank you!"

Then, at the end, came an impassioned call for revolt:

> . . . The name of Germany will be disgraced forever unless German youth rises up, in both atonement and vengeance, to crush its tormentors and to build a new and nobler Europe . . .

Leo Samberger examined the envelope the leaflet had come in. He thought it faintly ironical that the red stamp in the upper right-hand corner had Adolf Hitler's face on it. The address had been typed on the same machine as the text of the leaflet. Why had it been sent to him? How was his address known to the sender? There was no indication at all of where it had come from or who had sent it. It had been folded over like a letter, and now Samberger folded it over once more. He took a thick book from the top shelf in his study and tucked the folded-over leaflet deep inside it. As he was putting the book back on the shelf he automatically swiveled his head around, even though he was alone in the room. That was the gesture which, in Hitler's Germany, had become known as "the German look"— *der deutsche Blick*—a swift, furtive glance over the shoulder to be sure nobody was watching.

The leaflet, as Leo Samberger knew, was yet another sign that something strange and possibly explosive was stirring under the surface in the city of Munich, something unprecedented in all the ten years that National Socialism had been in power. Samberger himself had seen evidence of it one recent morning at the university. Charwomen were scrubbing away at some huge, sprawling words that had been painted on the walls and pavement around the main entrance. The scrubbing began at dawn in the hope that the words would be erased before the students arrived, but a thick, tarry paint had been used and the letters stubbornly resisted the effort to eliminate them. They were dimmer when the students began to arrive for their classes, but the outlines were still visible and the words could be deciphered. What they said was FREEDOM! and DOWN WITH HITLER!!! The university authorities reacted with mingled outrage and bewilderment. The local headquarters of the Secret State Police, the Gestapo, were immediately notified, and an investigation promptly launched. But worse was to come.

Two days after he received the subversive leaflet, Leo Samberger was attending his regular seminar in law at the university. It was February 18, 1943, a date he and many others would always remember, though the significance of what was happening would not become clear until long afterwards. All Samberger knew at the time was that shortly before noon a commotion was heard in a hallway outside the lecture room, a scurrying and a scuffling. When the seminar was over, agitation and alarm were sweeping the school.

The story circulated that some students had been caught scattering leaflets along corridors on the stairway between floors, and in the central hall under its high, domed skylight. The leaflets had been swiftly gathered up and spirited away by custodians before they could spread their corruption among the students. Copies were being closely examined in the rector's office to which, again, the Gestapo had been summoned. The names of the perpetrators were not immediately made known, nor was their fate. No mention of the occurrence appeared in the newspapers, but the suppression of news was no novelty in a society where the Ministry of Propaganda alone decided what should be printed and what should not.

Only by accident did Leo Samberger stumble on the aftermath of the incident that had caused such excitement at the university. Four days later, on February 22, he was buying cigarets at his usual shop not far from the law courts. The shopkeeper, passing along the gossip of the day, told him that an unusual case was being tried that morning in the Assize Court and that a judge had been specially flown down from Berlin to preside.

"Which judge?" Samberger asked. As a beginning barrister he was naturally interested in such matters.

"Freisler."

Samberger gave a low whistle of astonishment. Roland Freisler was the Chief Judge of the notorious People's Court, which was assembled only in cases of treason and subversion.

"Who is being tried?" Samberger asked.

"Some university students, I hear."

Samberger stuffed his cigarets in his pocket and hurried toward the forbidding neo-Gothic pile known as the Palace of Justice where, he knew, the Assize Court would be sitting. He mounted the stairs to room number 216. The trial was in progress, the room was packed, and he found no seat. He had to stand in the doorway, and even this was allowed only because of his credentials as a barrister.

He saw at once that though the courtroom was crowded, the trial had not been thrown open to the public. Admission was by invitation of the authorities only, and uniforms in three different styles predominated in the audience. The field gray of the *Wehrmacht,* the regular army, contrasted with the black of the *SS,* the elite Security

Corps, and with the brown of the *SA*, the Storm Troops who were the bullyboys of the National Socialist Party, the Nazis. From the number and variety of uniforms Samberger could tell that the proceedings, for reasons he did not yet understand, were of intense concern to all echelons of the German government.

The scene was dominated—overpowered—by the figure on the bench. Judge Roland Freisler was dressed in a robe of flaming red which his constant gestures and movements kept flowing and rippling, like a banner in a wind. On the upper left side of the robe was the same symbol which decorated all the military tunics before him: an eagle whose streamlined wings were spread wide and whose claws clasped a wreath enclosing the basic emblem of the National Socialist state, the swastika. Under his biretta his face was fixed in a permanent scowl, the mouth set in an unchanging snarl. He choked with fury as he read out the charges in the indictment:

> . . . *treason against the Fatherland and preparation for High Treason* . . .

> . . . *calling for sabotage of war industry and subversion of the armed forces* . . .

Now it became clear why the Chief Judge of the People's Court had been hastily flown from Berlin to preside at this trial and why the courtroom was so liberally seeded with representatives of the armed power of the state. The charges that Freisler had read from the indictments were among the gravest that could be brought against a German by his government in wartime.

It appeared from the evidence that the infamous deeds cited by the prosecution had been perpetrated over a period of many months by an organization with the curiously incongruous name of "the White Rose." Page after page told of the activities of this group which had secretly and subversively produced thousands of leaflets attacking the government and the war effort and circulated them in many different cities, thereby threatening the very survival of the Reich.

Freisler made no pretense of being judicial. He ranted. He bellowed. He encouraged the prosecution and ignored the defense. At his post in the doorway Leo Samberger turned his eyes from the flaming figure on the bench to the defendants. There were three of them. Though he didn't know them, he recognized their faces from seeing them many times in the concert halls of Munich which he himself frequented. They were college students, young, educated, clean-cut—his own sort. It seemed hardly credible that they were sitting in the dock with a death penalty over their heads as a consequence of what had happened at the university only three days before.

But what then seemed like a minor incident of no more than local importance had, in fact, caused consternation in the highest quarters in Berlin. Now the state itself was reacting as if the whole National Socialist system were suddenly in mortal danger. And not from the massive assaults of the Red armies in the East, or from the invasion that was sure to come in the West, but from these three—a girl and two young men—who looked as if they ought to be sitting in a classroom with their notebooks instead of in room 216 of the Palace of Justice flanked by armed police.

What was most disturbing to the judge and the prosecution was that all three of the accused had grown up under the aegis of National Socialism and had been schooled, trained, and nurtured by it. The National Socialist state had indoctrinated them from their earliest youth, shaping their views of the world and saturating their minds with the philosophy of Adolf Hitler and his political movement. Two of them, the two who were brother and sister—Hans and Sophie Scholl—had been enthusiastic members of the Hitler Youth organizations. Hans was once such a sterling young Hitlerite that he had been chosen to carry the swastika banner of his troop at one of the great Party rallies in Nuremberg. The girl, Sophie, had been a member of the League of German Girls and had even been a leader in it. The third member of the indicted trio, Christoph Probst, was a medic in the German army and a sergeant, as Hans Scholl also was.

To Freisler, to the whole National Socialist hierarchy, it was a shock, a scandal, and also a mystery that three such purebred products of the Hitlerite Age should be sitting where they were, branded as traitors to the Fatherland, aiders and abettors of their country's enemies.

It was the girl, Sophie, on whom most eyes were centered as Roland Freisler bellowed his denunciations and abuse from the bench. The whole auditorium was waiting for her to wince or cringe, to recant and beg for the mercy of the court. She did not. All three maintained their self-possession in a way that won a grudging admiration even in that room, but Sophie made a particular impression. Not only did she stand out as the lone female caught up in these proceedings but she had an indefinable quality of her own. She was twenty-two years old, dark, and with a curious aura of mingled girlishness and gravity. Now and then during the trial her brow would crease into a quick, musing frown which those who knew her would have recognized as characteristic. Even here, in the courtroom with her life at stake, the frown did not signify anxiety or dismay. It meant that she was turning over in her mind a point, an implication, or a shading and weighing it to get it right.

She was wearing a rumpled and rather mannish sort of coat which contributed little to her appearance. She had endured three days of nearly unbroken interrogation in a Gestapo prison, and she looked worn and tired. But her quiet appeal, hovering always between girl and woman, was unimpaired. It was overlaid, now, with a kind of subdued defiance apparent in the cast of her features and the set of her head. Once Roland Freisler, squirming with fury inside his scarlet robe, demanded to know how any German could possibly do what the indictment charged against the trio in the dock. It was Sophie who responded, clearly and coolly:

"Somebody, after all, had to make a start. What we wrote and said is also believed by many others. They just don't dare to express themselves as we did."

There was a stir in the courtroom and Roland Freisler was momentarily taken aback. Hans Scholl gave a sideways glance of approval at his sister and a slight nod of his head. He, too, was dark, but there was more resemblance in manner and personality than of facial features between these two. He was a strikingly good-looking young man of twenty-five, his black hair brushed back in a wave from a broad forehead. He, too, had spent the past three days under harrowing interrogation. Afterwards, when it was all over and too late, the Gestapo agent assigned to him confided to a colleague: "In

that young man I encountered a keener intelligence than any other I
ever met. I was sorry that circumstances made it impossible for me
to do anything for him.''

Side by side in the dock, Hans and Sophie were continuing the
nearness of a relationship that had existed all their lives. There was
a sibling warmth between them that combined affection with a re-
ciprocal respect and admiration. For Hans it was an agony that she
should be sitting beside him now. He had never wanted his sister to
become involved in the tensions and hazards of working underground against the regime of Adolf Hitler. It should not have happened, and it would not have happened, if she had not learned the
secret of the White Rose by accident and then insisted on participating.

Even after her arrest, ways had been opened for Sophie Scholl to
escape the fate that the court was sure to impose upon her. The Gestapo, in an uncharacteristic lapse into compassion, had suggested
that it would treat her gently if only she expressed regret and repent-
ance for her treasonable activity against the National Socialist state.
But since that would have meant turning her back on her brother and
repudiating what she most deeply believed, she rejected the entice-
ment instantly and completely.

Next to Hans and Sophie sat Christoph Probst, called Christel.
He, too, had volunteered to serve under the invisible symbol of the
White Rose whose leaflets had spread among the Germans a motto
that was also a program: *"We will not be silent. We are your bad
conscience. The White Rose will give you no rest."* Christel Probst
shared friendship, interests, and ideals with Hans and Sophie, and
now he was sharing their doom as well.

It was only through a fluke that Probst was sitting in Roland
Freisler's court. It was a matter of some scraps of paper that the Secret State Police had seized on, matched up, and figuratively woven
into a noose to hang him with. Unlike Hans and Sophie, Probst had
never succumbed to the lure of the swastika, even in his boyhood
when the marching and the uniforms had swept so many into the
ranks. He had always preferred climbing mountains by himself to
keeping step with the others. He was tall, broad, and athletic, but
there was about him an air of abstraction, as if he were thinking of

something other than what immediately occupied him. While Freisler ranted and the damaging evidence mounted up, Christel Probst seemed often to be elsewhere.

He was the only one among the White Rose students who was married, and at twenty-four he had just become the father of his third child. His wife was still in bed with puerperal fever. Of all those being gathered up in the Gestapo net, which was daily being cast wider and wider, Christel Probst's ordeal was perhaps the most desolating. But like Hans and Sophie Scholl, he had come where he now was because for him there was something worse than arrest, trial, and execution. What was worse was living without protest under a system which, by its nature, was the enemy of all the decencies on which civilized intercourse among human beings rested.

As the proceedings wore on, it became obvious that no defense worth the name would be offered. The court-appointed defense attorneys scarcely troubled to conceal their aversion to their task or to disguise their approval of the charges. The verdict itself was never in doubt. Berlin had not sent Roland Freisler winging down to Munich to preside over an acquittal.

Yet there was, as Leo Samberger noted, a pronounced tension in the courtroom as the words were about to be spoken that would, quite literally, cost three young people their heads. Such a thing had never happened before even in a Nazi courtroom. And the words came from the bench as expected: *". . . for the protection of the German people, and of the Reich, in this time of mortal struggle, the Court has only one just verdict open to it on the basis of the evidence: the death penalty. With this sentence the People's Court demonstrates its solidarity with the fighting troops!"* With this, Roland Freisler rose from the bench and left the room in a swirl of scarlet, trailed by his entourage of subsidiary judges, none of whom had contributed anything to the proceedings.

Even before the auditorium was drained of its gray, black, and brown uniforms, the condemned trio was hurriedly surrounded by a cordon of police, put in manacles, and led away. The three of them were taken directly from the court to the place of execution, to Stadelheim, on the outskirts of the city. There, that same afternoon, all three were beheaded, the girl, Sophie, going under the guillotine first. It was all done with a speed and brutality that signaled something like panic in high places.

This was not the reaction of a normal government which had merely caught a few of its young citizens agitating against the status quo, as young people so often do. It was, rather, as if the authorities, to their horror, had accidentally uncovered a coven of witches and warlocks capable of bringing the whole structure of the state crashing down with the dark magic of their abominable incantations—those forbidden words that were being scattered to the four winds of Germany on scraps of paper called leaflets. The executions of Sophie and Hans Scholl with their friend Christoph Probst—so callously quick, so brutally hurried—were the equivalent of an auto-da-fé, a medieval witch-burning, in the most technically advanced nation of twentieth-century Europe.

What made the shock to the Nazi hierarchy so jolting was that this was the first opposition to the rule of Adolf Hitler that had broken through to the light of day. It was the first public break in the universal lockstep imposed on German society by its leaders. And it came from a source particularly galling to a movement that preened itself inordinately on winning over the youth of the nation. The universities were supposed to be hotbeds of National Socialist fervor; but here at the University of Munich—in the "Capital of the Movement," where it all began—a fissure had opened. A crack appeared where the solidity of granite was looked for. Who knew but that the foundations were crumbling?

And, as events that were even then unfolding would shortly disclose, the students were not alone in their rebellion.

Five days after the executions, on the morning of February 27, a girl named Birgit Huber was awakened by the doorbell in her home in the middle-class suburb of Gräfelfing. It was 6:30 and still rather dark outside. When she looked out the window, Birgit could dimly make out three men standing at the garden gate.

"Who's there?" she called.

One of the men called back: "Please come down."

Birgit was only twelve and she was a little frightened. But her father was still asleep, her mother was away in the country, and so it was up to her to see what the men wanted. Still in her nightgown, she went downstairs. There she saw that the men were standing one behind the other, not side by side, and this somehow added to her uneasiness. But she was a polite little girl and she asked the first man, "What do you wish, Sir?"

The men ignored her and pushed through the gate toward the house. Birgit was used to visitors, mostly students, coming to the house and she wanted to take these men to the living room, too. But they went straight up the stairs. She squirmed around them and ran on ahead to her father's bedroom.

"Pappi!" she cried. "The Gestapo!"

Her father started awake, and the first thing Kurt Huber saw that morning was three strange, bulky men entering his bedroom. One of them said, *"Heil Hitler,* Herr Professor. Please send the child away."

The men from the Secret State Police searched every room of the house methodically, and it took several hours. They paid special attention to the study, opening all the drawers, pawing through files and letters, stuffing various papers into large manila envelopes, discarding others. As they went about their work they continually asked Kurt Huber questions, but they did so quietly and with respect. Kurt Huber, after all, was a professor at the university and as such was clearly entitled to courtesy and deference, even under these disagreeable circumstances.

Finally one of the Gestapo men said: "Now, then, if the Herr Professor will be so good as to come with us."

Kurt Huber called to his daughter to take his leave of her. He tried to make it seem like a normal parting, giving her a fatherly kiss, patting her on the head, and saying *"Auf Wiedersehen,"* as he always did. Then they took him away and Birgit Huber, age twelve, was left alone with her dread in the empty house.

A generation separated Kurt Huber from the young rebels of the White Rose. He was fifty-one years old. In addition there was the gap between them that always exists between professor and student, teacher and the taught. It was all the more of a shock to the authorities, then, to discover that he had made common cause with the Scholls and their friends and come under the same indictment of subversion and disloyalty as they had. Here was another gross rupture in the ideological underpinning of the system. The function of a professor in the National Socialist state was, surely, to "strengthen the young in unquestioning trust and confidence in the *Führer*, the people, and the Reich," as the indictment that was drawn up against him put it. But what had Professor Kurt Huber done? *"The exact opposite!"* said the indictment in italics and with exclamation point.

There would be more arrests, many more, but of them, two especially were heavy with import because they resulted in two more victims for the blade at Stadelheim. In the end six would die there for attempting, in the words of one of them, "to make a breach in the wall of terror" which enclosed them and their country.

When the Gestapo came for Willi Graf he was sitting in his small student's apartment in Munich discussing philosophical and religious ideas with his sister, hardly the typical pastime for a soldier on leave from the front. But if Willi Graf was not the typical German noncom, he was also quite unlike the popular idea of a dangerous agitator and a threat to the state. Willi was more like the legendary character of whom it was said that his strength was as the strength of ten because his heart was pure. What made an underground activist out of a character so mild and meditative was, as a friend explained it, "the unbearable pressure of being forced to live contrary to his innermost convictions." He would be the last to die, his agony a long one.

Temperamentally at the opposite pole from Willi Graf was his fellow dissident Alexander Schmorell. Alex had a light and stylish way about him which not even the drabness of the field-gray uniform could entirely obliterate. There was more of the laughing cavalier about him than of the hot-eyed enemy of society. But there was iron in his rebellion and, together with Hans Scholl, it was Alex Schmorell who first made the voice of resistance audible in Hitler's Germany.

Those, then, were the six who banded together to defy the swastika under the symbol of the White Rose. They did not for a moment imagine that they could, by their own unsupported efforts, demolish the mighty National Socialist state, which half the world in arms strained to bring down. They could not know what effect their ob scure efforts would have on the course of events or if any results at all would ensue. What they did know was that they could not, like so many millions of their countrymen, remain silent and, by their silence, acquiesce in a system that was brutal, corrupt, and immoral to its core. What drove them to act as they did was the moral imperative behind Sophie Scholl's retort to Roland Freisler in the courtroom at Munich:

"Somebody, after all, had to make a start."

It would never have occurred to them while they were making their doomed beginning that one day streets and schools and public squares would be named in their honor. They would have greeted the idea with incredulity and derision. But when the tumult and clangor of larger events had subsided, serious scholars would write words like these about what they did:

"As examples of moral heroism, the actions of 'The White Rose' are unsurpassed in European history and worthy of our highest admiration."

And these:

"They fought against the giant conflagration with their bare hands and their faith, and with their puny duplicating machine they challenged the all-powerful State."

Two

While Hans and Sophie Scholl were undergoing their first interrogations at the Gestapo headquarters in Munich, the all-powerful state was staging an entirely different kind of question-and-answer ritual in the Sports Palace in Berlin. The date was February 18, 1943, and the Berlin rally and the jailing of the young students in Munich were linked by more than the mere coincidence in time.

The two events were, each in its own way, definitive illustrations of the twin fundamentals on which every dictatorship is based: the suppression of the individual and the manipulation of the masses. The crowd at the Sports Palace was assembled for the set purpose of delivering a resounding "Yes!" to the regime and its policies. Hans and Sophie Scholl were in their cells in Munich because they had dared to say "No!"

What prompted the mass meeting was that the Nazi oligarchs were feeling the first quivers of dread about a future that once had seemed so certain. The four years of war had been an almost unbroken string of German victories, but now there was Stalingrad—an entire army wiped out, obliterated, gone, and the whole German position in the East threatened with collapse. The government was shaken, the public dismayed. No comparable crisis had confronted Adolf Hitler's regime in the ten years since he had come to power.

Hitler himself being absent in the East where he was playing King Canute to the rising Soviet tide, the regime turned to Paul Joseph Goebbels, the second most redoubtable demagogue, to resuscitate morale and restore confidence in the leadership. He rejoiced in the title of Minister of Public Enlightenment and Propaganda and saw no paradox in the two opposing parts of his function. A little man, hardly higher than five feet, he had one crippled foot and features that struck many as ratlike. He was a failed poet and novelist, but he was also wickedly brilliant at his job of putting the Nazi cause in the best possible light no matter how much objective fact might indicate the contrary. He was diabolically adroit at twanging the emotional strings which made a crowd stir and rumble and shout. Two of the self-made sets of precepts he habitually applied in his writings and speeches were: "Propaganda has nothing at all to do with truth" and "We must appeal to the primitive instincts of the masses." He used both of these guidelines, especially the second, with telling effect in the Sports Palace.

In a voice surprisingly rich and strong, Paul Joseph Goebbels flooded the huge arena for two-and-a-half hours with oratory that set off repeated explosions of roaring applause and patriotic frenzy in his 15,000 listeners. The Sports Palace was an established platform for Nazi rhetoric, and here Joseph Goebbels was in his element.

He was far too intelligent to attempt to minimize the significance of Stalingrad. He gave it its full weight as a national calamity, calling it "the alarm-signal of fate to the German people," but he contrived to transform the disaster from a cause of despair into a source of inspiration. The nation, he said, had been "purified to the depths of its being" by the ordeal of Stalingrad and now the nation would come surging back more powerful and confident than ever.

But, said Goebbels, the danger was not over. The menace of the barbaric hordes from the Asiatic steppes increased with every hour. Two thousand years of western civilization were in danger of annihilation if Germany did not stand fast in this, her hour of mortal peril.

By alternating dire threat with appeals to the manhood and patriotism of his listeners, the minister's speech generated paroxysms of response that shook the walls of the auditorium. In speaking here, he said, he was addressing the whole nation face to face; for did he not have a cross section of all Germany before him? He described the composition of the audience row by row: "Wounded soldiers from the eastern front, men with scarred bodies, with amputated legs, men blinded in action who have come with their Red Cross nurses, men in the prime of life with their crutches beside them . . . Behind them a block of armaments workers from Berlin's armored car factory. . . . And farther back, men of the various Nazi Party organizations. . . . Then physicians, scientists, artists, engineers, architects, teachers, civil servants. . . . Thousands of German women. . . . Youth. . . . '' Was not this, he asked, a true representation of the entire nation, front and home front and both?

The audience rose to its feet and sent a thunderous "*Ja!*" reverberating through the Sports Palace. It was the first of many, for Joseph Goebbels had designed ten questions, each one shrewdly calculated to evoke roars of affirmation. Did they still have utter and unquestioning confidence in their *Führer* and his policies?

"*Ja!*"

Did they still believe in the complete and final victory of German arms?

"*Ja!*"

The fervor of response mounted with every question, and soon the speaker could hardly complete a sentence before the answering "*Ja!*" was bellowed back at him. The audience was especially tumultuous when he put the question that was the core of his psychological assault on the emotions of his listeners:

"*I ask you. Do you want total war? If necessary, do you want war more total and radical than we are even capable of imagining today?*"

The stenographer making the official record of the meeting noted that a "veritable tornado" of assent engulfed the speaker here, equaling anything ever heard even in this place where so much political frenzy had been vented in the past. Then Goebbels put to the gathering another question which, again, fetched a howl of *"Ja!"* from the arena. He asked:

"Do you agree that anyone who goes against the war effort in any way should pay for it with his head?"

It was the most brutal and unmistakable warning possible to dissidents, a threat in the authentic Nazi manner to all internal enemies of the Reich. But it came too late to affect the young people of the White Rose, who would not have heeded it in any case. They had already committed themselves. And against Adolf Hitler's total war, that commitment was also total. They had said it in one of their leaflets with a few quiet words that spoke louder than all the frantic roaring in the Sports Palace: "It is a *moral duty* to put an end to this system."

The italics were theirs.

When Adolf Hitler came to power, Hans Scholl was fifteen years old and Sophie, twelve. They were living in the town of Ulm, on the Danube, with their parents and two sisters and a brother. A new Chancellor was not necessarily thrilling news in the Germany of the time, there having been a jumble of them, one after the other. No matter which one took office—Bruening or von Papen or von Schleicher—nothing seemed to change for the better. The worldwide depression was getting worse, and in Germany it had struck with particular virulence. More than twenty percent of the population, some 15 million people, was living at a bare subsistence level. Workmen could scarcely afford the price of a glass of beer. In Germany that was the terminal symptom of economic paralysis and social disintegration.

In Ulm it was no more clear than anywhere else how Adolf Hitler had come to be Chancellor at just this time. Few had expected it, including his own followers. His Party, the National Socialists, had the largest representation in the Reichstag, but though he had been campaigning furiously up and down Germany for years, he himself had never been elected to any public office. He was widely regarded as either an upstart or a joke. In no national election had his Nazis achieved more than thirty-seven percent of the popular vote. And yet the President of the Republic, the venerable Field Marshal Paul von Hindenburg, had appointed him Chancellor and thereby put the conduct of the Republic's affairs in his hands.

It was known that von Hindenburg, who was eighty-five, was easily manipulated by those around him, including his dubious son Oskar; but why he had made this unexpected move remained obscure not only to the ordinary citizen but to many of the most seasoned observers of public affairs. In government circles it was known that only a few months before, the president had dismissed Hitler as "that little Austrian corporal." The remark had been delivered in a tone that made everyone aware of the astronomical difference between a German field marshal like himself and a mere ex-noncom like the outlander Hitler. Count Harry Kessler, an intellectual of parts and an acute follower of public events, wrote the word "astonishing" in his diary on January 30, 1933, the day of the appointment.

When later he learned what was behind the appointment, the count was less astonished. Forces familiar to him, and to every other observer of high-level politics, had been at work in familiar ways. Political, industrial, and military interests had contrived to foist the ex-noncom on the Field Marshal, and thus on the nation, because these interests considered that such a move would be most profitable for themselves, collectively and individually. For one thing, the appointment would resolve, at least temporarily, the continuing cabinet crisis that was paralyzing the government. For another thing, Hitler was a handy expedient who, if he didn't work out, could easily be removed. The political, military, and industrial interests were confident they could keep Adolf Hitler under their control and, if not, dispose of him whenever the situation required it.

They would turn out to be grievously mistaken.

So, too, would be the many who thought that, odd as the appointment might be, it had no great significance because the upstart Hitler and his brown-shirted rabble could not possibly last for any length of time. At any rate, Hitler could not really mean what he had been saying in his speeches about the Jews, about his intention to destroy the Republic, and his determination to avenge Germany's defeat in the World War. Not many took seriously the statement to newspaper correspondents by one of his spokesmen: "You must realize, *meine Herren*, that what has happened in Germany is no ordinary change. Parliamentary and democratic times are past. A new era has begun!"

In towns like Ulm, and in families like the Scholls, the New Order did not at first alter the established way of life in any drastic way. The lapels of neighbors and acquaintances, and sometimes surprisingly, of friends blossomed with swastika pins that proclaimed their owners to be members of the National Socialist Party. The black-red-gold flag of the Weimar Republic was hauled down from poles on municipal buildings and in public parks. It was replaced by the black-red-white of the imperial Hohenzollern banner, usually to the cheers of bystanders. It was under the Hohenzollern Kaisers, after all, that Germany had reached its greatest puissance and prestige as a world power. The flag of the Republic, on the other hand, represented defeat in war and the political chaos that came with Germany's first experiment in democracy. Next to the old imperial flag, and very often without it, flew the swastika banner of National Socialism which now became so ubiquitous that it soon overwhelmed all other national emblems.

The initials NSDAP became more prominent everywhere. They stood for the new power in the land, the *National-Sozialistische Deutsche Arbeiter Partei*—the National Socialist German Workers Party. It was a contrived and labored title. The "Socialist" in it was bait inserted to catch the workers and to suggest that the Party was the enemy of the landed gentry, the rich, the aristocrats. No connection with the socialism of Marx and Engels was intended. The "Workers" in the title reenforced the Party's political concern for the humble toiler, though only a fraction of the membership was laborers. The NSDAP was, actually, a movement of the lower middle class, "a revolution of mailmen and school teachers," as one Munich scoffer described it.

The word "National" was the most sincere and genuine in the title. In the context it meant, and was intended to mean, rightist, ultra-patriotic, with strong implications of anti-Semitism. The true believer of the National Socialist German Workers Party might care nothing for socialism or the proletariat but he was a nationalist to his marrow.

A new ruling class surfaced in German society and made its presence felt in the town of Ulm as elsewhere. Fortified by the Party emblems in their buttonholes, the swastikas on their armbands, and the NSDAP membership cards in their wallets, the hitherto obscure and overlooked began to assert themselves. Shop clerks donned their Storm Troop uniforms and took charge of local governments without the formality of an election. The fire chief who was not a member of the Party was elbowed out by somebody who was. Hotel doormen with brown credentials began to speak sharply to the management which began to listen respectfully. On every level of social and political life the Brown Revolution manifested itself in a kind of seepage upward from below.

By means of the mesmeric oratory of which he was the unequaled master, Adolf Hitler had saturated the minds of millions with the idea that he, and only he, had the cure for the disasters and distresses that had reduced postwar Germany to near anarchy. Where other politicians exhibited only hesitation and indecision in confronting the problems of inflation, unemployment, and political confusion, Adolf Hitler offered ringing certainties and the promise of unwavering leadership. To the judicious his program seemed simplistic, reactionary, and dangerous. But, as Nietzsche knew, in times of great distress "the feeling of insecurity at last becomes so great that men fall in the dust before any sort of will power that commands." Hitler exerted this power of the will over the masses to a superlative degree. Though he had never yet achieved a majority of votes in a free election, Hitler's genius for mass agitation had built a broad base of support from which he could operate. Within weeks of his appointment as Chancellor of the Reich he had swept aside the democratic restraints of the Weimar constitution. He abolished the rights of free speech, press, and public assembly.

All political parties except the National Socialist were suppressed. Before his first year was out Adolf Hitler had transformed Germany from a republic into a dictatorship. But far from causing alarm and protest in the world, his feat of consolidating his regime so firmly in so short a time evoked general approbation. Germany at last was steadying down under a leader who knew what he was doing and where he was going.

For the majority of nonpolitical citizens going about their usual occupations, things seemed to be vastly improved. The American correspondent William Shirer, new to the German scene, was surprised and somewhat puzzled by what he saw. "The people of this country," he noted, "did not seem to feel they were being cowed and held down by an unscrupulous and brutal dictatorship. On the contrary, they supported it with genuine enthusiasm. Somehow it embued them with a new hope and new confidence and an astonishing faith in the future of their country." With a terrible irony whose dimensions would not become fully apparent until later, approval for Adolf Hitler's government at the outset was so general that it numbered Jews among its supporters. An organization called the Jewish National Union publicly signified its support for the new National Socialist regime.

Among the millions of Germans who thought that Adolf Hitler's coming to power was cause for rejoicing was Inge Scholl, the older sister of Hans and Sophie. She was sixteen when she heard the news from a classmate on the steps of her school in Ulm. Inge was a girl with intelligent, inquiring eyes and a lively interest in what was going on in the world around her. The new administration had not been in office very long before she and her brothers and sisters sensed that a fresh and invigorating wind seemed to be blowing where only stagnation and apathy had prevailed before.

"Everywhere—at school and from the newspapers and radio— we heard that Hitler had only one goal," Inge Scholl remembered long afterward, in the years of her maturity. "What he wanted, everybody said, was to make our Fatherland strong and prosperous again, to make us all proud of a new Germany that could hold up her head in the world. We young people found that good. We were eager to do whatever we could to bring it about."

A surge of patriotism swept the land, an emotion which had been largely muffled under the Republic. The Scholl children, all five of them—Inge, Hans, Elizabeth, Sophie, and Werner—needed no government propaganda to urge them to love their country. Like most children everywhere, they were patriotic by instinct and the country they loved was their immediate surroundings. It was a region easy to fall in love with. Whatever was to happen to them and their country afterwards, the hills and fields and woods around the town of Ulm would remain infinitely dear to them. There, in the region called Swabia, the Danube flowed through a fruitful countryside where farmland blended into orchard and where vineyards made the slopes and hillsides sweet with their fragrance. For the young Scholls the Fatherland always had the smell of grapes and loam, apples and moss.

A natural playground without boundary or limit stretched away in every direction. There were hills and caves and mountains nearby that offered endless enticements to clamber, camp, and explore. The young Scholls made full use of it, the girls as well as the boys and Sophie in particular. Once her school class was taken on a geological expedition among the caves and rocks of the area. Here and there high rocks shot up out of the valley, some to intimidating heights. To the consternation of the teacher and the alarm of the rest of the class, Sophie was suddenly discovered, all alone, atop one such rock. Going her own way, unheeding of teacher or class, she had nimbly and fleetly clambered to the top. The rock was there, it had challenged her, and she had responded. Only when she looked down and saw her teacher and classmates frantically signaling her to come down was she aware of her total isolation on the height. She descended from the rock a good deal more cautiously than she had mounted it, and when she was on the ground, her teacher made her promise never to undertake such breakneck climbing in the future. Sophie Scholl promised. She was fourteen then, but when much greater risks for far better reasons confronted her later in her life, she could accept them as readily as she had responded to the challenge of the rock in her native valley.

Swabia was perhaps a good region for future freedom-fighters to grow up in. The place traditionally bred rugged types with a disrelish for authority, a trait not especially typical of Germans in general. When in medieval times the rest of Germany was shorn of every semblance of personal freedom, Swabia alone maintained certain rights and privileges that were hers alone. In addition to philosophers and poets like Hegel and Schiller, the place prided itself —and still does—on more earthy personalities. One such delivered himself of a saying that, though once unprintable, became known as the "Swabian greeting."

It was Goethe himself who wrote the line that has been repeated uncounted times by uncounted Germans, many of whom would be hard pressed to quote any other line from Goethe at all. It occurs in the third act of the drama *Götz von Berlichingen* and is spoken by the eponymous hero, a knight who led rebellious peasants in a sixteenth-century uprising. Beleagured in his castle, Götz received a demand from the opposing commander to surrender. Götz's reply anticipated in a more vivid and scatological phrase the celebrated reply of the American General McAuliffe at Bastogne in the Second World War. Where McAuliffe contented himself with a curt "Nuts!" to a similar surrender demand, Götz's reply was more detailed and elaborate but just as dismissive and impolite. The nub of it loses nothing in translation. What Götz von Berlichingen conveyed to the enemy commander, as Goethe recorded it in his drama, was: "Kiss my ass!"

Goethe had second thoughts about the propriety of the retort and struck it out after the early performances of the play, but it was too late. The expression achieved an instant resonance and could not be withdrawn or canceled. Its utility as a ready response to all sorts of provocation embedded it so firmly in the general consciousness that, after a time, it was necessary merely to snarl "Götz von Berlichingen" at an opponent. The message could be conveyed without actually using the indecent word. Such prissy circumlocution was rarely employed in the place of the phrase's origin. In Swabia the saying is cherished as the definitive example of the native style of expressing defiance and contempt for whoever, or whatever, threatens one's personal integrity and self-esteem.

The attitude of the rebellious Götz von Berlichingen was part of the environment in which Hans Scholl grew up. Born in the small town of Ingerstein, which was nestled in the heart of the Götz country, Hans must have heard innumerable repetitions of the "Swabian greeting" in his boyhood. When the family moved to Ulm in 1930, the children on the streets used to chirp an eight-line jingle which was a local variation of Götz's immortal remark but even more indelicate than the original.

The Scholl children were seldom seen tumbling about the streets and were never heard singing improper songs in public. A close-knit clan with a strong sense of each other, they usually provided themselves with enough companionship to make the presence of outsiders unnecessary. With Werner as the youngest and Inge as the oldest, there was little more than a spread of five years among the five of them, and no great gap between any two. They varied in traits and temperament, but the sibling bond between them was warm and firm and remained so all their lives. When they moved into the big, sunny house on Cathedral Square in Ulm there was not the faintest sign that three of them—Hans, Sophie, and Werner—were fated for violent death and that tragedy would engulf them all.

Hans Fritz Scholl was the dominant personality among them, and not only because of his status as older son and big brother. He had the dark good looks not uncommon in south German males, but a certain Italianate cast to his features refined the modeling of his face and made him handsomer than most. He was tall for his age, slender, and with a kind of tautness that came from energy seeking its outlet. His friends, remembering him, described him sometimes as *glühend,* glowing, and sometimes as *strahlend*, beaming. He bent a little forward as he walked, as if eager to get where he was going.

The windows of the big, sunny house looked out on the local cathedral which had the highest steeple in all Germany, an imposing 162 meters. Inge and Sophie used to like to watch the pigeons strutting importantly around the square. Sophie's lively sense of the ridiculous was gratified when a particularly pouty specimen would, in all its gravity, tumble over the horse droppings which littered the square. Life in the big house was comfortable and sheltered. Inge remembered it as an island that offered isolation from the increasing turmoil of the world around it. If the headlines outside were strident and threatening, here one could find escape in the rich imagery of Johann Christian Friedrich Hölderlin, a Swabian poet who had gone romantically mad when young. Or in the mystical lyricism of Rainer Maria Rilke. Or the Bible. Mother Scholl, whose name was Mag-

dalene, had been a member of a Protestant nursing order, a deaconess, before her marriage. She was gently insistent that the way of Jesus was the sure way. No pressure was put upon the children to ad-
here to any sect or even to attend church regularly, but the Bible was
there to be read, and it was read.

Hans early picked a favorite passage. He chose the verses from
Corinthians that include the sentence: *"And though I have the gift
of prophecy, and understand all mysteries, and all knowledge, and
though I have all faith, so that I could remove mountains, and have
not charity, I am nothing."* The word translated as "charity" in the
King James version is *Liebe*, love, in the German. It was a curious
choice for an active young boy, but with it he made a kind of choice
of priorities in his life and in his view of the world. He carried the
verses with him all his life.

The house on Cathedral Square could not long escape the tremors
of change that the Hitler regime was bringing to Germany, and for a
time the Scholl household was violently shaken by them. Swabia
was not a stronghold of National Socialism, and once when Adolf
Hitler came to speak in the district, a local hero cut the cable of the
public address system. Hitler never came back. An organized Nazi
group had existed in Ulm since 1922, however. When the Party
came to power its decrees, measures, and constraints went into
effect there as they did everywhere else in Germany. The impact of
the New Order was felt soonest and most generally in the schools,
since National Socialism strove to be the Party of youth. To control
the young and command their allegiance was a fundamental goal of
the movement. "Whoever has the youth has the future," said Adolf
Hitler.

The swastika flags were hoisted in every classroom and up on the
walls went the portraits of the *Führer*, the leader, the guide, the pilot, of the nation. School libraries were cleansed of subversive literature, which meant any book, whether fact or fiction, that expressed
a liberal idea or suggested that the people themselves—rather than
the leader, guide, or pilot—should have charge of their destiny.
Such books were replaced with texts and tracts glorifying nationalism and militarism, with emphasis on the heroic achievement of the
National Socialist German Workers Party in rescuing the Fatherland

from the abyss into which the Weimar Republic had plunged it. The outworn notion of objectivity was discarded along with the theory that the school was there only for the purpose of transmitting knowledge. Now the school was there to "make out of growing youths men and women such as the National Socialist state will require in the coming struggle for national greatness." The new guidelines were accepted without significant protest by both principals and teachers, most of whom hastened to join the National Socialist Teachers League as soon as Hitler came to power. To make sure that nothing heretical would be taught, or even hinted, in a German classroom henceforth, the children were expected to report any deviation from National Socialist ideas on the part of their teachers to the nearest Party official for punitive action. All classes were to open with the Nazi salute and the cry of *"Heil Hitler!"*

But the Nazis were well aware that emotions are seldom stirred by what happens in a classroom and they resorted to more stimulating methods to win over the rising generation. The *Hitler Jugend*— the Hitler youth—was created as one of the earliest organizations in the National Socialist system and the only one to which Hitler lent his name. What he wanted to achieve with this program of training and indoctrination was, he said, "a youth that will be slim and lithe, fast as greyhounds, tough as leather, and hard as Krupp steel." It was an ideal to which the young themselves responded with joy and dedication. The ranks of the Hitler Youth swelled by thousands and tens of thousands in the wake of Hitler's rise to power.

The young male was rare who could resist joining the smartly uniformed columns of his peers swinging along to the rhythmic thump of the drums, the piercing blare of the bugles, and the snap of swastika banners in the wind overhead. The pull to become part of it, to fall in step beside the others, was powerful. The banners and bugles spoke to the young and what they said was: "Come. Join in your country's surge toward greatness. Do not stand apart. March with us." To stand aside while others marched was to mark oneself as a milksop, a malingerer, a pariah.

Hans Scholl joined the Hitler Youth with the intensity that was characteristic of him when he found a cause. For him it was a rite of passage, the primal act of the adolescent who makes his break with boyhood and his entry into manhood by defying the authority of the father and going his own way.

Robert Scholl was hurt and dismayed when all his children, led by Hans, succumbed so readily to the appeal of the Nazis. He himself had been wary of them from the start and with time he came to regard them as a blight and affliction. One of his friends said afterwards that Robert Scholl had an accurate compass inside his mind that charted Hitler's course correctly from the beginning. His own outlook was broad and liberal, an attitude rare enough to set him apart from his associates, some of whom kept him at a distance for his suspected pacifism and lack of nationalist fervor.

Robert Scholl had served as mayor at various small towns in southwest Germany like Ingerstein at the foot of the Alps, where Hans was born, and in Forchtenberg, Sophie's birthplace. He had managed to bring his family virtually unscathed through the harassments of a grinding depression, astronomical inflation, and political disarray, a feat that testified to his character and intelligence. After losing an election, and sensing that the coming of the Nazis would end his political career in any case, he set himself up in Ulm as a tax and business consultant. Mustached, cigar-smoking, sometimes gruff, he left his children in no doubt about who was in command in the household, but he respected them as individuals and granted each of them the right to his or her own personality. He was instinctively democratic and there was no arbitrary imposition of opinion in the Scholl family. But there were differences and disputes which sometimes led to tears. The break with Hans was especially painful.

The dissonance of opinion between Robert and Hans Scholl, a repetition of the father-son discord common to family life in every generation, was made more acute by the urgency of the political situation that engendered it. To Hans and his brothers and sisters it seemed that the father was being hopelessly old-fashioned and reactionary to set his face so woodenly against the new dispensation in Berlin. How could he be so blind? They strove to enlighten him. Inge Scholl remembered how the talk went and recorded it.

—Look at the statistics in the newspapers, they said. Hitler is actually ending the depression! Unemployment is dropping spectacularly! The German workman can afford his stein of beer again. A great achievement, surely.

"Yes," said Robert Scholl, "but think how it's being done. The wheels of industry are turning again— war industry. Workmen are busy building barracks. And those famous *Autobahnen*—the new thruways—they'll be very useful to Herr Hitler for moving his troops about when the time comes."

—But he's making Germany strong again, isn't he?

"Strong for what? Don't you see how it all will end?"

—Why, the *Führer* is even being praised abroad! Here in the paper is an interview with Lloyd George, Britain's prime minister during the last war. He calls Hitler a great leader. He says he wishes that England had a statesman of her own like him.

"I know the Nazis better than Lloyd George does. Believe me, they are wolves and wild beasts, and they are misusing the German people abominably."

—But, Father, the people support him!

"That makes me think of the old German fairy tale of the Pied Piper of Hamelin who lured the children to perdition by playing pretty tunes on his flute. No, it cannot end well."

For Hans Scholl joining the Hitler Youth meant breaking out of the enclosure of school and family and taking his place in a wider world. The sound of action and heroics was in the air, and he felt that he himself was being summoned to act heroically. Here was a cause founded on youth and vitality, and Hans Scholl was young and vital.

There was in him, besides, a deep strain of idealism which demanded that life have a meaning, that activity have a basis in purpose, that something of substance be included in the daily round. The program of the Hitler Youth responded to these demands. Its slogans and catchwords were shrewdly calculated to prod slumbering emotions awake and bring into play the energy and enthusiasm which are the natural gifts of youth. The keynote was self-sacrifice for the good of the cause, the suppression of the "I" of the self for the "we" of the group. There was an exaltation bordering on the mystic to be told, "You are nothing—your nation is everything!" and to accept that as a verity.

Hans' induction into the ranks of the Hitler Youth was solemnized by the presentation of a dagger with the words "Blood and Honor" etched on it. It was a sign that the Hitler Youth meant to prepare him, as the manuals said, for a "future role as a defender of his country." This seemed natural and right to him, for he loved his country and would willingly defend it if called upon. The uniform— brown shirt open at the throat, black shorts, knee-length gray stockings—was not more martial than the Boy Scout suit, and aside from the dress dagger, no weapons were issued or used. But the goal of the program was stated without disguise by the Hitler Youth official who informed German parents: "We train and educate your son and mold him into a man of action, a man of victory. He has been taken into a hard school, so that his fists may be steeled, his courage strengthened, and that he may be given a faith, a faith in Germany."

Hans' faith in his country was already strong, and he threw himself into the training with the dash and drive that he brought to any undertaking that engaged his interest. He learned the prescribed manner of giving the Hitler salute, the "German greeting," by raising his right arm at the correct angle while placing his left hand on his belt buckle. He was told that the salute derived from the old German warriors who raised their spears in greeting, though in fact the origins of the greeting are obscure, and in any case it was already being used by Mussolini's Fascists in Italy. He was instructed in the symbolism of the National Socialist flag which now seemed to be flying in clusters everywhere he looked. The red background, so it was expounded by Hitler himself in his book *Mein Kampf*, represented "the social idea" of the movement. The white circle at the center spoke of the purity of its nationalistic goals and the black swastika within the white circle denoted the racial superiority of the "Aryan" race, the Nordic breed, to which the Germans belonged.

Not only was the swastika flaunted on the flag, but it decorated every possible appurtenance in the Nazi scheme of things: armbands, lapel buttons, helmets, cockades, guidons, cufflinks, tie pins, and every sort of insignia. Hitler's choice of it as a racial symbol was quite arbitrary since a variety of meanings had been attributed to it over the centuries, including the idea that it represented the passage of the sun through the heavens. The swastika was not exclusively German or "Aryan," having appeared in almost every age and civilization and even on the artifacts of the American Indian. Its origins are unknown and its meaning a mystery. But on Hitler's banners it caught the eye of the world.

Hans wore the swastika armband of the Hitler Youth with pride. It made him feel part of a vast, pulsing organization that was including him, personally, in the future it was shaping. Its racial dogma did not, at first, disturb him. There was, in fact, something gratifying in being told, with all the emphasis that authority could impose, that one was racially superior, a member of the master race.

The training program tested him continually. Wishing to prove himself to the movement and to himself, he welcomed the testing. With his troop he made 20-kilometer marches under heavy field pack, pacing them off to conform to the time limits set by the manuals. He learned to use a compass, to read maps, and to make the most of "available cover in open terrain." The zest with which Hans and his companions threw themselves into these activities was not lessened by the fact that school classes were suspended for Hitler Youth events and the lost time was not required to be made up. Schooling was subordinated to political indoctrination which, of course, was a kind of schooling itself. Minds as well as bodies were being groomed for the New Order in which, as one of the marching songs said:

> *The old must perish*
> *The weak must decay* . . .

The Hitler Youth provided education for conquest and bred a readily recognizable type. Exercise, the open air, indoctrination, and discipline shaped a generation of young Germans into tanned, sturdy, smiling specimens who won the admiration and respect of foreign observers and made Hitler exclaim: "My magnificent youngsters! Are there any finer in the world? What material! With them I can make a whole new world."

Hans Scholl was the very model of the magnificent youngster with whom Adolf Hitler was going to make a new world. His performance as a Hitler Youth was so exemplary that he was promoted to the rank of *Fähnlein*, or ensign, which permitted him to sport the green-white braid of a squad leader and wear three small stars on his shoulder. When the Hitler Youth paraded through the streets of Ulm, the squad leader with the dark good looks and the special swing to his stride was likely to excite ripples of admiration among the girls watching on the sidelines, including his own sisters. More and more, however, his sisters were not on the sidelines watching the parade go by. They were marching themselves.

The Scholl girls, all three of them, joined the counterpart of the Hitler Youth with the same enthusiasm that inspired their brothers. Inge, Sophie, and Elizabeth enrolled in the *Bund Deutscher Mädel*, the League of German Girls, another branch of the Nazi Party. The girls of the *BDM* also marched and drilled and did calisthenics, physical fitness being as basic to this program as to the boys'. On parade the girls too wore a kind of uniform which was not quite military but which identified them as members of the *BDM*. It consisted of a brown coat, a white blouse with a loose black tie and swastika pin, and a navy blue skirt. The outfit was not notably attractive, the shapeless skirts falling almost to the top of white ankle socks and the coats being nearly shapeless. The girls were also required to give the raised-arm salute, cry *"Heil Hitler!"* repeatedly, and subscribe without reservation to National Socialist dogma, especially as it applied to females. How it applied was made abundantly clear. In *Mein Kampf* Hitler devoted thirty pages to the education of boys and seven lines to the education of girls. "The one goal always to be kept in mind when educating girls," he wrote, "is that some day they are to be mothers." Spiritual and mental considerations, he added, were secondary.

Yet the Nazi leadership, with its unfailing knack for manipulating the emotional responses of crowds and groups, made membership in the *BDM* a bracing experience for tens of thousands of German

girls. Songs and slogans created an esprit, a zeal to serve the Fatherland and a pride in being called upon to do so. Though the training
was closely supervised and regulated it was often great fun as well.
Long after National Socialism had revealed itself to Inge Scholl for
the barbarous system it was, she well remembered the innocent relish when she and her sisters participated in the program of the
League of German Girls.

"We went on long hikes together and camped overnight in the
open country, in the woods and hills, which we loved," she has
said. "It was a joy to be thrown together with so many lively young
people we might otherwise never have met and to share new adventures and challenges with them. We felt we were part of a process, a
movement, that had welled up from the people to embrace us all.
Our group held together with the closeness and intimacy of friends,
not just club members. The comradeship was something beautiful."

Sophie, too, marched and sang and saluted in unison with her
comrades, reveling in the physical activity in the open air and the
sheer exhilaration of it. She had a tomboy streak that had her swimming across the Kocher, the river that flowed past her birthplace,
when she was still a child. She had clambered up fir trees to heights
that few of her playmates matched, and in racing and wrestling she
was usually ahead of her sisters and never far behind her brothers.
In walking, her body was strikingly erect and there was something
in her bearing that prompted a friend of the Scholl family, an artist,
to say that she had the carriage of an Old Testament maiden.

This was not the way the ideal *BDM* girl was supposed to look.
The ideal was blonde and blue-eyed and Teutonic, with a coronet of
golden plaits upon the head or twin pigtails bobbing behind. Sophie's hair was dark and her eyes dark and deep. She was delicately
formed with nothing of the Valkyrie about her. Her hair was often
boyishly short with unruly strands falling down over her left eye.
No artist from the Youth Leadership Office would have chosen her
as a model for a *BDM* recruiting poster.

But like her brother Hans, she could not be lax or lukewarm once
she had committed herself to an activity or idea. Her intelligence
was quick and she always seemed more adult than her years. She
soon achieved the same rank among the girls that Hans held among

the boys. Sophie was made a group leader and wore the appropriate decorations of that rank, the braid and the stars. Sophie Scholl was, like her brother, an ornament of Adolf Hitler's youth movement. Participation in the *BDM* was, for her, a way of joining her comrades in what was officially called "the rejection of an outmoded past and the shaping of something new."

They were young and they were not alone in failing to read the signs of their times. They were not alone in failing to see that they, and their nation with them, were being manipulated for monstrous ends. Many who were older and presumably wiser would never see it. But there were some signs and symptoms that were read aright even by the young and even that early. One night a group of *BDM* girls, of which Sophie and her sister Inge were a part, was stretched out in sleeping bags under the stars after a day-long bicycle tour. They were pleasantly tired and the talk was of what a day it had been and how splendid it was to be together on such agreeable excursions. In a pause one of the group, a fifteen-year-old girl, said with no apparent relevance: "It would all be so lovely if it weren't for that business with the Jews. I can't seem to swallow that . . ." There was an awkward silence until the adult leader of the group spoke up to assure everyone that the *Führer* certainly knew what was best for Germany and it was wisest to overlook disagreeable details and concentrate on the big picture. It was not an answer that satisfied Sophie. She herself had raised the same question more than once.

When she first joined her *BDM* group at the age of twelve— "with girlish enthusiasm," as she said—something bothered her almost at once. She had a good friend named Luise N. who was not allowed to join because she was Jewish. This seemed absurd to Sophie, and she said so. If one were going to be logical, she pointed out, Luise was the one who ought to be accepted. Luise was blonde and had blue eyes, which were the accepted signs of the racially superior Aryan, whereas Sophie was both dark-haired and dark-eyed. It made no sense to Sophie.

Her habit of seeing clearly and speaking frankly was rather surprising in a winsome young girl, especially in a society where conformity and submission were expected of everyone and the young

most of all. She once upset her school teacher by insisting that whoever did not know Heinrich Heine did not know German literature.
This was an obvious truth but not many were daring to express it at a
time when the incomparable lyrics of the Jew Heine were officially
declared both forbidden and nonexistent. But Sophie had read
Heine's enchanting *Buch der Lieder* (*Book of Songs*) whose pages
glitter with some of the loveliest and lightest lines ever composed in
the German language. It seemed an absurdity of a piece with barring
Luise from the *BDM* to contend that a great poet was not a great
poet because he belonged to the wrong race.

Teachers hardly knew what to make of Sophie Scholl. One of
them, taken aback by the airy and offhand way in which she voiced
her often startling opinions, called her *frivol*. Sophie asked at home
what the word meant and was told that it referred to people who
were frivolous and flippant. It was an odd word to apply to Sophie
who struck others as being thoughtful and knowing beyond her
years. A long-standing family joke was that Robert Scholl once
said, only half joking, "She is the wisest of my women." But Fräu-
lein Kretchmer was not the first teacher to misread the character of
a pupil and Sophie's was less easy to fathom than most.

Part of the appeal of the *BDM* was that it offered a variety of activities in which girls could participate on their own, giving them a
feeling of independence and self-reliance which few of them had
ever experienced before. Sophie responded to this. She had an early
and instinctive bent toward what is now called feminism, reserving
whatever awe she had for the male sex for her brother Hans whom
she not only loved but adored. Like Hans, she felt at first that the
youth movement was going to provide new outlets for her energies
and offer her possibilities as a person. It would not merely tuck her
away in the conventional niche reserved for German girls in previous generations and forget her. The youth movement told her she
mattered.

Her zest gradually diminished as it became more and more clear
that the *BDM*, like all other National Socialist programs, was designed for conformity rather than liberation. The three K's which
traditionally marked off the boundaries for the German female—
Kinder, Küche, Kirche, children, kitchen, and church—would re-

main fully in force under the Nazis despite the exertions of the Ideological Training Division to persuade everyone that a new day had dawned.

The shoulder-to-shoulder marching, the continual sloganeering that emphasized the group rather than the individual, came to have a suffocating effect on Sophie, who always had a sure sense of herself which she never wholly lost even when the marching, singing, and saluting were at their height. The constant pressure to give herself over to organized activity became less and less tolerable. "How can one find oneself," she onced asked her diary, "if one is forever under the compulsion to pay attention to other people?"

That was hardly the attitude expected of a group leader of the *BDM*. It ran counter to the National Socialist insistence on unquestioning conformity in every branch and phase of German society. But Sophie Scholl's temperament was too independent to be confined for long in an ideological straitjacket. Her alienation from the League of German Girls and everything it stood for was inevitable.

Adolf Hitler's movement had a passion, a madness, for flags. Tens of thousands of them—"a sea of flags"—rippled over the vast Zeppelin Field at Nuremberg when the annual Party Day rally was held there in 1936. In the speech that brought the rally to its climax, the *Führer* paid special tribute to those who were carrying the flag of National Socialism in the immense throng that roared itself raw in the throat at every sentence he uttered. "I salute you, my banner carriers," said Adolf Hitler, and he called them "the hope of the present and the guarantors of our future." They were, he said, "the standard bearers of a new history." One of the standard bearers at the rally was Hans Scholl.

Hans was holding the flag of the Hitler Youth contingent from Ulm. It was a great honor, but he had been the obvious choice because he was the most ardent, and the handsomest, boy in his unit. For Hans—for any member of the Hitler Youth—the trip to Nuremberg on a special train bedecked with bunting and gay with flags was a tonic experience. He had never been so far from home before or involved in such a stirring event. The town of Nuremberg, when he got there, was a breathtaking turmoil of Nazi uniforms, beery revelers, and blaring bands which rattled the windows of gabled houses and almost raised the red-tiled roofs. On the street the hawkers were selling picture postcards showing portraits of Frederick the Great, Bismarck, and Hitler. On the cards was the legend: *"What the King conquered, the Field Marshal defended, the Soldier saved and unified."* Here in Nuremberg Hitler was not only on a level with Frederick the Great and Bismarck but pictured as their culmination.

Once a year, in September, the National Socialists took over the sedate medieval town and turned it in a combination of jamboree and shrine. Some 200,000 Brown Shirts of all ages and ranks poured into Nuremberg, on the seven railroads that converged there, to celebrate another glorious year in the reign of Adolf Hitler and to pledge their allegiance to him anew. A miracle of planning and logistics was needed to get them all there, and to house and feed and manage them when they got there, but the Party considered the results well worth the effort and expense. The profit in propaganda was huge, and besides, it provided the transportation system with an annual rehearsal for its future function in the movement of troops.

Nuremberg's seven railroads were decisive in the city's being chosen for the annual Party Day, but there were other reasons as well. The place was steeped in German history and tradition. Nuremberg was the home of the immortal cobbler Hans Sachs and of the *Meistersinger*. Albrecht Dürer was born there and his frescoes decorated the 17-century town hall. It was quaintly famous for its toys and gingerbread and for the invention of pocket watches, which were once known as Nuremberg eggs. In a way rather less quaint, Nuremberg was famous as the bailiwick of Julius Streicher, the *Gauleiter*, or district leader of Franconia, who was one of Hitler's earliest and most rabid supports. He was also a ravening anti-Semite, and a notorious pornographer whose newspaper, *Der Stürmer*, touched depths of obscenity that sometimes offended even his fellow Nazis. Hitler never missed an issue.

Second only to Munich as a mecca of National Socialism, Nuremberg provided a suitable backdrop for the parade of Nazi brawn staged every year to intoxicate Germans with pride in their own resurgence and to impress the world. No one could mistake the menace inherent in the robot-like procession of one brown phalanx after the other through the twisting streets of the town and in the massed formations on the Zeppelin Field. At night, in the blaze of searchlights, the Storm Troops were marshaled in patterns that no ballet or opera could surpass for theatrical effect and emotional impact. The triumphs of the Caesars of imperial Rome, the martial splendors of Napoleon, the ostentation of Red Army Day in Moscow were mere charades compared to the scope and flamboyance of the shows put on every year by the Nazis in Nuremberg.

Hans Scholl and his young comrades were caught up in this week-long frenzy of national self-celebration and unbridled chauvinism. They lived in a tent colony of their own, consisting of acres of spotless white canvas arranged in rows with T-square precision, as everything at the rally was. Hans and his friends got up, ate breakfast, exercised, sang, marched, skylarked, and went to bed in unison on rigid schedule. All day long martial music beat against their ears—the *Horst Wessel Lied*, the marching song of the Storm Troopers; the *Badenweiler*, favorite march of Adolf Hitler; and over and over the national anthem, *Deutschland Über Alles*. The bellow of "*Heil!*" was incessant—"*Heil Hitler! Sieg Heil!*"—and everywhere arms were being automatically raised and lowered in the Nazi salute like semaphores gone mad. Hour after hour Hans was either marching or standing by to watch others march. A kind of contagious delirium was generated in which personal identity was absorbed into the sheer mass of brown humanity that pressed in on all sides without remission.

Holding his banner high, Hans Scholl marched into the arena to the sound of fanfares. He was one of the elect, part of the vanguard of 50,000 young Nazis singing their song of the future:

> *We are not citizens, farmers, workers.*
> *Strike down the barriers, Comrades!*
> *Before us all waves one flag only—*
> *The flag of the young soldiers!*

The rally crested on its last night with a speech to the massed battalions by the *Führer*, Adolf Hitler himself, an awesome event whose grandeur was accentuated by every device of ritual and stage-craft that the Ministry of Propaganda could conceive. The ceremonies and staging tended to dwarf the central figure, who was not physically impressive. Adolf Hitler was only five feet nine inches tall and weighed about 150 pounds. His skin was pale and he was rather shapeless. His smudge of a mustache, hardly wider than the breadth of his nostrils, made him look to irreverent foreigners like Charlie Chaplin. An unseemly forelock kept falling over his forehead and he had a tendency to sweat.

But he was history's greatest demagogue and could dominate a mass audience like no other orator. To millions of Germans he was *der schöne Adolf*, handsome Adolf, and women sometimes swooned in his presence and females listening to his speeches often went pale and gasped as if in the throes of orgasm. His voice was harsh and oracular and, for millions of Germans, had a hypnotic effect that was impossible to analyze when he was alive and has not been explained since. What he said with it was openly, nakedly, barbarous. This only seemed to inflame rather than repel his audiences in the most technically advanced nation in Europe. "Only force rules," he said. "Force is the first law." And: "Conscience is a Jewish invention. It is a blemish, like circumcision." And: "In eternal peace mankind perishes."

On this occasion Hitler's speech was untypically mild. His cause was prospering and he could afford to bask in his unbroken string of successes. In only four years of power he had all but nullified Germany's defeat in the 1914–1918 war. The Saar, with its immensely rich mining area, had been recovered for Germany. He had introduced compulsory military training and thereby made a scrap of paper of the Versailles Treaty. Two recent coups further added to his stature as leader at home and a figure to be reckoned with abroad. First, he had with impunity defied both the French and English by sending his troops into the demilitarized Rhineland. Second, in the last national elections his candidates had won ninety percent of the votes. It was no wonder, then, that roars of adulation shook the stadium when he appeared on the podium to begin his annual address to the Party faithful.

Aside from an ugly threat to any who might be foolish enough to attempt to overthrow the regime, the speech was a rather sentimental discourse on how far he and the movement had come together, *"You once heard the voice of a man and it struck your hearts, it awoke you, and you followed that voice . . ."* For Hitler it was a brief speech and it culminated with yet another salute to youth— German youth, Hitler youth. Hans Scholl and his comrades stiffened to even more rigid attention when, in the midst of that vast assemblage, the *Führer* directed his most moving passage to them. *"I greet especially the young who are drawn up before me here in parade formation,"* said Hitler. *"Let them become men like the men they see before them. Fight the way those men have fought! Be upright and determined, fear no one , always do what is right and always do your duty. Then the Lord God will never forsake our people. Heil Deutschland!"*

At this, as a newspaper reported the next day, "a tremendous wave of exultation swept over the nocturnal field," and the 1936 Reich Party Day was over.

There was every reason for Hans Scholl to return from Nuremberg with his enthusiasm for the Hitler Youth heightened and intensified. The gigantic spectacle of which he had been a part was geared to its last detail to create a renewed fanaticism for the National Socialist cause. At its very peak the *Führer* had singled out Hans' contingent and charged it with the high mission of being the hope of Germany's present and the guarantor of her future. Those chosen to carry the Party's flag had special responsibility and special honor, the *Führer* had said, and Hans Scholl was holding one of those flags. Adolf Hitler might well have been talking directly to him. He should have gone back to Ulm aglow and exhilarated.

He did not.

Afterward, Inge Scholl remembered how surprised and puzzled she was at her brother's appearance when he returned from Nuremberg. He had gone off to the rally joyously, and he came back morose and moody. Neither Inge nor Sophie, nor his parents, pressed him, but they all sensed that something had gone wrong. Normally open and outgoing, Hans was capable of withdrawing abruptly into himself and shielding his thoughts from exposure until he had sorted them out. Nuremberg had become a turning point for him, but he was not yet ready to acknowledge its full implication for his future. In chats with his sisters Inge and Sophie, he let them know little by little what was bothering him.

He had looked forward to an experience that would be stimulating and broadening, with new vistas opening for him and rewarding new friendships begun. Instead of stimulus and excitement there had been only drill and routine. Instead of bracing new contacts and vistas there had been only stereotypes. His mates in the tent colony had been embryo Storm Troopers and the adults at the rally were full-blown Party fanatics to a man. The talk had had the sameness of the uniform. The blustering clichés had been repeated with suffocating monotony—the greatness of the *Führer*, the marvel of Germany's revival, the virtues of the *Volk*, the German race, and the perfidy of the Jews. It was a glut of shibboleths and catchphrases which soon bored and irritated him and which eventually would so offend and disgust him that one of his leaflets would charge the Nazis with *"choking the German people in a fog of empty phrases."* At Nuremberg, Hitler himself had commanded him and his comrades to model themselves on the men they saw around them at the rally, the stalwarts of the Party. Something in Hans Scholl cringed at the prospect of living his life according to the Storm Troopers' credo which, in Hitler's words, demanded "blind obedience and absolute discipline." It was a repellent notion to anyone bred in the tradition of Götz von Berlichingen.

Hans was for a time guarded and evasive about his disappointment with the rally, but his sisters surmised the doubts and misgivings that were at the root of his moodiness. "After Nuremberg," Inge observed, "there were powerful rumblings stirring inside our brother Hans." A lingering sense of loyalty to the movement he had joined, and the pull of the commitment he had made to it, postponed his final break with the Hitler Youth and its principles. He was also obligated by the fact that a unit of the *Jungvolk*, which included boys from ten to fourteen, had been put in his charge. In the end, this only served to deepen his disillusionment.

To make his *Jungvolk* (Young Folk) unit feel special and distinctive, Hans proposed that they make a flag of their own to supplement the usual swastika banners that all the other units carried. He helped the boys with the design which featured a mythological beast gloriously rampant at the center. The boys themselves sewed the flag together and mounted it on a staff. In a solemn ceremony it was dedicated to the *Führer*, and each of the boys in turn pledged his loyalty to it. The homemade banner made a brave display when carried in the van of the little troop, and the boys were inordinately proud of it.

One evening they were lined up smartly on the field they used as a parade ground, awaiting the arrival of a senior Hitler Youth leader who was to inspect them. The banner with the strange device was snapping overhead in the breeze, and it immediately caught the attention of the visiting leader. He regarded it coldly for a long moment.

"What's that?" he asked.

"Our Troop banner," Hans replied.

"Give it here," the leader said to the boy who was carrying it.

The boy, an eager twelve-year-old, was rattled by the unexpected demand and the preremptory tone of it. He stared straight ahead and gripped the staff more tightly, his knuckles showing white.

"Hand it over," said the leader, more sharply this time. "You people have no right to a flag of your own. You are to keep strictly to the flags prescribed in the manuals."

A ripple of protest went through the ranks of the little troop, and the flag-bearer tensed. Hans, standing by, was indignant. Couldn't the man see what the banner meant to these boys? To them it was not just another flag but their own special symbol. They had pledged their fealty to it.

As the leader made a motion to reach out and wrest the flag away, the boy holding it wavered and looked to Hans for help.

Hans stepped between the boy and the leader, pushing him back. "Let the boy keep the flag," he said. "Stop bullying him." There was a scuffle and Hans struck the leader a blow on the ear. It was an unheard-of act of insubordination.

Hans Scholl's days as a troop leader in the Hitler Youth were over.

The incident of the flag, added to the impact of Nuremberg, accelerated the shift in Hans' attitude toward National Socialism and the world it was creating around him. Changes were taking place in him which, though gradual at first, were irreversible. From now on, each new experience would only confirm him in his scepticism of what he had previously held to be true. Events would, one after the other, lead him to conclusion at the opposite pole from where he started. What was happening to him was also happening to his brothers and sisters, but there was something in his temperament that made the change in emotional climate more drastic for him. Once he found his direction he was not going to turn back or stop halfway.

One day in the summer of 1937 Hans Scholl and his sister Inge made an excursion to Munich to visit the newly opened House of German Art which Hitler himself had helped design and in which a selection of paintings approved by him were on display. It was not unusual for any of the Scholl children to be visiting an art museum. Culture was taken seriously in the family. Books were regularly consumed, passed around, and discussed. Sophie liked to draw and had a gift for it. Elizabeth was musical and played the piano. Inge, always sensitive and observant, could write. Werner loved to read and collected books. Music and song, often supplied by Hans and his guitar, were part of the daily round in the household.

He and Inge were more stunned than impressed by their first look at the House of German Art which was a showpiece of the new Nazi architecture. The museum was brutally stark and severe, a heavy mixture of ultra-modern and semiclassical. Across its façade was spread a clutter of square columns which gave the impression that matters had somehow gotten out of hand and too many had been put up before a halt was called. The wits of the town promptly labeled the building ''Palazzo Kitschi'' and ''the Munich Art Terminal.''

Inside Hans and Inge found some 900 examples—paintings sculptures, drawings—of what Adolf Hitler, a failed artist himself, regarded as art. He had expressed his ideas on the subject in a speech at the opening of the exhibition—a raging denunciation of modern art and all its practitioners. There was something almost maniacal in his vituperation of ''this clique of babblers, dilettantes, daubers and betrayers of art who,'' he promised, ''would be rooted out and destroyed" in the new Germany. "With the opening of this exhibition," he said, "has come the end of artistic lunacy and the artistic pollution of our people."

The pictures themselves had been selected by Professor Adolf Ziegler, the President of the Reich Chamber of Visual Arts. He was a painter himself, a specialist in nudes which he painted in such detail that he was dubbed the "Master of the Pubic Hair." Reflecting the taste of the *Führer* throughout, the pictures were mostly cartoon-heroic and calendar-realistic—sturdy peasants on their farms, idealized German girls braiding their hair, Teutonic females giving breast to their young, and muscular Storm Troopers. The level of the exhibition could be gauged from a statement by one of the judges, a Count Baudissin, who said: "The most perfect shape, the subtlest image, that has recently been created in Germany has not come from any artist's studio. It is the steel helmet."

Hans and Inge were bored and depressed as they trudged from one uninspired and uninspiring painting to the next. They were also bewildered. Where were the pictures that had made Munich famous as a center of innovative art and attracted painters from all over Europe—Vassily Kandinsky and Paul Klee, for instance? Where were the great German contemporaries—Kokoschka and Dix and Kollwitz and Beckmann? Hans had early discovered, and responded to, the outré imagery of the Expressionists, especially Franz Marc of the Blue Rider school which originated in Munich. Blue riders and red horses seemed to Hans thrilling eruptions of the human imagination by which a new kind of beauty was brought into the world. As such he applauded them without reservation. His enthusiasm for the Expressionists was of a piece with his relish for anything that stirred and expanded his mind.

For Inge, too, the exhibit was stale, flat, and unprofitable. She was an admirer of the work of Walter Gropius, the modernist architect, and of the functional beauty of the designs of his *Bauhaus*, now banished from Germany. To her the House of German Art and what it contained were an offense to eye and spirit; one day she herself would work in the *Bauhaus* mode.

But, as Inge and Hans discovered, the Nazis had not entirely ignored the modernists and their art. There was another exhibition running in Munich which they also visited. It was conceived by Dr. Joseph Goebbels and staged by the Ministry of Public Enlightenment and Propaganda. This was a collection of what was called "Degenerate Art" and it was intended to create revulsion and contempt in the public. Here the paintings of the modernists were hung with captions like "Thus Did Sick Minds View Nature" and "Peasants Looked At In The Yiddish Manner." Drawings from an insane asylum were hung to show that they differed little from the surrounding works. All the great names of contemporary German painting were exhibited in the "Degenerate Art" show, but on Hans and Inge the paintings had the opposite effect of the one intended by the Propaganda Ministry. The pictures here were far more stimulating and had infinitely more to say than the sanctioned display at the House of German Art. Hans and Inge studied them for hours and left reluctantly. They were not alone in their reactions. The "Degenerate Art" attracted far more viewers than its reactionary rival. The exhibit had to be withdrawn as one of Dr. Goebbels' more embarrassing blunders.

But the policy that inspired the show persisted. In the Third Reich of Adolf Hitler any artist, however gifted, could be put under *Malverbot* for "political unreliability." That meant that he was no longer allowed to paint. He could also be put under *Ausstellungsverbot*, which meant that his paintings could no longer be exhibited. Artists who declined to paint sturdy peasants and muscular Storm Troopers were leaving Germany one by one: Klee to Switzerland, Kandinsky to Paris, Kokoschka to England, Georg Grosz to America. The word *Verbot* was taking on increasing significance for more and more Germans in every phase of intellectual life. It was not necessary to be an artist or sculptor or writer to feel the weight of it. No one of inquiring mind or active intelligence could escape its impact.

Hans Scholl could not.

His favorite book as a boy was not a boy's book but a collection of article-essays by Stefan Zweig called *Sternstunden der Menschheit*, a title that loses something in English—"Stellar Hours of Mankind." In it Zweig described a variety of crucial moments from which some enduring significance for coming generations flowed. The scheme gave Zweig great freedom of selection and his choices ranged from the discovery of the Pacific to the moment when Georg Friedrich Handel sat down to write the *Messiah,* from Napoleon at Waterloo to the laying of the Atlantic cable. Common to all the pieces was Zweig's vigorous prose and his gift for imparting a sense of actuality, of drama, to each of his episodes. The book can be taken as an early example of what much later was to be called the "new journalism" in that it blends fact with color and interpretation in a way that impinges on fiction. Even with his sometimes dubious embellishments, Zweig evokes his chosen moments convincingly and often thrillingly. The book had great success and is still in print.

Hans Scholl read *Sternstunden* over and over. Every chapter opened another vista, another view of life's possibilities beyond his own immediate place and time. Here were men functioning at the top of their bent and making their passage through life grand and memorable. They showed what the human spirit was capable of in a lifetime or in a moment.

Like the homemade troop flag, the book caused an incident that soured Hans further on the regimentation that the Hitler Youth insisted on imposing on its members. During a pause in one of the exercises, he was sitting on the ground absorbed in a favorite passage in *Sternstunden* when a group leader approached and asked what he was reading. Hans handed him the book.

The leader scowled as he read the title page and leafed through the book. Slamming it shut, he said: "You are forbidden to read this stuff."

Hans was taken aback.

"Why?" he asked. It was the first time he had been rebuked for reading a book.

"Look who wrote it," said the leader, pointing to the name of the cover. "A Jew. He's on the list. There is a *Verbot* on Stefan Zweig and all his works. Don't let me catch you reading him again."

It was a new and disturbing development for Hans. A flag might be forbidden, perhaps, for the sake of uniformity within an organization. One might come to accept that. But a *book*? What did that have to do with the organization? And a book by the great Stefan Zweig at that!

He had heard dimly of the book-burnings which had occurred

years ago, shortly after Hitler came to power, but that had merely
seemed to be some sort of political demonstration to which not
much attention was paid outside of Nazi circles. Now he learned
that not only was *Sternstunden* on the Nazi list of forbidden literature but so was all the rest of Zweig's work—the great biographies
of Erasmus and Tolstoi, the brilliant essays and commentaries. The
man himself had fled to London, beginning an exile that would end
only with his suicide. When Hans inquired how this could happen to
a man whose books had been translated into thirty languages on five
continents, he was told: Zweig was a Jew, a pacifist, and a demo-
crat. In the National Socialist state the Jewishness was reason
enough by itself. The other two blemishes only compounded the
crime. For Hans the scorning and suppression of his favorite book
was one of those experiences that take root in the mind of the young
and bear their fruit later in unforeseen ways.

If the flag and the book were incidents which involved the boy
Hans Scholl directly, tampering with his beliefs and wounding his
sense of what was reasonable and right, there were now innumerable pressures and compulsions which were distorting everyday life
for everybody under the New Order that had come to Germany.

"Bit by bit the world we wanted to believe in began to crumble,"
said Inge Scholl afterwards, remembering. "What were they making of our Fatherland? Not a place where a new and happy life could
flourish for everyone, as they had promised. No, instead they imposed one clamp after the other on our country until, gradually, all
of us were sitting in a huge jail cell, prisoners."

The "German look," the furtive over-the-shoulder glance to see
if anyone was watching, became universal and with reason. Somebody always *was* watching. In the town of Ulm now, as in every
other German town and city, an agent of the Nazi Party was stationed on every block, in every apartment house, wherever people
lived in numbers. The *Blockwart* was the lowest functionary in the
system, but he was the one who was in direct contact with the people. He was a licensed snoop charged with keeping watch on his
neighbors and reporting any breach in the social discipline which
the state was imposing on the people. The warden noted any failure
to put out the swastika flag on gala occasions. He checked on how

much each individual contributed to the latest Party collection and how willingly, or reluctantly, the contribution was made. He was ever alert to detect suspicious actions by anyone within his bailiwick and to record any careless talk he might chance to overhear. Everything was regularly reported to the nearest Party headquarters for punitive action.

The *Blockwarte* were usually insignificant on the social scale—gardeners, janitors, handymen—but they were everywhere, and collectively their power was formidable. Unfavorable reports from a street warden could wreck a career or cost a life because above and behind the wardens loomed the Secret State Police. To the Gestapo every citizen was automatically suspect and the omnipresence of its 40,000 agents shadowed every phase of German life on all levels. It was not necessary to commit an overt act of defiance or subversion to risk arrest and imprisonment. An ordinance called the "Treachery Law" made the mere expression of repugnance for the regime, or discussing it critically with others, a punishable offense, a crime that could result in imprisonment, torture, or even death. The rule of law that had prevailed for centuries in every civilized country of the western world had been negated in Germany and replaced by an ideology that was summed up in two sayings of its principal exponent, Adolf Hitler: "We must put a stop to the idea that it is part of everybody's civil rights to say, write, publish, or paint whatever he pleases"; and "Everyone must know that if he raises his hand to strike at the State, then certain death will be his lot."

As the clamps came down and were locked into place, one by one, the Germans for the most part held still and let it happen. Every fourth adult was a paid-up member of the National Socialist German Workers Party, the NSDAP. Most of them subscribed enthusiastically to the opening assertion of the Party manual: *"Der Führer hat immer recht"* —"The Leader is always right." But among the 66 million inhabitants of the Third Reich there were some who did not hold party cards and who thought that the Leader was frequently wrong and sometimes appallingly wrong. Millions of old-time liberals and former Social Democrats, the decent conservatives, and the sincere Christians were all too painfully aware of what was happening in their country, but went their daily round as before and did nothing. The American correspondent William Shirer mingled with them, talked to them, questioned them, and wondered about them. "What could they do?" he wrote. "They would put the question to you, and it was not an easy question to answer." Not with a network of informers watching and listening and the Gestapo looming in the background everywhere.

In the big house on the cathedral square in Ulm the doubts and disillusion that Hans Scholl brought back from Nuremberg had spread to his brothers and sisters. The marching and singing and saluting had abated. Except for the minor collisions with the system in which Hans had been involved, the Scholls had not suffered materially from the new measures imposed by the regime. For them there was no difficulty with the *Ahnenpass*. This was the certificate of ancestry which every German had to obtain to prove that there were no Jews among his forebears going back to all grandparents on both sides. Under the Nuremberg Racial Laws anyone lacking such proof was branded an outcast from society, stripped of his social and economic rights, and threatened with being deported to a prison camp at any time. But as certified Aryans no such menace hung over the Scholls. The family could have drifted through the Hitler era wrapped in the protective anonymity of countless other German families where even the most exteme measures of the regime were accepted with equanimity, indifference, or outright applause. But inbred in the Scholls, parents and children alike, was a rugged decency, an unwavering fealty to the tested values of the past, and this did not permit indifference to what was happening in the world around them.

What was happening changed their own immediate world and their relationship with each other. The breach between Robert Scholl and his children closed as they came to see for themselves what had been clear to him from the start. Even amid the din of official propaganda about the glories of the New Order, whispers and rumors constantly filtered through to confirm Robert Scholl's forecast of the corruption that the Nazis would inflict on German society. A popular young teacher they all knew disappeared; no one could say where or why. It was said that he was hauled up before a squad of Storm Troopers who paraded past him, each one spitting in his face on command in passing. When his mother was asked what offense he had committed, she cried, "Nothing! Nothing at all! He refused to become a Nazi. He wouldn't conform. He couldn't bring himself to go along with them. That was his crime."

The rumor was that the young teacher had vanished into a "KZ," two initials which were coming into increasing use and which were usually spoken in whispers. They were an abbreviation of the German word for concentration camp, and before long their significance would become all too clear. The first of the camps was established not very far from where the Scholls were living, at a place called Dachau, only 15 miles from Munich. This had been a pleasant market town until the Nazis made it the prototype for all the camps that came afterwards—Buchenwald, Sachsenhausen, Auschwitz, and the others. Dachau, as a historian would later write, was the "godfather of the system, with the curse of eternity upon its creation."

When the Scholl children asked their father what the camps were there for and what went on in them, he did his best to explain though not much was known about them at first by anyone. "They are a crime against the people," Robert Scholl told his children as they strolled together on an evening along the Danube. "They are part of the war that the regime is already waging—inside Germany and against its own people." In the camps, he said, were political enemies of the system, Socialists and Communists, union leaders, pacifists, some dissident clergymen and priests, but mostly Jews. They were all penned behind barbed wire like cattle and guarded by SS men who wore the death's head insignia on their helmets.

The children were appalled.

"Does the *Führer* know about the concentration camps?" they asked. In retrospect it seems an absurdly naïve question but it was one many Germans were asking. Some of them kept asking it to the end.

"How could he not know?" Robert Scholl answered. "They could not have been built without his consent. His closest associates run them. Hitler could abolish them any time he wished, but they continue, and there will be more of them." Though Robert Scholl could not know it, Adolf Hitler in private conversation had left no doubt about why the KZs were established. "People will think twice before opposing us when they hear what to expect in the camps,'' he said, and he had added: ''Terror is the most effective political instrument.''

The evening walks and talks together reconciled Hans Scholl with his father. The warmth that had existed between them before their quarrel was restored. The whole family was drawn closer together, and if the house had seemed an island before, it now took on something of the air of a rampart. The Scholls, all of them, felt themselves to be on the defensive against the encroachments of the society around them. The house on Cathedral Square became an enclave, a haven, in what increasingly seemed like hostile territory. ''All of us,'' said Inge Scholl, ''felt that we had to stand together to shield what we believed in and cherished. What began among us as doubts and misgivings about the Nazis had turned into indignation and outrage.''

But they were young, and life was not all indignation and outrage. None of them was inclined to sit indoors and fume while the summer sun was shining on the river or when the nearby hills glistened with cover that invited sled and ski. The Nazis had not abolished school, and there were classes to attend, lessons to learn, and examinations to pass. There was enough normal childhood activity to make growing up in Ulm a happy experience for the Scholl children. They all had their own friends and playmates, read their own books, and met the new day with the zest of the healthy young. In the early years of the Hitler regime there was little that was furtive or conspiratorial about the Scholl family.

In the evening, at the dinner table, political events were often discussed, with Robert Scholl clarifying for his children what the newspapers and radio concealed or distorted. He allowed his children full freedom of expression in these family forums. They could say whatever they wished and they all had opinions. This was far from customary practice in German households where, by long tradition, the authority of the father was seldom questioned or his statements challenged. Father Scholl's way was rare enough to be cited against him when, later, he fell afoul of the Gestapo and again when two of his children were put on trial for their lives. A Nazi Special Court would charge him with the politically intolerable defect of having a "liberal, cosmopolitan attitude." This was a surprising accusation to be brought against a man who had grown up as a peasant boy in a forest area where the possibilities of becoming either liberal or cosmopolitan were remote. Robert Scholl's intelligence and his avidity to learn had attracted the attention of the local pastor who saw to it that the boy could advance beyond his backwoods schooling and acquire a higher education. Robert Scholl's moral sturdiness was such that during the First World War, despite the patriotic frenzy and nationalist hysteria which only the rarest spirits could withstand, he refused combat duty and would serve only as a medic.

As World War II approached, his aversion to mindless nationalism was not only unchanged but stronger than before. In his dinner-table discussions with his children he could interpret events for them with an insight unblurred by current prejudices or official pronouncements.

At the end of a meal he would often get up and announce: "Now, if you'll excuse me, I'll go and earn a jail sentence." They all knew what he meant. He was going to listen to a forbidden radio station— Radio Strasbourg perhaps, or a Swiss broadcast where the news would be given with some semblance of accuracy and honesty. "Black" listening of this kind was a crime, and to prevent it the government issued receivers which were capable of bringing in Nazi broadcasts only. But these "people's sets" could be tinkered with to increase their range, and black listening was widespread. Robert Scholl earned himself many a jail sentence before the one that would actually be passed on him.

All of the children, but especially Hans and Sophie who would one day need it most, learned a quotation from their father which they never forgot. From time to time, when stress and aggravation threatened to become unbearable, Robert Scholl would mutter, *"Allen!"* The whole family knew what that meant. It was the first word of a Goethe saying that went: *"Allen Gewalten zum trotz, sich erhalten!"* In English it means, "Despite all the powers, maintain yourself!" The saying sank deep into Hans Scholl's consciousness and it was there to sustain him when, in the worst of circumstances, he needed to call on it to steady himself. It was, in fact, a more literate and elegant version of the Götz von Berlichingen phrase and could be used almost interchangeably with it, according to mood. Sophie too treasured the line and, like her father, could be heard uttering the single opening word *"Allen!"* under her breath or between her teeth in moments of trial or exasperation.

Until the war came, and until she made the commitment that led to Stadelheim, Sophie Scholl had little occasion to steel herself against adversity. She seldom encountered any. The winding and wooded valley of the Danube was always there to turn to when the world was too much for her. "We know where to go when things go badly," she once wrote to a friend, and she meant the mountains and fields. It amazed her, she said, to discover how a tiny flower "could fill one up so" that no room was left for any other thought or emotion. She could feel fresh, merry, and free—*frisch fröhlich frei*—on an overnight bicycle trip with her friend Lisa, and write a lively letter about it to another friend, Lisl. "It was glorious to be rolling along the highway in the April sunshine, and we seemed to ourselves to be a couple of gods who had blundered onto earth one fine day and found that they liked it there. The one thing that wasn't very godly about us was our behinds which weren't used to such a long bike ride . . ." They reached a little town called Untermarchtal and debated whether they should spend the night in the convent there but decided against it because they didn't much like nuns. Instead they pedaled on to Obermarchtal and found a charming old castle with an inn attached. There they ate fresh eggs and country sausages and, for an additional treat, had glasses of mulled wine while the regular customers of the place grinned at them hospitably. Then they climbed into their beds in the castle inn. "It was princely," Sophie reported.

The excursion to Obermarchtal was only one among many in Sophie's girlhood, and the chatty letter was only one way of expressing her joy in being at large in the open. To her diary she revealed a deeper and more poetic strain in her feeling for nature:

> *I could shout for joy that I am so alone with the wild rough wind drenching my body. I'd like to be on a raft, standing upright above the gray river whose hurrying water the wind cannot disturb. I'd like to stand there and shout that I am so gloriously alone.*

The wind tears the blue sky open, and the sun comes out and kisses me tenderly. I'd like to kiss it back, but I forget my wish immediately because now the wind has leaped upon me. I sense the wonderful firmness of my body. I laugh aloud for joy, because I am a resistance to the wind. I feel all strength within me.

The house on Cathedral Square, the atmosphere of it and the people who lived in it, attracted kindred souls for whom the place became a kind of retreat and anchorage. Nearby were the Hirzels, the family of the respected pastor of the Martin Luther Protestant Church. Young Hans Hirzel liked to visit the Scholl house to listen to Robert talk about what was going on in the world and to be around Hans Scholl whom he looked up to and admired. Quick to grasp the implications of what he heard, Hans Hirzel early felt the same rumblings of rebellion that had seized Hans Scholl. In his own way and own time, he came to the same conclusion: "Something has got to be done." It was a decision that one day would bring him, too, before the People's Court.

His sister Susanne, called "Suse," was blonde, pretty, and pert and learning to play the cello. She also spent much of her time in the house on Cathedral Square, being of Sophie's age and her good friend. But not all the visitors were from Ulm. Some came from farther away.

Ernst Reden came from Cologne. He was doing his compulsory military service and hating it. For him the Scholl house and the people in it were a grateful escape from drill and barracks. To the girls, especially Inge and Sophie, he was a romantic figure. Dark and rather saturnine, Ernst Reden carried himself with an air of brooding remoteness which only added to his appeal for young females. He made the Scholl girls think of Rainer Maria Rilke whom he resembled and who was then greatly in vogue with the intellectual young. Reden himself wrote and composed poetry. He could speak with flair and fire about contemporary books and writers that were new to Inge and Sophie, and they hung on his words. Between Reden and Inge, who was closest to him in age, a warm and intense relationship developed while Sophie, too, cherished him as one of the most stimulating men she had ever met.

Ernest Reden was a source of fresh ideas and impressions for Hans as well. Reden was the first to tell him of the sensational lecture given in the great hall of the University of Munich by the novelist and playwright Ernst Wiechert. The subject was "The Author and His Time" which had seemed academic and innocuous enough to the authorities. But in cool, measured language Wiechert had attacked the government's treatment of the arts, especially literature. He denounced the "authors' training camps" which the Propaganda Ministry had set up to groom writers for their role as exponents of National Socialist ideology. Wiechert called this manufacture of mass art by the government "murder of the soul." He branded it unworthy of the German literary tradition and fatal to the spiritual life of the nation. Without calling for outright revolt, Wiechert had made comments like: "Nothing so corrodes the marrow of a man and a people as cowardice." And he added: *"Youth must not be seduced into silence when conscience demands that it speak."*

Those were words which reverberated through the hall packed with college students. They echoed in the mind of Hans Scholl when they were repeated to him. The Wiechert lecture was copied down and circulated in secret in one university after the other. Early one morning three Gestapo agents in civilian clothes appeared at Ernst Wiechert's home and took him off, first to jail in Munich and then, chained to another prisoner, in a mass tranport to the KZ at Buchenwald.

Ernst Reden's distaste for drill and regimentation matched that of Hans Scholl. Together they organized a group of like-minded boys and attached themselves to a movement that called itself, in cryptic lower case, *d.j.1.11.* The *d.j.* stood for *Deutsche Jungenschaft* (Young Germans) and the *1.11* denoted that the organization was founded on the first day of the eleventh month. Lower-case letters were used because that was the way the *Bauhaus* did it, and the group wanted to seem modern and progressive. In spirit and style *d.j.1.11* was at the opposite pole from the Hitler Youth.

There was no marching and saluting, no drill. The idea was to allow for free play of personality and a wholesome enjoyment of sport and comradeship. On weekends the boys, ranging in age from twelve to seventeen, made expeditions into the woods or mountains, sometimes for exploration but usually for the joy of being active in the open. There were similar groups all over Germany with branches in most population centers and in smaller towns as well. They had their own kind of tent, called a *Kothe,* which was made of heavy black cloth and, like a wigwam, came to a point at the top which was open to allow the smoke of the fire inside to escape. The *Kothe* had been brought back from Lapland by the founder of *d.j.1.11,* a wanderer named Eberhard Köbel whom the Laplanders named "Tusk," their word for German. From his treks through Scandinavia, Tusk brought back the folk songs which became part of the repertory of every *d.j.* group. He also introduced the balalaika to supplement the guitar which was already standard in every gathering.

Hans Scholl was good on the guitar and had a voice that was both robust and pleasing, which made him a natural leader of the song sessions without which no meeting was complete. His repertory was long and varied and included Cossack songs and Balkan ballads, and he was always on the alert to add to it. One of the things that had turned him away from the Hitler Youth was its rule that only German folk songs were to be sung. The snarl of "Aren't our songs good enough for you?" was sure to cut off any rendition of a foreign ditty, however melodious or innocuous. With the *d.j.1.11* Hans could play and sing whatever he liked. That the government should want to interfere with the choice of a song had seemed both absurd and offensive. The lack of freedom to indulge their own tastes and follow their own bent was making the National Socialist system increasingly intolerable to him and his comrades.

The *d.j.* groups evolved a style of their own in which free-wheeling behavior and a touch of swagger were characteristic. They adopted touches of dress—a way of lacing a boot, a knot in a scarf—that made them recognizable to each other. They invented phrases and catchwords which they used among themselves but were meaningless to outsiders. They made a point of taking up foreign fads, like the banjo and American cowboy songs, knowing such antics to be frowned upon and provocative. Their style included the youthful tendency to deride and mock, and they dabbled dangerously in repeating forbidden jokes which could have gotten them jailed. "What is an Aryan?" one of them would ask the group, and the answer would come hooting back in unison. "Blond like Hitler!"—who was dark. "Tall like Goebbels!"—who was short. And "Slender like Goering!"—who was fat. They wrote poems and kept journals and passionately discussed life, God, and the mysteries of the female. They were fervent and eager and restless.

There was a long tradition among German youth of hiking and camping in groups and turning to nature as a way of escaping the banalities and boredom of middle-class life. Early in the century the *Wandervogel*—"Birds of Passage"—caught the imagination of young Germans who tramped in clusters over the countryside with books of poetry in their rucksacks and made a cult of nature. For them the campfire became a shrine and gathering around it a ritual. They composed and sang their own songs which were often exalted and hymnlike:

> *We reach to the heavens,*
> *Reach to the horizon,*
> *With our arms. . . .*
> *We dance joyfully, locking arms,*
> *All of us are one.*

The theme of communion with nature and the mystical oneness of the group answered some need in the psyche of many young Germans and it ran through the various movements that succeeded the *Wandervogel*. In all such alignments there were moral and transcendant components which, however callow or mistaken, set them apart from mere boy-scouting or college-fraternity fellowship. The Hitler Youth itself took over some of the ritual and mystique of its predecessors but hardened and coarsened everything for the set purpose of shaping the young in the image of the state. "In that period when the young people of Germany were more intensely involved in the life of their nation than at any other time," one Hitler Youth leader wrote afterwards, "they were forced into a mold which to a great extent destroyed the specific magic of adolescence." It was intolerable to Hans Scholl that the state should rob him and his comrades of that magic, and his activity in the *d.j.1.11* was another effort to fashion his life nearer to what he believed it ought to be and could be.

The *d.j.1.11*, too, had its deeper and more somber songs and purposes. For all its schoolboy strut and exuberance, it was in fact an underground group, virtually a secret society. The Hitler Youth had ceased to be a voluntary organization and had been made an obligatory stage in the growing up of every German girl and boy. As an apparatus of the government it no longer tolerated any rivals. The days of clubs like *d.j.1.11* were numbered. The Nazi scheme of things did not allow for the assembly of any group where opinions could be exchanged and ideas discussed without the supervision and guidance of the government. The system boasted, and believed, that it had anchored itself in history for 1,000 years, but it quivered with alarm at every hint of doubt and defection.

For the members of the *d.j.* the element of secrecy and defiance of authority had a pronounced appeal. But beyond the zest and excitement of belonging to a forbidden enterprise there was, for Hans Scholl and the more mature members of the group, a constant sense of clouds and thunderclaps to come. There was the awareness, never wholly quiescent, that a time of testing for all of them was in the offing, that sooner or later decisive choices would have to be faced. They would be involved in moral confrontations which their peers in more open societies would be spared. This was brought home to them in one of the verses they sometimes chanted in chorus:

The time is coming when you'll be needed.
See to it that you're prepared and ready.
And into the fire that threatens to go up in smoke
Cast yourself as the final log that keeps
the flame alive.

These were apocalyptic visions for growing boys who otherwise spent much of their time in sport and skylarking, who followed the careers of favorite movie stars and indulged in the normal capers with available girls. But they were German and they were trapped by history in a time and place where the normal ways of life, including the rites of passage, were being systematically warped and perverted by a system whose Leader could say: "Our training will breed a youth that will appal the world. An overpowering, domineering, fearless, terrible youth is what I want. There must be nothing soft or tender about them. In their eyes I want once more to see the gleam of the spendid and unbridled beast of prey." For Hans Scholl the idea of turning human beings into beasts of prey was barbarism. It warred with his every instinct and inclination. It was a concept he could never come to terms with; nor could he with the system that produced it.

But there was a life to be lived. There were things to be learned. There were girls.

Attending the upper school at Ulm, Hans Scholl was preparing for his *Abitur,* the examination that would qualify him for admission to a university. The *Abitur* was a more advanced version of the high school diploma and was a milestone in the life of every young German who aspired to a professional career. It was a caste mark signifying that the recipient was a permanent member of the white-collar community with the possibility of unlimited academic achievement open to him. Hans passed the examination without difficulty. The year was 1937, and on September 22 he celebrated his nineteenth birthday.

It was a comparatively calm year for the German people, devoid of the shocks of some of the preceding years and something of a breather before the more violent ones to come. The German air force, the *Luftwaffe,* which was not supposed to exist, was flexing its muscles by intervening on the side of the Franco insurgents in the Spanish Civil War. In April the *Luftwaffe* had bombed the town of Guernica, an event that would have been lost to memory in the thousands of bigger bombings to come except that Pablo Picasso made a terrifying painting of it. Not many understood the significance of Guernica as clearly as the artist did. It was an omen for those who could read it. The Second World War had begun, obliquely but surely.

Studying for his *Abitur* left little time for *d.j.1.11* activity, which he was outgrowing anyway, but Hans' interests were not entirely confined to his books. He was attractive to girls and one of them, the sister of a friend, spoke of "something unexplainable about his personality that makes him irresistible." Much could be explained simply by his looks. He was handsome in a way that bordered on the movie-actor style. His face could be thoughtful and intense or winning and warm by turns. His black hair was brushed back in a pompadour and when neatly combed it formed itself into a wave above a broad brow. The eyes lay deep and there was a permanent glow in them that testified to the alert and active mind behind them. Few who came into his orbit remained indifferent to him. Even the authorities who condemned him to death included in their formal indictment the observation that Hans Scholl's personality exerted a "strongly suggestive effect" on those around him.

The girls who came to the Scholl house to visit his sisters usually found themselves paying more attention to the brother. One of them was the same Lisa who was Sophie's companion on her overnight bicycle trips and her best friend. Lisa was ripe beyond her years and had a bubbling temperament and a merry way of talking. Hans had known her since she was a child but, in the immemorial way, made a sudden discovery of her during one vacation when she was fifteen and blooming into womanhood. Lisa was enchanted at being discovered but as time went on made a discovery of her own. It was one that others would share with her. For all of Hans' eagerness and openness in entering into new relationships with women there was always something held back, something kept in reserve. The same girl who called him irresistible also detected a strain of stubborn independence in him which would not wholly dissolve even in the warmest moments of affection. Lisa, as well, found to her grief that Hans insisted always on preserving a little distance, a part of himself that he kept to himself. Romantically, he made no unalterable commitments. Once, in a letter to another girl, he tried to explain the inner restiveness that would not allow him to put down emotional stakes too deeply anywhere.

"I love these transitional stages," he wrote. "It's the same feeling that makes being in a big railroad station so stimulating to me. I know a man who, so to speak, never takes off his overcoat no matter where he goes. He always remains a transient, a guest stopping for a moment, though he doesn't cloak himself in silence or try to make a mystery of it. You get the idea when talking to him that he might take his watch out of his pocket at the end of any sentence and say: 'Now it's time.' This man appeals to me strongly.''

Hans himself was in a transition stage.

In the normal course of events he would have been moving on from secondary school to university and choosing a profession for his future. But here, too, the new system decreed otherwise. Now every German, male or female, had to enter the National Labor Service at the age of nineteen and spend six months on a construction project or a farm. This was another device of National Socialism to keep the young under its supervision as long as possible, but the National Labor Service also served other purposes. The program removed thousands from the labor market, thus reducing the unemployment statistics, and kept idle youth off the streets where they might cause trouble. With shovels substituted for rifles, the usual Nazi drill and discipline prevailed in the labor service, which made it a form of military training as well. A more beneficent and enlightened aspect of the program was that it applied to everybody and so tended to break down social barriers, putting everyone on the same level and making manual labor a common denominator. The Nazi Party, having risen high from low beginnings, made a point of scorning class distictions and extolling the virtues of the common man as long as he conformed and behaved himself.

Hans Scholl was assigned to road building near a place called Göppingen which was located, agreeably for him, in the familiar Swabian countryside. The project was part of the *Autobahn* system, the network of auto roads across Germany which was one of Adolf Hitler's top-priority innovations because it was both eminently practical and a source of favorable propaganda for his regime. Working outdoors at a pick-and-shovel job was hardly cruel and inhuman punishment for a robust nineteen-year-old like Hans Scholl, but the labor service was yet another measure by which the state was controlling his life and another limitation on his range of choices as to how his days should be spent. At the end of his term as a highway laborer the prospect was not a resumption of his private life but further regimentation. After the labor service came the army.

Two years before, in 1935, Adolf Hitler had reinstated compulso-

ry military training and thereby "swept away the last remaining rags
of illusion from the naked truth of German rearmament," as a later
historian phrased it. The military restrictions imposed on Germany
after its defeat in the First World War were now totally expunged.
Under National Socialism the German armed forces—the *Wehrmacht*—increased fourteen times over in four years.

Hans Scholl had always loved horses and spent a good deal of his
time around them. He rode whenever he got the chance and made
himself into a more than competent horseman. His skill as a rider
offered a way of making army duty more palatable for him. There
were still mounted formations in the German armed forces, and
since by volunteering he could choose his branch of service, Hans
signed on for the cavalry. The unit he was assigned to was stationed
at a spa called Bad Cannstatt, another agreeable location hardly
more than 50 miles from Ulm. The routine was not especially trying; he enjoyed the horses; and he had reason to hope that his two
years of military training might turn out to be less of an ordeal than
he had anticipated. There was time to read books, and the army was
more indulgent about what was read in the ranks than the Hitler
Youth had been. He could choose what he wanted, and he read av-
idly. He also kept in touch with his former comrades of the *d.j.1.11,*
exchanged letters with them, and occasionally saw them.

This was a mistake. The Secret State Police, in one of its periodic
outbursts of paranoia, suddenly launched a sweeping operation
aimed at stamping out, root and branch, all club and group activity
which was not a part of the Hitler Youth program. All over Germany boys and young men—members, former members, and suspected members of illicit organizations—were collared without warrant
or warning and thrown into jail.

The recent cavalry recruit Hans Scholl was high on the list of suspects. They arrested him at his barracks and delivered him into a
cell at Gestapo headquarters in nearby Stuttgart. The shock of it was
numbing and inflicted an emotional wound which would never entirely heal. Nothing that had yet happened to him under the National
Socialist system had so grossly affronted his sense of his own worth
as a human being. A curious detail in the process of being imprisoned stuck in his mind and it recurred to him from time to time af-

terwards. On the door of his cell was a red sign with one word on it: *Jugendlich*—"Juvenile.'' It seemed especially demeaning for the state to classify a grown man in uniform as a juvenile while treating him like a criminal.

The Gestapo did not stop at the arrest of Hans Scholl. The house on Cathedral Square in Ulm was also invaded, and Sophie, Inge, and Werner were taken off to jail while their parents stood by, the father protesting and the mother holding back tears. Of the Scholl children only Elizabeth escaped the indignity and dread of being confined in a Gestapo cell. Sophie, who was then sixteen, was released almost immediately and allowed to go home the same day. She seemed too young and girlish to be a menace to the state; but in releasing her the Gestapo was letting slip a potential enemy with whom it would later have to reckon in a far more serious situation. There is no way of establishing the precise moment when Sophie Scholl decided to become an overt adversary of the National Socialist state. Her decision, when it came, doubtless resulted from an accretion of offenses, small and large, against her conception of what was right, moral, and decent. But now something decisive had happened. The state had laid its hands on her and her family and now there was no longer any possibility of reconciling herself to a system which had already begun to alienate her.

Inge and Werner were held for days and repeatedly interrogated. The Gestapo was probing for additional names and any evidence of any culpable activity among those known to be indifferent or hostile to the regime. Werner had in fact been a member of *d.j.1.11* with his older brother and was therefore suspect. Inge was arrested on the basis of guilt by association. Her closeness to Hans was known through the activities and interests they shared. The police assumed that her outlook was the same as his and in this they were right. But nothing concrete could be uncovered against either Inge or Werner, and they were both released when the Gestapo, after about a week, decided they had been sufficiently intimidated and that nothing was to be gained by further questioning.

Inge's close friend Ernst Reden did not fare as well. Basically unconcerned with politics and never an activist, Reden was held for more than six months, part of the time in the KZ at Welzheim. It was ironic, and an instance of how misguided and arbitrary the Gestapo could be, that the member of the group least motivated by hostility to the regime was dealt with most severely.

The Gestapo was thorough. It searched the homes of its suspects, including the Scholl house, and confiscated diaries, journals, poems, essays, folk song collections, and all other evidence of youth activity that was not Hitler Youth activity. This material was amassed in stacks and pulped before it could futher undermine the New Order. Nothing so disturbed the watchdogs of National Socialism as uncontrolled thought, uncurbed opinion, and unsanctioned emotion.

The questioning of Hans Scholl went on for weeks. The State Police sensed that in him they had a potentially dangerous adversary, but hard evidence against him was scant. What they were after was information that would lead to the arrest of more members of the *d.j.1.11* and other suspect organizations. Hans disclosed nothing of use to them. Between interrogations there were empty hours of boredom when he sat in his narrow, vaulted cell seething with resentment. To pass the time he spelled out the names of girls with bread crumbs. The name he spelled most often was "Lisa."

He might have been held in custody indefinitely if pressure had not been brought to bear for his release. Hans regularly attracted friends and supporters, usually without any conscious effort on his part. He had impressed the captain of his cavalry unit who considered him a valuable addition to the troop. The captain also regarded the Gestapo investigation as unwarranted political meddling in army affairs. The Gestapo, for its part, was not inclined to irritate the army unduly on what was not an issue of major consequence. The captain's intervention resulted in Hans' being released and returned to his unit with a warning. But from then on he would be subject to sharper surveillance than a citizen who had never come under Gestapo scrutiny would be. His mail could be censored. He had been jailed. He had a record.

The effect on Hans was to increase his contempt for the system and cause him to ponder what he could do about it. Action did not yet seem imperative. He did not think that a political arrangement so crude and primitive as National Socialism could last very long. That the Nazi regime was doomed to early collapse was a belief shared by thousands of Germans who still thought of Adolf Hitler as an alien upstart whose domination of their country was a temporary aberration of history. It was a belief also held by some foreign statesmen and many journalists. The story of Adolf Hitler, someone would say afterwards, was the story of how he was underestimated.

No one who has been arrested and jailed is ever quite the same person afterwards, and the Gestapo cell in Stuttgart left its mark on Hans Scholl. His resentment of the regime could no longer be classified as *Jugendlich*, juvenile. It had matured, hardened. His service in the cavalry isolated him to a degree from activities he would normally have participated in and it left him time to brood over what the state had done to him, to his brother and sisters, to his parents. It was not something that could be either forgiven or forgotten. But he rode his horses and did his drill and saluted his officers— the traditional army salute now, not the Nazi gesture—and he conducted himself in a way calculated to get him through the rest of his military service with the least possible difficulty. The Gestapo, however sharp its eye, would have nothing further to pin on him. Not yet.

But his sister Inge got a glimpse of what he was privately feeling when she opened one of his books and read what he had written on a flyleaf: *"Reisst uns das Herz aus dem Leibe—und ihr werdet euch tödlich daran verbrennen."*

"Tear our hearts from our bodies—and one day they will fatally burn you."

Three

In March of 1938 there was a new topic of discussion around the Scholl dinner table. Adolf Hitler had marched into Vienna and, to tumultuous applause, annexed Austria to the German Reich. The official word for the maneuver was *Anschluss,* which meant "union" and was intended to convey that two German-speaking nations who were neighbors had amicably decided to merge. A natural and plausible procedure.

The German armored columns had crossed the border unopposed. No shots were fired. It had been a bloodless operation, if one discounted the political murders that preceded it and the terror that followed it. Adolf Hitler had made his first conquest of territory beyond his own borders without warfare, thus registering another of those coups which made his countrymen acclaim him as the wonder man of contemporary statesmanship. For him personally it was the headiest of triumphs. He returned as a conqueror to the town of Linz, where he grew up, and was received with a wild jubilation intensified by local pride. The unregarded boy who had played cowboy-and-Indian on the streets of Linz—Hitler had devoured books on the American West by the German writer Karl May—was now the dominant statesman of Europe with all of Austria at his feet. In

Vienna the reception was even more turbulent. Crowds roared, church bells rang, and swastikas fluttered from every building, including the steeple of St. Stephen's Cathedral whose Archbishop-Cardinal greeted him with the sign of the cross. In this ancient capital, now wild with adulation, Adolf Hitler had once been a homeless drifter, a vagabond, an outcast. Now the place and the country attached to it were his. Little wonder that he often spoke of his career as "a miracle, an absolute miracle. . . . To posterity it will appear like a fairy tale."

The *Anschluss* surprised the world, but it had all been written down and published long before by Hitler himself. In his book *Mein Kampf (My Struggle)* the opening paragraph told of his determination to unite Austria with Germany; but like almost everything else in the book, that bold announcement had been ignored or dismissed as fantasy. Everything else he intended to do was also plainly set forth in the book. Had it been heeded, *Mein Kampf* might not have cost, as has been estimated, 125 lives for every word: 4,700 lives for every page; and 1 million lives for every chapter. Robert Scholl had read the book. Unlike many others, he understood it. So did Hans Scholl, one of whose leaflets would describe it as being written "in the worst German I ever read"—an opinion of its style held by most literate Germans.

Hitler's unimpeded success with the *Anschluss* confirmed him in his belief that destiny was with him and that his further undertakings, too, were fated to succeed. At one stroke, he had brought about a decisive shift in the continent's balance of power and immensely improved his strategic situation. His army was now on the threshold of the Balkans. He was positioned for aggression, and as he told an associate, "There is no solidarity in Europe. There is only submission." The road to conquest was open.

Robert Scholl understood the pattern that was unfolding and he explained it to his children for whom politics had become a matter of passionate concern. A letter arrived from Hans, written in his cavalry barracks at Bad Cannstatt and postmarked March 14, the day Hitler rode into Vienna. It was addressed to his parents and was passed around, and discussed, in the family circle. He was plainly disturbed by the turn of events. "We are certainly rattling the sabre at a great rate,'' he wrote. ''I don't understand people any more. When I hear that enthusiasm on the radio I feel like going outside to some wide, empty space where I can be entirely alone, away from everybody.'' Later, as political tensions mounted and Hitler's designs became clearer, he wrote about the talk of war that was rife in his outfit. ''Hardly anybody considers the idea: Why have a war at all? Most of them are blind or dumb, moved by a certain curiosity or a lust for adventure that makes them eager to begin marching. The idea of it is more and more hateful to me all the time.''

Sophie Scholl's rapport with her brother was such that she hardly needed his letters to know how he was feeling and how he would react to political events. She approved of his attitudes and shared them, but she was often uneasy about his frankness in expressing them. Friends who knew them both well often noted a cooler and more precise intelligence in Sophie than in her brother. Less fervent and impetuous than Hans, she sometimes tried to be a restraining influence on him. What she loved most about him was his gaiety, the liveliness of his mind, and the fire of his convictions. She did not want him to get into trouble, but if he did she would be at his side without thinking twice.

Sophie sometimes worried that her intense interest in what was going on in the world would make her seem unfeminine to others. She was corresponding with a young soldier of whom she was fond and it bothered her that he might think it ridiculous for a girl to concern herself with politics. ''Girls,'' she wrote him, ''should let their emotions govern their thinking . . . at least, that's the general opinion.'' Such misgivings were fleeting, however. She could not for long disguise the fact that she had an active mind nor suppress her inclination to use it.

She, too, aimed at making her *Abitur* and one day entering a university and establishing herself away from home as an independent personality. Meanwhile she attended the secondary school at Ulm where she did well in her studies while berating herself for not doing better. ''I work too little . . . I don't achieve what I should,'' she wrote in her diary. She scolded herself for daydreaming and vowed to stop it. Her moral sense was strong, but not overpowering, and her self-severity was offset by her habit of wearing a flower behind her ear and her love of laughter—"the salt and pepper of life," as she called it. Those who knew her little were sometimes put off by a reserve that was taken for conceit, an idea nobody who knew her well ever entertained. Sophie Scholl looked at the world testingly, inquiringly, but with no sense of superiority.

She took English at school and had a gift for it. She liked to sprinkle her letters with English expressions, and one of her favorite books was Thornton Wilder's *The Bridge of San Luis Rey,* a novel whose plot of the coming together of a group of people doomed to die together had a certain rough relevance to what was in store for her, her brother, and their friends. No such foreboding of personal disaster would have occurred to her, however, since there was nothing clouded or grim in her outlook on life. Her view of her own future included no hint of coming heroism or martyrdom. She once told her sister Inge with great amusement of a dream in which she, Sophie, saw herself as a typical "Omi"—grandmother—with youngsters clustered around her knee while she told them tales of her girlhood. In the dream one of the grandchildren interrupted her to say: "Come now, Omi, you're making that all up!" Had she been permitted to live she would, indeed, have had tales to tell her grandchildren.

At school she continued to upset some of her teachers with her candid and clear-eyed comments which repeatedly ran counter to the prevailing Nazi doctrine. More than once she was summoned before the principal of the school and admonished to change her attitude on pain of being barred from making her *Abitur,* which would have been fatal to her dream of entering a university. It says something of Sophie Scholl's independence of mind that she dared to speak out even at such a risk.

The school, she discovered, was not entirely infested with the National Socialist spirit. Some of the female teachers were what was known as "politically reserved," which meant that they were slightly less fanatical than the majority of their colleagues or were even, perhaps, closet doubters. In oblique and roundabout ways such teachers sometimes made it possible for their pupils to examine ideas which were otherwise under strict *Verbot* in the new educational guidelines. In studying Schiller's *Maria Stuart* one class was permitted to discuss some of the moral aspects of the intrigues that led to the death of Mary Queen of Scots and of Queen Elizabeth's involvement in her execution. The passionate National Socialists among the students argued that whatever Elizabeth may have done was right since, as head of state, she was responsible for its welfare and, hence, above any consideration of petty morality. The leader of a nation was justified in being unjust, the good of the state superseding whatever harm may come to individuals in the process. In arguing on these lines the students were following the concept of government inherent in Hitler's 'leadership principle''—the *Führerprinzip*—which held that authority was never to be doubted or disobeyed. Other students, like Sophie, tried to defend the opposite view in which a higher and more humane morality prevailed over naked political expediency and the state was required to acknowledge the worth and dignity of the individual.

Such topics, otherwise taboo, could be debated only by removing the issues from the twentieth century to the sixteenth and transposing them from current reality to the realm of literature. Even so, the debates sometimes became so heated and unambiguous that they had to be abruptly cut off, the teacher fearing that her touch of liberalism was getting dangerously out of hand. For Sophie such interludes were an indication that even in the most rigidly regimented groups in Germany there were those who, privately, thought differently and harbored private doubts and heretical convictions. The tide was running strongly against them, but it had not succeeded in washing them away.

The pressure point at which dissent and resistance became moral imperatives had not yet been reached. It was still possible to go through the routine of a day more or less normally by paying only lip-service to the demands of the New Order and avoiding any head-on collisions with its supporters. The accustomed mechanisms of society functioned as before and often more efficiently than before. Citizens and visitors both were impressed with how competently the National Socialists were managing Germany after the disarray that preceded them. There seemed little for anyone to dissent from if one overlooked some of the Leader's more virulent speeches. These were easy to condone as the usual bluff and bluster of a statesman bent on making his name in the world. Germany was, after all, still in the process of asserting itself in the community of nations after its long wallow in defeat and despair. Not many Germans saw any valid reason to doubt that their regime was pursuing the legitimate ends of national ambition and that, at bottom, National Socialism was as acceptable a form of government as any other.

Then, in November of 1938, the façade cracked.

A young man named Herschel Grynszpan, whose father had been transported to Poland in a freight car with hundreds of other Jews, went to the German embassy in Paris and announced that he had an important document to give to the ambassador. He was shunted to the office of the Third Secretary, Ernst von Rath, who invited him in and asked to see the paper in question. Instead, Herschel Grynszpan pulled a revolver from his pocket and said: "You are a filthy boche and here, in the name of twelve thousand persecuted Jews, is your document." He then shot the Third Secretary five times. This was a cruelly ironic mischance because vom Rath was not only not anti-Semitic but was under surveillance by the Gestapo for his lack of enthusiasm for the Nazi regime.

Herschel Grynszpan was an hysterical boy of seventeen and clearly not responsible for his actions. At first his act was reported routinely as a not too sensational item of crime news. But Dr. Joseph Goebbels was seized with the inspiration to treat it otherwise. He used Herschel Grynszpan's pistol shots to instigate the first pogrom in a western nation in modern times.

The shooting was played up in the press as part of a "Jewish world conspiracy" against the German people. The cry was for retaliation. With the consent of Hitler himself, the Propaganda Ministry organized a series of "spontaneous" demonstrations which spread across the entire country like an epileptic convulsion. Anti-Semitism, always latent in some levels of the German population ("The Jews are our misfortune!"), had been deliberately aggravated and intensified by years of Nazi propaganda designed to spread the racial obsessions of the *Führer* throughout the population. Now it exploded like a powder keg to which a torch had been applied. Spurred on by Storm Troopers and joined by packs of hoodlums, raging mobs swarmed through the German streets. They smashed the windows of

Jewish stores, businesses, and homes. They looted. They set fire to synagogues. In one night they destroyed forever the idea that Nazi Germany was a state dedicated to law and order and that National Socialism was as acceptable a form of government as any other.

It came to be called the "Crystal Night" because the streets of every town and city glistened with broken glass. The destruction went on for days. Witnesses described the crowds as "rampaging like wild dogs," and there were Germans who turned their faces away from the spectacle and wept. Not only were Jewish shops wrecked and ransacked but their proprietors were mercilessly hounded and beaten. Not only were synagogues burned and the Sacred Scrolls publicly desecrated, but their rabbis, some of them old and infirm, were abused and tortured. While the police stood by— "regulating traffic and making wholesale arrests of Jews 'for their own good' "—the toll of destruction mounted into the tens of millions. The physical savagery was not exhausted until some 2,500 Jews were dead, a stark foreshadowing of the holocaust to come. The correspondent for the *New York Times* cabled that no such wave of mass terror and destruction had been seen in Germany since the Thirty Years' War.

In Ulm and the neighboring towns—even in the university towns of Heidelberg and Tübingen—the flames of burning synagogues reddened the night sky. The *National Socialist Courier*, the regional newspaper, headlined its account of the affair with: JUST VENGEANCE OF OUTRAGED CITIZENS. The paper gloated that at last the unspecified crimes of the Jews in Germany were being avenged.

A few days later the paper reported with mingled indignation and bewilderment that, apparently, not everyone applauded the mass violence of the Crystal Night. The paper deplored the "soft-hearted squeamishness" of some spectators. "Swabians are reputed to be sentimental, but this does not mean they are delicate," the *Courier* commented in a Dialogue With Our Readers. "I have heard of a few people whimpering and complaining about operations against the Jews in the past few days. . . . We can scarcely believe that in 1938 there is still anyone so blind. . . . Such simpletons are beneath contempt." The article ended with the admonition: "Be thankful to live in such glorious times!"

Gratitude at being part of such times was far from universal. Something profoundly disturbing had happened and many sensed it. Now, said one German commentator, "the cowed middle classes stared at the Nazi monster like a rabbit at a snake. A general psychosis had been created under which the populace was reduced to absolute submission; and this effect was valuable to the Nazis." Gerhart Hauptmann, Nobel laureate and Germany's most celebrated dramatist, was among those who were appalled. "This scum will bring war to the whole world," Hauptmann lamented to a friend. "This miserable brown comedian, this Nazi hangman, is rushing us into a world of war, into destruction!"

"Then why don't you protest or emigrate, like Zweig and Thomas Mann?" his friend asked.

"Because I'm a coward!" the dramatist replied. "Do you understand? I'm a coward!" He spoke in private, but he spoke for thousands of others.

The glittering shards of Crystal Night which littered the streets of Ulm only confirmed the prediction made years before by Robert Scholl that Hitler's first war would be waged internally, inside Germany itself. The burning synagogues, the looted shops, signified more than merely an outburst of unrestrained hooliganism. "The Third Reich," as the American reporter William Shirer noted, "had deliberately turned down a dark and savage road from which there was to be no return." If the situation was not phrased so sweepingly around the dinner table in the house on Cathedral Square, the feeling was strong that something crucial had happened and that even more dismaying events were in the offing.

With the irrepressible élan of youth, Sophie Scholl clung to the idea that the world she was living in could not be as menacing and ill-omened as so many signs and circumstances indicated. She held resolutely to the notion that she could still fashion a satisfactory and rewarding life for herself and that the fundamentals necessary for such a life could never be wholly destroyed. She saw proof of this in her own family, in her circle of friends, and in her own daily round of school, play, and companionship which had not as yet been radically disrupted. The sheer momentum of living kept her spirits high and her optimism intact. "After all," she wrote in her diary, "one should have the courage to believe only in what is good. By that I do not mean that one should believe in illusions. I mean one should do only what is true and good and take it for granted that others will do the same, which is something that can't be done by intellect alone . . ."

Curiously, another young girl caught up in the disasters of her time in another way confided almost the identical sentiment to the diary she was secretly keeping in an attic in occupied Amsterdam where she was hiding, with her family, from the German police. "It's really a wonder I haven't dropped all my ideals," wrote Anne Frank, "because they seem so absurd and impossible to carry out. Yet I keep them because in spite of everything I still believe that people are really good at heart. I simply can't build up my hopes on a foundation consisting of confusion, misery, and death."

Neither could Sophie Scholl or her brother Hans, though like the Dutch-Jewish girl they never met or heard of, they too were fated to learn that their faith in the future was an illusion and that the times they lived in would make no concessions to the innocence and gallantry of the young.

The Neckar is a river that comes out of the Black Forest and meanders pleasantly among orchards, farms, and vineyards for several hundred miles before losing itself in the Rhine. On its way it flows past two universities. The one at Heidelberg is the most celebrated because a frothy operetta, *The Student Prince,* was written about it with captivating songs by Sigmund Romberg about the drinking, duelling, and loving that went on there.

The other university, Tübingen, has some distinctions of its own, none of them quite so gaudy. It boasts a respected school of theology and an intellectual history that includes such heavyweights of German culture as Johann Gottlieb Fichte, Georg Wilhelm Friedrich Hegel, and Philipp Melanchthon, the friend and collaborator of Luther. Besides philosophers and theologians, Tübingen can also point to Wilhelm Schickhardt, who devised the world's first calculator in 1623, and Hans Geiger, inventor of the Geiger counter. The place—"this quaint Swabian town"—is also dear to the hearts of literate Germans for its connection with Friedrich Hölderlin whom

Rilke himself hailed as "the glorious enchanter." Hölderlin was born near Tübingen and spent forty years of his life there dreaming in his long madness of a mystical fusion of Christ and Apollo.

Hans Scholl, his military service behind him, enrolled at Tübingen in the spring of 1939 to study medicine. Afterwards he confessed that he was never sure why he chose medicine beyond a rather vague inclination for the natural sciences and a lack of zeal for any other profession at the time. "I chose medicine and I didn't know why," he told a friend, but for what he would do with his life the choice turned out to be fortunate.

After two years with the cavalry, he found Tübingen an agreeable interlude. The nearby Black Forest invited exploration, the Neckar was there for swimming and boating, and the town itself had a drowsy charm with its gabled marketplace, its castle, and its Renaissance atmosphere. If his medical books did not rivet his attention, there was readily available a profusion of other books that did.

For all his energy and exuberance, Hans Scholl was a young man who could write in a notebook: *"Ich suche Läuterung. Ich will, dass all Schatten von mir weichen . . ."*—"I seek clarity. I want all shadows to depart from me . . ." His pursuit of light in an increasingly clouded and confused world took him further and further back in time, away from the clangor of contemporary argument and dispute. Not even the poets of his time—not Rilke or Stefan George, dazzling as they were—provided answers equal to his askings. He tried Nietzsche and found nothing to quench what his sister Inge called the "burning emptiness" inside him. He read the Socratic dialogues on the commitment to morality in the face of death and felt he was getting closer to what he was groping for. He discovered Pascal and the great wager on the existence of God: "Let us weigh the gain and loss in choosing 'heads' that God is. Let us weigh the two cases: If you gain, you gain all. If you lose, you lose nothing. Wager then unhesitatingly that He is . . ." He noted another of the *Pensées* that conformed with his own maturing outlook: "Thought makes the whole dignity of man. Therefore, endeavor to think well; that is the only morality."

Hans Scholl was endeavoring to think well.

At home, early, his mother had gently guided him to the Bible, and now he turned to it again and absorbed it with a new intensity. In it he found passages that astonished him with their aptness for the time he was living in. He looked for further anchorage among the Church Fathers and found it. In Augustine there was assurance bordering on certainty that the barbarians could not, in the end, prevail. It had seemed a satanic triumph beyond remedy when Rome, the Holy City, was sacked by the Visigoths; Augustine himself had seen the desolate refugees come streaming by the thousands into Africa. Augustine was still at his post when the Vandals—another Germanic tribe, as Hans Scholl may have noted—laid siege to the Bishop's own domain at Hippo. As Augustine knew and proclaimed, neither Vandals nor Visigoths could in the end triumph over the City of God—the *Civitas Dei*, a phrase that Hans Scholl would one day use in the leaflets that cost him his life. The tidal wave of barbarism crested and receded, and Rome remained.

For a warranty he could accept that the universe was a cosmos and not a chaos, Hans immersed himself in the luminous common sense of Thomas Aquinas, and here too he found rich material and motivation on which to base his coming rebellion. Aquinas' sublime blending of reason and belief provided Hans Scholl with spiritual support for the rest of his life. In a world being menaced and corrupted by Germans it was something of a comfort that Aquinas was German too.

Though it was the concern of Aquinas to fortify men and women in their faith in God, he also wrote about life on earth in a way that Hans could respond to without reservation. Society and the state, said Aquinas, existed for the individual, not he for them. Though sovereignty derived from God, it was invested in the people. The people may grant power to a prince but it is always revocable by the people—"the prince holds the power of legislation only so far as he represents the will of the people." Should the ruler become a tyrant, he can be disposed of by the orderly action of the people. He must always subject himself to the law and be its servant, never the master. The state, said Aquinas, should be an analogy of the divine order. This saying too would be embodied in one of the leaflets of the White Rose.

Hans Scholl's reading solidified his conviction that National Socialism, the way of life imposed on Germany by Adolf Hitler, was at every point inimicable to the spiritual and social concepts that the civilization of the West had evolved over millennia. In a world that had heard Christ's new commandment—"That ye love one another"—Hitler's "force is the first law" was an ideological defilement that could not be tolerated, that would have to be opposed. The Christian scheme of grace and redemption, of a loving Father offering salvation to mankind through the sacrifice of His Son made incarnate, seemed to Hans Scholl the one possible bulwark against the dark that was closing in on his world and threatening to extinguish whatever of light still remained in it. The Christian ethic, the word of God, became his mooring for all the time that was left to him, and he expressed what it meant to him in a vivid passage in his diary: *"If Christ hadn't lived and hadn't died, there would truly be no way out at all. Then all the weeping would be horribly meaningless. Then one would have to run against the nearest wall and smash one's skull. But as it is, no."*

In this there was no element of the born-again convert to whom a sudden revelation brings a transformation of personality. With Hans Scholl the diary entry was the result of a slow accretion of ideas and convictions, a distillation of the religious legacy of his mother, the inborn probity of his father, and his own quest for a shield against the assaults of a system which was trampling on his most treasured moral certitudes and affronting his every instinct for what was right, just, and decent.

Hans' absorption in the Church Fathers did not bring with it any tendency to accept without challenge whatever might be offered him on the subject of religion and faith. His native Swabian scepticism hardly ever deserted him and he was stubbornly cool to the pronouncements of contemporary priests and pundits—"I usually know what they're going to say before they say it." He once expressed a strong preference for the conversation of a bright sixteen-year-old girl to that of any theologian he could think of. He would make scathing fun of books in which he detected foolishness or fraud. A particular target of his contempt was Ward Price of the *London Daily Mail* whose books, like his newspaper, always presented Hitler in the best possible light. Hitler often used Price to spread his diplomatic ploys through the world press. "Germany's problems cannot be settled by war," Hitler told Price who duly printed the observation, along with Hitler's further assertion that "war will not come again." Hans Scholl knew better and it angered him that a Ward Price, who should have seen through Hitler's remarks, would print such stuff. Hans was inured to the distortions of the Nazi newspapers but it seemed intolerable to him that deliberate untruths should also occur where the press was free.

Tübingen was only about 50 miles from Ulm and there were opportunities for Hans to shuttle back and forth between the university and home for visits with his family and evening strolls along the Danube with Lisa. With the family, and particularly with his father and Sophie, there was a good deal to talk about that summer, some of it disturbing and much of it puzzling. In May the "Pact of Steel," the military alliance with Italy, was signed with much pomp and circumstance in Berlin. This solidification of the tie between the two Fascist powers was hailed by Hitler's supporters as yet another in his unbroken series of political achievements. Hardly three months later came what one historian has since called "the biggest bombshell in Europe's long diplomatic history." On August 23, 1939, Nazi Germany and Communist Russia signed a Non-Aggression Treaty in the Kremlin.

All through his six years of power, and long before, Adolf Hitler had made it a basic tenet of his creed that Russia and its bolshevism were mortal threats to Germany, to Europe, and to western civilization. No vituperation was too extreme, no excoriation too savage, for the Nazi press to pour out on Josef Stalin and the system he represented. For the Kremlin the Nazis were "Fascist beasts" and "bloody assassins of the working class" who deserved nothing less than extermination at the hands of an outraged proletariat. Now, in a reversal that sent a gasp of astonishment around the world, the Brown tyrant Hitler was fraternizing with the Red tyrant Stalin. Two powers that had vowed undying enmity for each other were suddenly cheek by jowl in complete disregard of the opposing ideologies which gave them their being. Something unimaginable to any true-believing Communist, and inconceivable to every dedicated Nazi, actually took place: Josef Stalin lifted his glass in the Kremlin and toasted Adolf Hitler.

For the two leaders the agreement was an act of frank cynicism prompted by naked expediency. Stalin needed time to shore up a system that had been undermined by a series of bloody purges, political and military, and by a faltering economy. Uncertain of the reaction of Great Britain and France should Hitler decide to attack him, Stalin had chosen to fend off Hitler's aggressive drive by joining him and thus diverting it elsewhere.

For Hitler the treaty was a stroke of calculated *Realpolitik* to clear the way for the next phase of his design for conquest. By neutralizing Russia he had canceled the threat of a two-front war should hostilities develop in the West. For most Germans this was another dazzling example of his statesmanship. But for Germans like the Scholls the Non-Aggression Pact was as disturbing as it was surprising. Robert Scholl was not alone in resorting to the black radio in an effort to make sense out of what was happening by listening to foreign commentators. This was seldom helpful, since political analysts everywhere were equally confused. The only certainty was that whatever Hitler's motives might be, they were necessarily suspect and sinister.

In fact, what the Nazi-Soviet Non-Aggression Pact meant was war. Hitler had long since chosen his target: Poland. This time he did not want to gain his ends by diplomacy and negotiation. He was determined on war. A secret protocol divided eastern Europe into two spheres, the German and the Soviet, which meant that Stalin had given Hitler a free hand for the assault he was preparing.

Even before the agreement was formally signed Hitler had assembled his generals in conclave and told them: ''The destruction of Poland has priority. . . . I shall give a propagandist reason for starting the war, no matter whether it is plausible or not. The victor will not be asked whether he told the truth or not. When starting and waging war it is not right that matters, but victory. . . . Close your hearts to pity! Be steeled against all signs of compassion! Whoever has pondered over this world order knows that its meaning lies in the success of the best by means of force.''

The propagandist reason Hitler invented to justify his war was like something out of a cloak-and-dagger paperback written by a hack. Twelve or thirteen condemned criminals were given lethal injections and then dressed in Polish uniforms. Their bodies were scattered in the vicinity of a German radio station at Gleiwitz on the German-Polish border. Then *SS* and Gestapo men staged a fake attack on the station, fired some shots, and briefly broadcast from the station in Polish before disappearing. Behind them they left the dressed-up corpses as evidence that an attack by Polish troops had occurred. This crude charade was then used by the Nazi Foreign Office to inform the world that "In defense against Polish attacks, German troops moved into action against Poland at dawn today."

The day was September 1, 1939.

Two days later both Great Britain and France declared war on Germany, honoring previous pledges of support for Poland in the event of a German attack. The Second World War was under way, begun with a primitive hoax at an obscure border town in central Europe. From there it would gather its frightful momentum, spread around the globe, and claim its 55 million casualties, military and civilian, before it ended.

Sophie Scholl was eighteen years old when the German troops marched into Poland. She heard about it over the radio in the big house on Cathedral Square in the town of Ulm.

She went to her room, to her night-table, and took out her diary. She wrote:

I cannot grasp that now human beings will continually be put in danger of their lives by other human beings.
I can never grasp it, and I find it horrible.

And she added:

Don't say it's for the Fatherland.

Four

The Poles came to the defense of their country literally at a gallop. The Pomorska Cavalry Brigade charged into battle with lances leveled at the oncoming German tanks, and the brigade was of course wiped out. The incident typified a campaign in which quixotic gallantry out of the past beat itself to death against the mechanized efficiency of a new way of war that the Germans brought to an astonishing pitch of perfection with their first use of it.

With the first dispatches from the battlefront a new word embedded itself in the vocabulary of combat: *Blitzkrieg,* lightning war. This radical scheme of attack combined maximum shock with maximum speed by means of racing armored columns which shattered conventional defenses on impact, spreading havoc at the front and demoralizing the rear. There was also a new word for the unstoppable German tanks, *Panzer*; it too became part of the language of war. With every German advance came a hitherto unknown terror from the skies, the *Stuka*, the dive bomber with sirens built into its wings so that the wild scream of its earthward plunge added pure panic to the damage done by its bombs and machine guns.

In little more than a week the best Polish divisions were either routed or surrounded, and German tanks were prowling the outskirts of Warsaw. Before the month ended the war was over, and 23 million more of the people of Europe came under the sway of Adolf Hitler. The film that the Propaganda Ministry made of the campaign was called "Baptism of Fire"; it showed no German corpses but stressed the élan and efficiency of the *Wehrmacht* in action as a source of pride for the German people and a warning to Germany's enemies.

The campaign had put so little strain on the Third Reich that thousands of young men eligible for military duty were not called up. Hans Scholl was, like many others, allowed to continue his studies. The army had no immediate need of men but it would certainly have use for medically trained personnel in the future. Hans had already put in his two years with the military. His basic training had been seen to. For months he had reason to hope that he might never have to practice on the battlefield what he had learned in training.

The phase that became known as the "Phoney War"—the *Sitzkrieg* —had set in, the period when Hitler held his hand and there was no overt aggression on either side. Men in better positions to judge than Hans Scholl also nursed the notion that perhaps Hitler's thirst for conquest had been slaked. In this euphoric mood Europe, including most Germans, carried on with business as usual, fingers crossed.

The lull allowed Hans Scholl to journey northwest to the town of Göttingen to take several courses at the university there. This, too, was a pleasant enough place with its impressive medieval architecture and the unhurried way it went about its business, which was scholarship. The most famous occurrence at the university may have caused Hans some moments of sardonic reflection on the progress of academic freedom with the passage of time. In 1837 the King of Hanover had issued a decree which infringed on the basic rights of the university. An uproar ensued and seven of the foremost professors issued flaming letters of protest which caused the king to have them all dismissed. Among the seven were the brothers Grimm, Jacob and Wilhelm, widely known not only for their fairy tales but for their philological research. In defense of the expelled scholars a storm of indignation broke over the king and university. The letters of protest became collectors' items and people fought to obtain copies of them. The professors' salaries were paid them by popular subscription. The "Göttingen Seven" became national heroes. Nothing of the sort, Hans could not help remarking, had occurred in twentieth-century Germany when Hitler and his Nazis abolished academic freedom at every university in the land. No Göttingen Seven had risen up anywhere in protest and no surge of public outrage had welled up to protect scholarship from interference by the state.

There was, as well, another legendary figure connected with the place to whom Hans could respond with warmth and admiration across the years. This was Heinrich Heine who had attended classes at Göttingen but left behind no sentimental remembrances of his alma mater. He once called it *"that accursed hole"* and one of his most popular books opened with a mock defense of the local women against the charge that they all had big feet. This humorist, poet, and ironist had been an uncommonly acute observer of the German character. A hundred years before Hitler, he issued a warning to Germany's neighbors, especially the French, in words that were uncannily applicable to the very time of Hans Scholl's stay at Göttingen.

Christianity, wrote Heine, had somewhat suppressed the German lust for battle but had not banished it. Should the restraining talisman of the cross ever be broken, said the poet, then:

> . . . the savagery of the ancient warriors will blaze up again, the mad berserker fury about which the Nordic bards said and sang so much. . . . And when one day you hear a crash like no other crash in the history of the world you'll know that the German thunder has been loosed. At the sound of it eagles will fall to earth dead and lions in the remotest African wastes will put their tails between their legs and slink off into their royal lairs. A drama will be played in Germany that will make the French Revolution look like an innocent idyll . . .

With the invasion of Denmark and Norway, on the ninth of April, the berserker fury of the ancient warriors blazed up again in an outburst of conquest such as Europe had never before witnessed. In weeks the rampaging *Panzer*, the screaming *Stuka*, and the superb infantry overran Denmark, Norway, Luxembourg, Belgium, and the Netherlands, and then rendered France's cement bulwark, the Maginot Line, ridiculous by simply outflanking it. The British army was driven off the continent and into the sea at Dunkirk. France itself, with the largest land army in the West, collapsed. Adolf Hitler rode into undefended Paris as its master, completing what *Time* magazine in neutral America called "the most prodigious military performance in modern history."

Four days after the formal French surrender at Compiègne on June 22, 1940, Sophie Scholl was writing a letter at her nighttable in her bedroom in Ulm. There was no rejoicing at the German victory in her letter. She wrote:

I would have been more impressed if the French had defended Paris to the last shot without consideration for the valuable art treasures it contains, even if—as was certain—that wouldn't have been of any use, at least of no immediate use. But in these times expedience is everything, and understanding doesn't exist any more. And honor doesn't exist any more either. The main thing is to escape with your life. If I didn't know that I shall probably outlive many older people, then I could sometimes shudder in horror at the spirit that governs history today . . .

Hans Scholl had been called up for active duty with a medical unit during the Battle of France. Fresh from his books, he had reason to recall the comment of Blaise Pascal as the troop transport rolled toward the Rhine and the French border: *"Can anything be more ridiculous than that a man should have the right to kill me because he lives on the other side of the water, and because his ruler has a quarrel with mine, though I have none with him?"* Hans, at any rate, had no intention of killing anyone and, as a medic, would not be required to. His choice of medicine as a profession was paying its first dividends.

He crossed the border with conflicting emotions. He was temperamentally eager for any new situation that promised to be exciting and challenging, but he had no desire to contribute to the expansion of the Third Reich. He agreed fully with the comment in his sister Sophie's daybook: "Don't say it's for the Fatherland."

Though a medic does not participate in the fighting he sees the consequences of it in close-up; the impact of war comes home to him as surely as to the combat soldier. In dressing stations and field hospitals in France Hans Scholl underwent his baptism of blood and saw for himself all the ghastliness that had been so carefully edited out of "Baptism of Fire." For a time he was stationed in St. Quentin, in Picardy, where the fighting had not been severe and duty was not especially onerous. He found prolonged inactivity behind the lines so boring, and somehow indecent, that even the occasional enemy air raid was welcome. What he was doing, or not doing, seemed to him "aimless and pointless." The most reasonable thing to do, he told himself, would be to go over the hill, but there was nowhere for him to go where the war was not.

He also felt guilty. The army had requisitioned the best houses, ousted their owners, and quartered German troops in the vacated rooms. "I liked it better when we were sleeping on straw," was Hans' reaction. "What am I—a decent human being or a thief?" Where points of decency in human behavior were at issue his judgments were severe, with himself as with others. A French doctor famous in the area committed suicide because he could not endure the prospect of life under German occupation. The incident elicited no sympathy from Hans. "What kind of patriotism is that?" he wanted to know. "This is a time when France needs all the strong men it can find."

Even when the fighting stopped the work of the medical unit did not. Hans' outfit took over a field hospital with 400 maimed and wounded soldiers in it. The place was in a deplorable condition, a circumstance that Hans blamed on the Prussians who had previously been running it. This was perhaps an outcropping of a regional prejudice, the Prussians being traditionally unpopular with south Germans; but the hospital *was* badly in need of proper management. It was averaging twenty operations a day and Hans always remembered one forenoon when two "high" leg amputations were performed, one after the other. There were times when he himself, though far from certified as a doctor, was called to perform minor surgery in the absence of qualified personnel.

A redeeming feature of duty at the field hospital was that a group of local nurses came to assist the German medical unit. Hans welcomed this development. Like other cultivated young Germans he had a curiosity about the French way of life that bordered on envy, and he seized every chance that came his way to learn more about the people among whom he was living. He found it difficult. The French were reserved and withdrawn, an attitude he understood. He had, after all, come into their midst in the wake of assaults by *Panzer* and *Stuka*. He was aware that most Frenchmen must regard him as a member of a barbarian host, the modern incarnation of Visigoth and Vandal.

Hans Scholl had cosmopolitan inclinations, wherever they may have originated, and French culture, including its cuisine, offered enlargements of life not available in Ulm. He cultivated every possible French contact. He set about learning more of the language than his previous schooling had given him. Stationed in Versailles, he formed a relationship with a fourteen-year-old girl who, he always afterward insisted, spoke the most beautiful French he was ever to hear anyone speak. The girl found nothing barbarous about the invader named Hans Scholl and gave him many hours of instruction in the language along with unwitting tutelage in ways of the French female. She taught him to read and savor Baudelaire, a gift for the rest of his life.

The ugliness of the German occupation could not be disguised or ignored for long. It could only be fleetingly tempered when occupied and occupiers, as with Hans Scholl and the girl in Versailles, made contact by letting human warmth seep through the partitions erected by chauvinism and war. In the wide march of German conquest much worse was to come in the way of brutality and oppression than what occurred in France. Hans Scholl saw enough to add another layer to the burden of distaste and aversion he was already carrying for the regime whose uniform he was wearing. He saw the dread Reich Security Service, of which the Gestapo was an arm, move in and establish itself wherever the army cleared the way. He saw the red posters edged in black go up everywhere. They regularly announced the number of French hostages executed in the Nazi program of terror designed to keep the French in subjection. He saw trucks and freight cars come from Germany loaded with military supplies and return bulging with booty pilfered from the French. He heard the stories of *Luftwaffe* officers in Paris using champagne as shaving water. He saw France, the last stronghold of freedom in Europe, transformed into a totalitarian state where all traces of *liberté, égalité,* and *fraternité*—concepts he himself cherished—were being systematically stamped out by German jackboots.

It was a source of satisfaction for Hans Scholl when he was put in charge of arranging transportation and shelter for French refugees who had been displaced by the German advance and were now being resettled. His new duties multiplied his contacts with the French people and set him apart from the more heartless aspects of the occupation. But he was never entirely comfortable in the field gray of Adolf Hitler's *Wehrmacht* among a people whose style in wine and women and poetry he so much relished. When, in the fall of 1940, orders came that recalled his unit to Germany he was ready to go.

In the family circle at Ulm the mood was one of subdued alarm and foreboding, and Hans' eye-witness reports from France did nothing to dissipate it. The sensational victories of the *Blitzkrieg* had strengthened Hitler's grip on the nation, and many who had opposed him, if only privately, were now caught up in the surge of national pride that followed on the fall of France. For weeks the radio had trumpeted one victory after the other with rousing fanfares that became regular features of the daily listening schedule. After Dunkirk the church bells all across Germany clanged joyously for three days. Millions thrilled to the newsreels of the French surrendering to Adolf Hitler in the same railway car, in the same clearing in the forest of Compiègne, where the Germans had capitulated twenty-two years before.

To the hard-core Nazis all this was granite confirmation of their belief in the military and political genius of the *Führer*. To doubters it was persuasive evidence of the strength and efficiency of the National Socialist system. No power on earth, it now seemed, could match the might of the German war machine or stay Adolf Hitler's march of conquest. Even anti-Nazis had to concede that the German triumphs had been achieved by brilliantly innovative tactics and techniques which not only assured swift success but kept casualties at a minimum. But for people like the Scholls who had looked for signs of strength and resolution from the western powers as a counterweight to Hitler, it was a time of disappointment and dismay.

Sophie Scholl, for one, was so discouraged by the course of the war that she was sometimes on the verge of "laying down my own arms and giving up." When this mood took her she stoutly repeated to herself the saying her father had taught her: *"Allen Gewalten zum trotz, sich erhalten!"* It was the attitude of the whole family— maintain yourself, hold on to your integrity. But how was that to be done under a system that became more restrictive and oppressive with every new day?

"We were living in a society where despotism, hate, and lies had become the normal state of affairs," Inge Scholl has recorded of this period. "Every day that you were not in jail was like a gift. No one was safe from arrest for the slightest unguarded remark and some disappeared forever for no better reason. Woe to the mother who tried to relieve her anguished heart by denouncing the war that had robbed her of a son! She would be made to regret that she had spoken out. Hidden cars seemed to be listening to everything that was being spoken in Germany. The terror was at your elbow wherever you went."

In Ulm, as elsewhere, there was now hardly a street from which someone was not missing. It became a more and more frequent sight to see little bands of people being herded through the ordinary pedestrian traffic of midtown toward the railway station. Occasionally a passerby would be startled to see a neighbor, or even a friend, in such a captive group and wonder what he or she was doing there. With time almost everybody came to know why people in increasing numbers—men, women, children—were being herded to the railway stations.

"Those?" the inquirer would be told, sometimes with a shrug. "Why, they're Jews on their way to Poland. KZ, you know."

In the hubris inspired by the great victories in the West, the Nazi leadership did not hesitate to expose its ultimate aims and purposes in rhetoric such as modern statesmen had never before used in public. "The German race—that is our faith!" proclaimed Dr. Robert Ley, leader of the National Socialist Labor Front. "It has higher rights than all others. We have the divine right to rule, and we shall assure ourselves of that right." The sentiment was widely applauded by Hitler's true believers, but there were Germans who did not believe it. In Munich an uprooted Prussian aristocrat was keeping a diary in which he expressed something of the revulsion that other Germans felt as the arrogance and presumption of the Nazis grew. "This gang of apes," was how Friedrich Reck-Malleczewen characterized his country's leadership, and he added: "Truly, a devil has broken loose from his leash in Germany—ah, and none of us knows how we are to get him back on the chain again."

For the Scholls the situation posed the same question that decent Germans had been asking themselves ever since the Nazis came to power: "What can one do?" Overt opposition, they knew, would be both suicidal and senseless. In long evening walks and talks together, the Scholl family weighed the possibilities of some kind of opposition if only of a limited, marginal kind. To be wholly passive and indifferent seemed unthinkable. It was not alone the maniacal racism and reckless adventurism of the regime that offended them; it was rather the massive Nazi assault on the decencies and traditions of the civilization they knew. What was happening, they saw, was a deliberate dismantling of the whole structure of established social and ethical values to make way for a new set of attitudes that would turn civilization around and send it reeling back into another Dark Age. The Nazis had gone far beyond the exercise of the legitimate authority allowable to the state. They had long since forfeited the allegiance ordinarily due a government from its people.

The gravity of the times pervaded the big house on Cathedral

Square, and to Sophie Scholl it sometimes seemed that politics and public events were crowding everything else out of life and she resented it. As usual, she took a rather stern line with herself, observing that since political affairs were in such a sorry and confused state it would be cowardly to turn one's back and ignore them. "I think I would be much happier if I could do that," she wrote to a friend, "but the way things are, everything else has to take second place." Nevertheless, at nineteen, she was seldom overwhelmed by the parlous state of the world for long. A two-hour bicycle ride with her sister Inge was enough to revive her spirits, and she always came back brimming with lively observations on what she had seen and felt along the way. "Even when you're sure everything is falling to pieces," she said after one such excursion, "the moon is always right back in its usual place the next evening, and the next day the birds are singing as sweetly and eagerly as ever. They never give a thought to whether it's of any use or not. How lovely that that is always there." Though her sunny confidence in the future was now often clouded by events, she did not abandon it. She looked forward with undiminished excitement to enrolling at the university in Munich. "Wouldn't it be wonderful if Hans and I could study there together for a time?" she asked her diary early in 1941. "We're always bursting with plans—irrepressible!"

She had won her college certificate after all, despite the misgivings of the upper-school principal who had doubts, fully justified, about Sophie Scholl's ardor for the National Socialist cause. She also took courses that qualified her as a kindergarten teacher which she intended to make her life's work after graduating from college. She hoped, too, that her status as a kindergarten teacher might exempt her from the six months labor service which all girls her age were obligated to put in. The prospect of being cooped up for half a year with a group of strange females while serving a system she detested was not alluring.

Brother Hans, still in the army, had been ordered to join a Student Medical Company in Munich where he was assigned to continue his studies. He pulled what strings he could to have Sophie deferred from the labor service so that she could enroll at the university immediately. But it was wartime and regulations of all kinds had been tightened; no one would be admitted to the university unless all conditions set by the state had been fulfilled, and these had more to do with regimentation than with academic standards. Her attendance at the university would, in fact, have to be postponed for an additional six months because she was obligated to the National War Assistance program after her labor service was over. She faced a full year of what she regarded as forced labor for the Nazi state before she could hope to realize her dream of joining her brother in Munich.

The bleak prospect required her to muster all the resources that had already won her a reputation among her classmates of being precociously self-contained and unflappable. This was the obverse of the open, laughing side of her that her close friends and family knew, and it would serve her well in ordeals yet to come. Her rule was to adapt herself to any new condition immediately, to come to terms with it, and get on with living her life. "That way," she once explained, "you achieve independence from circumstances, both good and bad." She sometimes thought, rather ruefully, that the couplet about her in her graduation book—it had been a rather teasing reference to her unemotional manner—had been right after all; but she abided by her rule nevertheless. Instead of pausing to sulk and fume about her summons to the labor service, she stoically packed her bag, said her good-byes, and set off, as ordered, to a place called Sigmaringen, which was about 45 miles southwest of Ulm.

There she found herself quartered with eighty other girls in a rambling old castle whose charm was the one redeeming feature of the situation. She slept in a room with ten others, and the giggling and chattering often drove her to pull the covers over her head and clamp the pillow around her ears. There was much awed and admiring talk about the *Führer*, who had the same effect on most of the labor service girls as movie stars had on young females in other countries. A good deal of sighing and twittering was also audible when photographs of dashing types from the Hitler Youth and the *SS* were passed around. Sophie kept her photographs to herself.

Sometimes she joined in the after-hours banter and jollity of the group but she was always vexed with herself when she did. It seemed to her a kind of betrayal of her principles. She was fiercely at odds with the attitudes and outlook of those around her, and she was bitter about the time and development that the Nazi state was robbing her of. Even when, with all good will, she participated in the sociability of the castle it did not go well. A surviving snapshot shows twelve of the girls, including Sophie, at an impromptu party. They are in their nightgowns around a festive table, with cups and glasses in their hands and smiling for the camera. Sophie is not smiling. She is serious and detached, as if she wished she were somewhere else.

More than most, Sophie could manage her emotions but she could not annul them. She was homesick and unhappy. Her natural reserve tended to isolate her from her surroundings, which was an advantage; but she found that being encapsulated within herself, and within the castle, numbed her to events which she would normally have followed with passionate concern. The capitulation of Greece that spring, and the occupation of Athens by the *Wehrmacht*, caused her only momentary distress where formerly she would have been devastated by such news. The distribution of the mail a few hours after she heard it seemed to be of more importance. That worried her.

She began to fear that the frivolous atmosphere of the castle was beginning to infect her but it did not happen. One evening in April she turned away from the chatter around her to look out of the window at the trees silhouetted, bare and stark, against a somber sky. It occurred to her, as it had to no one else, that this was Good Friday. "The sky, so distant and indifferent, made me sad," she wrote of that evening. "I felt myself shut out. Shut out from the mindless merriment around me that had no connection with that remote sky, and from the indifferent sky itself . . ." She found a refuge in reading.

Work for the girls consisted in doing a variety of chores on the farms in the vicinity. There was little public entertainment in that predominantly rural area and the girls were obliged to manufacture their own fun at the castle of an evening. Sophie found it hard to concentrate amid the almost incessant hubbub, but by putting herself in a self-imposed coventry she could enter a more congenial world of her own. In the mental regimen she had set for herself she had given up reading novels because, she said, they were a good deal like wine—pleasant enough while being consumed but often causing an unpleasant aftertaste or even a hangover. The choice of books at the castle was limited to National Socialist literature of the most stereotyped sort and private books were prohibited, but Sophie had managed to smuggle in a volume that sustained her through the empty evenings—a selection from the works of St. Augustine.

As with Hans, the alarms and confusions of the times had increasingly turned her to Christian doctrine for assurance that a divine order and purpose did indeed underlie a universe that seemed to be in the grip of forces both blind and irrational. In the *Confessions of St. Augustine* she found a sentence which seemed to have been written for her: *"Thou hast created us for Thyself, and our heart cannot be quieted till it may find repose in Thee."* It was a saying 1,000 years old, but it helped quiet the heart of Sophie Scholl and give her a measure of tranquillity.

She often brooded about life as a doorway to eternity and she worried that the distractions of the passing day might blind her to the purpose and meaning of existence. "My heart gets lost in petty anxieties," she once wrote in one of these moods. "It forgets the great way home that lies before it. Unprepared, given over to childish trivialities, it could be taken by surprise when the great hour comes and find that, for the sake of piffling pleasures, the one great joy has been missed. I am aware of this, but my heart is not. Unteachable, it continues its dreaming . . . wavering always between joy and depression."

But the same Sophie could begin a light letter to a young man she currently favored with: "You know how stupid girls can be, thank God . . ." And she could go on to say: "I pity people who can't find laughter in every little thing, some bit of amusement in the doings of the day. It has nothing to do with being superficial. . . . Yes, I believe that even in the most sorrowful moment I could find something ridiculous if necessary."

The young man was one of her circle of friends in Ulm, a frequent companion on hikes and picnics and often her escort at parties and concerts. His name was Fritz Hartnagel and he was now an officer on active duty with the army. He had come up through the Hitler Youth and was a loyal soldier, but a decent and attractive person for all that. He was also sensitive and intelligent, as Sophie's regard for him testified. In her letters she did not spare his feelings in airing her opinion of the regime he was serving and in the end she would be the cause of his break with National Socialism. Gay or serious, her letters were candid reflections of what she was thinking and feeling.

When he was stationed in Holland, she wrote to ask how the tulips were surviving the war. ("I hope those innocent things weren't completely destroyed.") She tells him she has adopted a French motto for the times: *Il faut avoir l'esprit dur et le coeur tendre*— "One should have a tough mind and a tender heart." She writes him, with some wonderment, of how overwhelmingly the fields, meadows, and woods affect her, dissolving away all thoughts of the war, her parents, politics, ". . . and you!"

She very much hopes he will survive the war without becoming its slave, and she reveals that she does not subscribe to the established idea that a soldier is obliged to serve his country's cause under any and all circumstances. She defends the then radical, and dangerous, idea that there are moral imperatives that outweigh traditional fealties. "I think," she tells him, "that right and justice are superior to other loyalties, which are often merely sentimental. It would certainly be better if, in a war, people could choose the side whose cause they felt to be the most just . . ." She rejects the German idea that subjective judgments are the best. A judgment cannot be valid for her without an objective basis. To Sophie the imposition of force by the strong on the weak was a horror to which she could never reconcile herself. As a child she would cry at the sight of a mouse in a trap and be distressed for hours afterwards. The mouse squealing in the trap became a metaphor that haunted her for the rest of her life. War, to her, was only a needless extension and heightening of the everyday pain and cruelty which she so much abhorred.

She could not conceive that anyone would find it good, and even applaud, when a more powerful country fell upon a weaker one and destroyed it. For her the situation was not altered when the more powerful country was her own. "If you believe in the victory of might," she wrote in another letter, "then you have to believe that men are on the same level as animals." To live without protest in a society based on the rule of force would, in the end, become impossible for Sophie Scholl.

One of the girls at the castle was a Nordic type who was both attractive and intelligent, which made her something of a rarity among the nondescript assemblage of labor service girls, most of whom were neither. Her name was Gisela Schertling, and she and Sophie Scholl struck up a warm friendship. They made a contrasting pair, the one of medium height and dark, the other tall and of light complexion. But they shared the personality traits of being reticent and undemonstrative without being dull and they were congenial. Gisela was interested in art and art history and intended to go to the University of Munich, which made another bond between them.

Every so often the labor service girls were allowed a "travel Sunday" for visits home, and on several occasions Sophie took her friend Gisela along to the house on Cathedral Square in Ulm. Once or twice it happened that Hans was there on leave on the same weekend. Always open to new encounters and as eager to test the possibilities of an attractive girl as the next young man, Hans took an immediate interest in Gisela. With time, gradually, a romance developed between them, and Sophie followed it with intense interest. (It was one of her observations that "entering a new relationship with a person is a great and important event. It is a declaration of love and a declaration of war at the same time.") Given the social climate in Germany, the relationship between Hans and Gisela held far more of hazard and mischance than an affair in a less hectic period would have. What began for them so normally and with all middle-class propriety—fond sister introduces her pretty friend to a favorite brother—would in the end bring Gisela Schertling, too, into a Gestapo cell and before the People's Court.

That was a time when almost nothing was easy and natural any more in the conduct of life in Germany. The war had ceased to be merely European and had become global with Hitler's attack on the Soviet Union in June of 1941 and his declaration of war on the United States in December of the same year. By breaking his Non-Aggression Pact with Stalin and sending his armies storming into Russia, Hitler had committed one of those incalculable acts that causes seismic alterations in the course of history and changes the world. It was Hitler's purpose from the start to change the world, to wrench society out of its established pattern and make it over according to his own designs; but now he had fatally misjudged the impact of the forces he was unleashing.

When Foreign Minister Joachim von Ribbentrop in Berlin summoned the Russian ambassador at four in the morning to hand him the declaration of war, Vladimir Dekanozov was stunned and outraged at the unexpected development. He said: "You will regret that you have attacked the Soviet Union. This is a base, treacherous, and unprovoked aggression. You will pay dearly for it." Hitler did not think he would. "We have only to kick in the door and the whole rotten structure will come crashing down," he told his Chief of Operations. He thought the Russian campaign would be over in four months.

At the onset it seemed that Adolf Hitler was right again. The feats of his *Wehrmacht* that had stunned the West were now duplicated in Russia on a scale that dwarfed all previous victories. In the first weeks of Operation Barbarossa the German army achieved penetrations and encirclements which gave new dimensions to the new kind of war called *Blitzkrieg*. Whole divisions of the Red army were routed or annihilated by deep-thrusting German armored spearheads and engulfed by waves of oncoming infantry. Soviet troops were captured, or surrendered, by the tens of thousands and then by the hundred thousands. Minsk, the capital of Byelorussia, was captured in five days, and the three-pronged invasion rolled inexorably onward—toward Leningard in the north, Moscow in the center, and the Ukraine and the Caucasus in the south. By the end of July even generals of the German High Command who had opposed the Russian adventure as foolhardy thought the war was as good as won and that Hitler was scoring yet another of the successes which everyone else had thought impossible.

At home, on the radio, programs were being interrupted with increasing frequency by announcements that special news was coming—"*Achtung! Achtung!* Please stand by." The silence that ensued would then be suddenly shattered by a choir of trumpets delivering what was known as the "Great Fanfare." With the attention of the nation thus arrested, the Special Announcement would be delivered in crisp, curt military language but with intonations signifying that here the voice of history was speaking. On July 29, 1941, a Sunday, no less than twelve special announcements came from *Führer* headquarters, each one revealing a separate and sensational victory or advance in Russia. Through the following weeks the special announcements, each with its exultant bellow of brass to reenforce the impact, came over the radio in almost daily succession to proclaim "the greatest victories in the history of the world." With them a new marching song rang out, and its title was *From Finland to the Black Sea, Onward, Onward!*

The developments in Russia reverberated adversely on the anti-Nazi opposition at home. For people like the Scholls, who yearned for the downfall of National Socialism, the situation was more hopeless than ever. Again it had been demonstrated that whatever the regime undertook succeeded, and succeeded spectacularly: France crushed, England driven from the continent, the Balkans subjugated, the swastika hoisted over the Acropolis, and now the mighty Union of Soviet Socialist Republics, with the biggest army ever assembled on the face of the earth, teetering on the edge of collapse under the lightning assault of German arms. Who could hope to shake, or even damage, a system capable of such enormous success? What sense did it make to try . . . ?

But an undercurrent of doubt and defiance persisted. There were still those who, like Sophie Scholl, could not reconcile themselves to the idea of brute aggression as a national policy, however successful, and who did not believe that a government merited allegiance on the basis of successes scored in blood and reeking of death. That was a parlous attitude to maintain in a society geared for

conquest and bursting with nationalistic pride at achievements un-
paralleled in its history. There was, as well, the often agonizing inner conflict over whether it was allowable, under any circumstances, to oppose one's own government in time of war.

The Scholl family felt itself increasingly alienated from the feverish nationalism which seethed around them in the wake of the
Russian triumphs. They kept themselves apart from the victory demonstrations—the organized explosions of mass emotion which the
Munich diarist Reck-Maleczewen described in words of contempt
that almost burned through the paper: ". . . this bovine and finally
moronic roar of *'Sieg Heil!'* . . . hysterical females, adolescents
in a trance, an entire people in the spiritual state of howling der-
vishes." In this world, this atmosphere, this Germany, the Scholls
and those like them fought to sustain their sense of themselves as
custodians of a culture once respected by the world. In their with-
drawal from a society with which they had less and less in common
as it became more and more distorted, the dissidents took refuge in
something that came to be known as the "inner immigration." They
became expatriots inside their own country.

The spread of the conflict to the Soviet Union caused the Secret
State Police to intensify its activities with a series of nationwide
raids and arrests. Hundreds of Germans suspected of harboring
Communist, or even liberal, sympathies were jailed along with almost anyone who had previously given any sign of opposition to the
regime or who had been in custody before. This made life more than
usually tense for the Scholl family where arrests had already been
made. Now that re-arrest was the order of the day, a knock on the
door of the house in Cathedral Square could be expected at any
time.

But it did not happen. Then.

Hans being away in Munich with his medical unit and Sophie absent with the labor service, the full family was together only on the
odd weekend when both the children were home on leave. A new
personality had joined the Scholl inner circle, a serious and intelligent young man named Otto Aicher whom everyone called "Otl."
He was about Inge's age and here, too, a strong initial liking would

grow into a warm and more binding attachment. Otl Aicher's outlook and convictions were the same as those of the Scholls. He and
Inge began putting their ideas on paper in the form of essays and
commentaries. These were expanded into round-robin letters which
were sent to a score or more of like-minded friends who, in turn,
passed them on to others. When the letters began to circulate with
some regularity, they were given a name and so took on the character of a publication. The name chosen was *Windlicht*—"Storm Lan-
tern."

Hans and Sophie, when they were home, also contributed to
Windlicht which, in a veiled and guarded way, became a form of resistance for the whole Scholl circle. The essays and commentaries
were all cultural in tone; there were no political pieces as such and
no direct attacks on the regime. *Windlicht* was, rather, a personal
and private way of achieving some kind of self-expression divorced
from the inhibiting hand of the state and beyond its reach. The paper
provided an escape from the miasma of Nazi thought-control and
was, at the same time, an assertion of intellectual independence.
Words had to be used gingerly and sentences shaped with hair-line
precision so as not to commit to paper anything that could trigger a
reaction from the Gestapo. (Even with these precautions, there was
hazard in the situation. Once Inge Scholl, returning from a visit to
Hans in Munich, was met at her doorway by an agent who took her
to Gestapo headquarters for immediate interrogation. In her travel
bag was a copy of *Windlicht*, with an article about Napoleon which
could be taken—and was intended to be taken—as a parallel to Hitler, with the implication: Remember what happened to Napoleon
and take hope! Had the Gestapo agent read this essay and drawn the
correct conclusion from it, Inge Scholl would have faced a long
prison term for circulating subversive literature. Fortunately, her interrogator left the room for several minutes and she was able to rip
out the dangerous page, crumple it into a tiny ball and secrete it in
her purse, which was not searched.)

The essays and commentaries were designed to reflect an attitude,
a cast of mind. *Windlicht* was a kind of signal to the like-minded to
let them know that they were not totally alone in the totalitarian

darkness. The authorities were lulled by the frequency of religious, and even theological, discussions in *Windlicht*, which made the paper seem more nonpolitical and innocuous than it actually was. But for the Scholl circle the study and practice of Christianity were themselves forms of protest, since the Christian ideal was at the furthest possible remove from National Socialism. To immerse oneself in Christian doctrine and belief was a way of putting distance between oneself and Nazism, immunizing oneself against the ideological contagion that held so many Germans in its grip.

A source of growing distress for Hans Scholl was that the church, in both its denominations, had accepted Adolf Hitler so readily in the beginning and remained so uncritical of him since. Once in the family circle he expressed his concern about the lack of protest, the general apathy, of the Christian leadership in Germany in the face of the manifest crimes of the Nazi regime. "It is high time that Christians made up their minds to do something," he said. "What are we going to have to show in the way of resistance—as compared to the Communists, for instance—when this terror is over? We will be standing there empty-handed. We will have no answer when we are asked: 'What did you do about it?' "

But a powerful impetus to his own progress along the road to active resistance came from a churchman.

It began with a directive of forty-five words from Adolf Hitler to a deputy in his Chancellery in Berlin. A panel of doctors would be appointed to determine which inmates of German hospitals, asylums, and nursing homes were incurably ill, either physically or mentally. This was to be done in order that the patients so designated "could be granted release by euthanasia."

The program launched by Adolf Hitler's forty-five words was given the label of *Aktion t 4* and put into immediate effect, without objection or protest, by the *Führer*'s subordinates. Before it was terminated some 70,000 men, women, and children were "granted release" by methods evolved by German doctors and administered by the bureaucracy of the National Socialist state. The 70,000 were only a beginning.

Hitler's directive was issued on the outbreak of the war against Poland, in September of 1939. His idea was that "persons unworthy of life"—also called "useless eaters"—should be eliminated in time of war when the beds they occupied could better be used by wounded soldiers. Also, the hospital space might serve the state better by accommodating unwed mothers whose offspring would tend to compensate for the losses on the battlefield. Further, the incurably ill, the hopelessly crippled, the senile, the retarded were of no use to society anyway; rooting them out would make for a healthier and more vigorous nation, one more racially fit.

This was unassailable reasoning to adherents of Nazi ideology and it had the effect of precept and law; in keeping with the principles of the *Führerstaat*, the leadership state, everything emanating from the Leader was beyond question or dispute. So the German doctors dutifully checked over their hospital and asylum lists, setting a red crayon mark next to the names of those whom they deemed to be of no further use to the state or society. Those permitted to go on living were checked in blue.

The useless eaters were then brought together at an assembly point and transported by bus—the crippled children thought the ride a treat—to various "release" centers scattered through the Reich. The younger children were disposed of mainly by lethal injections. For the older patients another procedure was followed. Everybody was made to undress, and an attendant in a white smock, who was not necessarily a doctor, pretended to give a physical examination. This was done to make everything look routine and legitimate and keep down panic. Then everyone was asked to open his mouth, and after looking into it, the attendant stamped a four-digit number on the patient's chest. This was a code which told whether or not the person so stamped had gold teeth. The patients were herded in groups, sometimes as many as fifty at a time, into shower rooms. Some were pushed in in their wheel chairs; others hobbled in on crutches; still others had to be carried on stretchers. Overhead were what looked like shower nozzles. But when these were turned on, it was not water but poison gas that came out. It kept coming out until everyone was dead. This could be determined by the attendants who looked into the "shower" rooms through peep holes provided for the purpose. It took between fifteen and twenty minutes.

Then the corpses were dragged out and separated according to the code stamped on the chests. The gold teeth were broken out of the jaws of those who had them and piled up in heaps to be melted down and used to enrich the National Socialist state. The next of kin of the victims were notified that they had died unexpectedly of heart failure, or stroke, or sudden hemorrhage, and that the bodies had been cremated. With the notices went a death certificate in duplicate with a form letter urging that the certificates be preserved in case they were needed in the future for official reasons. These notices all ended with *"Heil Hitler!"*

Eventually, out of Hitler's directive of forty-five words, the huge extermination factories of Auschwitz and Buchenwald and Belsen would grow. The methods and procedures of *Aktion t 4*, having been found eminently workable and efficient, were expanded beyond the scope of a mere 70,000 defective human beings to include 6 million more, whether defective or not. Out of Hitler's euthanasia program grew his holocaust.

The *Aktion* was intended to be a strictly secret operation, but it involved too many people—doctors, nurses, guards, bus drivers—to be kept hidden indefinitely. From the hospitals and asylums, around the "release" centers and the crematoria, rumors and whispers multiplied and spread. They came, finally, to the ears of a man who could not in conscience keep silent. Count Clemens von Galen, bishop of Münster, determined to speak out, no matter what the risk.

Count Clemens von Galen was of a noble Westphalian family and there was something intimidating in his look. His mouth was stern and unsmiling and his eyes, beneath bushy brows, had the cool self-assurance of the aristocrat. Like many other German churchmen, Catholic and Protestant, he had welcomed Adolf Hitler's regime as a bulwark against the spread of what he called godless Communism. Then Hitler's racial doctrine and the Nazi attacks on Christianity and the church gave him second thoughts. But it was not until the summer of 1941 that he raised his voice in a way that won him the name "Lion of Münster" and caused the Nazi overlords to consider having him hanged.

Outraged by the government's confiscation of church property and the ousting of monks and nuns from their cloisters and convents, Bishop Galen mounted his pulpit one Sunday morning and excoriated the National Socialist regime with a vehemence that astonished all those who heard him. He denounced the arbitrary and unlawful actions of the government and its Secret Police and he demanded that the rule of law be restored in Germany. "Unless this call for justice is answered," the bishop warned, "this German folk and Fatherland, despite the heroism of its soldiers and their famous victories, will perish from inner rot and foulness."

No such language had been heard in public anywhere in Germany since Adolf Hitler came to power. Here was the voice, bold and resonant, of a latter-day Savonarola being raised where only the sounds of conformity and acquiescence were allowed. People in the congregation looked at each other in fear and wonder as they nodded in agreement with what they were hearing. It did not take long for the local agents of the Gestapo to be alerted to the secular blasphemy that was being uttered from the pulpit of the St. Lamberti Church in Münster. It took very little longer for transcipts of the sermons to reach Berlin.

One thing only saved Bishop Galen from immediate arrest and this was his popularity among the people and their respect for him. "If anything is done against this bishop," it was pointed out when the more radical Nazis proposed hanging him, "all of Münster will have to be written off for the war effort—and the whole of Westphalia, as well." So Bishop Galen was marked for arrest and execution after the war, and his sermons continued.

His most virulent attack was reserved for Hitler's euthanasia program. He denounced it as an indefensible violation of natural law, divine law, and criminal law for which he cited the relevant paragraph in the German penal code. He made the breathtaking demand that the high-ranking Nazi officials responsible for the program be charged with murder. "Once it is allowed," said the bishop, "once it becomes permissible, to put to death 'unproductive' human beings, then we are all of us open to being murdered when we, too, are old and feeble and no longer productive . . . if such things are permitted, then none of us is safe in our lives." He particularly enraged the Nazi authorities with his warning that if the "unproductive" were to be killed by the state as a matter of policy—"then woe to our brave soldiers who come back home to us from the fronts grievously wounded, as cripples and invalids."

Nothing of the sermons appeared in any newspapers and it was perilous even to talk about them, but Bishop Galen's words circulated nevertheless. They were copied out and passed from hand to hand and achieved an audience far beyond the limits of the St. Lamberti congregation in Münster. They reached the town of Ulm. Copies of the sermons reproduced on a mimeograph machine began appearing in the mailbox of the Scholl family in the house on Cathedral Square. (How they got there the family did not discover until later. Hans Hirzel, son of the local Lutheran minister, brother of Suse, friend of Sophie Scholl, admirer of Hans Scholl, had begun his own activity as a dissident. He had secretly duplicated the sermons and mailed them anonymously to people he was sure would approve of them.)

The sermons made a profound impression in the Scholl household. It was heartening—exhilarating even—to know that such words had been openly spoken and were being spread abroad in Germany. "At last," said Hans Scholl, "somebody has had the courage to speak out."

The most sensational passages in the sermons, the revelations of the euthanasia program, only confirmed for the Scholls what they had already learned at closer hand. Mother Scholl had kept up her friendships from her days as nurse and deaconess. From a nearby institution for mentally defective children she had received disturbing reports of what had lately been going on there. Nurses told her of black SS trucks which drove up to the institution, took on groups of children, and drove off to a destination that was never revealed. The children did not return.

When the black trucks came back, the children who were then bundled aboard asked where they were being taken. The nurses, themselves terrified and desperate for a soothing answer, replied: "Why, the trucks will carry you off to heaven!" Thus reassured, the children were singing as the trucks drove away.

The spectacle of blameless and defenseless children going singing to their doom at the hands of the state epitomized for the Scholls the ultimate barbarity of a system which had taken their country out of the community of civilized nations and tainted its name forever. Such a state no longer had any claim on the allegiance of its citizens; it had drained words like loyalty and treason of their ancient meanings. In an earlier sermon, Bishop Galen had been unequivocal on that score also. Rejecting the demand of the totalitarian state for total submission, he said: "An obedience that enslaves souls—that is to say: penetrates to the innermost sanctuary of man's freedom where his conscience lives—is uttermost slavery." Hans Scholl read and reread the Galen sermons in his father's office in Ulm. "I remember seeing him standing there with the sheets in his hand, looking thoughtful," his sister Inge wrote. "After a while he said: 'One definitely ought to have a duplicating machine of one's own . . .'"

It was a thought that he took with him when he reported back for duty in Munich.

Five

"For me this is more than a city," Adolf Hitler once said of Munich. "I am devoted to it in boundless love." He had reason to talk that way.

He had come to the place a penniless drifter who was obliged to sketch picture postcards and hawk them on the streets to pay the rent on his dingy attic room. In Munich he found the first supporters for his political tirades among his fellow rejects and castoffs in the lesser beer halls of the town. Here his first Storm Troopers had marched in ski caps and windbreakers in lieu of uniforms. Here his followers multiplied until, in only a few years, he became known as the "King of Munich." And from here, his voice—coarse and guttural, throbbing with hate and malevolence, mysteriously compelling—resounded through all Germany and worked its mesmerizing effect on millions.

Berlin was the nation's capital but Berlin was a city he never liked. Munich remained his permanent base—the "Capital of the Movement," a title he bestowed on it with all the aplomb of one who regarded himself as its rightful proprietor. "This," he said on another occasion, "is *the* city of Germany closest to my heart."

Small wonder. Before Munich he was a human cipher. In Munich he became master of Europe and shook the world.

Others loved the place for other reasons, of which there were many. Thomas Wolfe's reaction to it was rhapsodic. "How can one speak of Munich but to say it is a kind of German heaven?" he asked in *The Web and the Rock*. Thomas Mann, who wrote some of the great novels of his time there, spoke of the place as "luminous" and "easygoing and charming," words which, taken together, apply with accuracy to few other cities of the world. Munich was profligate with gifts which were often in short supply elsewhere—art, music, and ambrosial beer. In looks it was an agreeable mix of Gothic, rococo, and baroque, with the whole sweep of the city dominated by the twin cupolas, 300 feet high, of the Church of Our Lady, the *Frauenkirche*. In the deep south of Germany, at the foot of the Alps, Munich was close enough to Italy to acquire a Mediterranean touch in many of its buildings and fountains, and in some of its attitudes. In the open-air victuals market, cozily nestled in the center of the town, statues had been erected in honor of two esteemed local characters, the comedian Karl Valentin and his partner in jocosity and satire, Liesl Karlstadt. A new form of art was born in Munich when, in 1910, Vassily Kandinsky painted the first nonobjective picture in his studio in Schwabing, the bohemian quarter of the city. Both Richard Strauss and Richard Wagner were regarded as native sons, the first having been born there and the second having composed some of his finest work there. Opera was looked upon as a typical local product, like the ambrosial beer and the *Weisswurst*, the little white sausages which tradition required to be eaten before the ringing of the noontime bells. "Athens on the Isar" the place liked to call itself, after the placid river that flowed through it.

But by the early 1940s, when Hans Scholl was stationed there, the luminosity had dimmed. Words like "charming" and "easygoing" seemed less and less apt. The name "Munich" had become synonymous with the triumphs of totalitarianism and the defeats of democracy. The word "appeasement" acquired a taint it would never lose when, in 1938, Great Britain and France signed the Munich Agreement which ceded Czechoslovakia to Hitler. The expectation, the wistful hope, was that he would then cease troubling and give the world a rest. But what in fact the agreement did was put him in strategic command of central Europe without the necessity of firing a shot or dropping a bomb. From Munich the British prime minister, Neville Chamberlain, returned to London waving the agreement and proclaiming that it meant "Peace in our time." Another English statesman read the signs more shrewdly. Winston Churchill saw in the concessions at Munich " a total and unmitigated defeat" and he called it " the first sip, the foretaste of a bitter cup," which it turned out to be.

Nothing more vividly illustrated what had happened to Munich since Adolf Hitler's adoption of the city than that Thomas Mann could no longer live there. The living symbol of German culture, a Nobel laureate applauded around the world for books like *Buddenbrooks* and *The Magic Mountain,* was in exile.

As a member of the 2nd Student Medical Company, Hans Scholl walked the Munich streets in the field-gray uniform of Adolf Hitler's victorious *Wehrmacht* and gave every appearance of being a credit to it. He was slender and energetic, his service cap sat smartly on his head, and his salute—still the army style, not the "German greeting" of the Nazis—was sharp and prompt. He attended classes at the university, listened to lectures at various clinics around the city, and made the rounds of the wounded from the Russian front at the hospitals. His conduct was so satisfactory that he was promoted to *Feldwebel,* sergeant.

He had come back from his service in France determined that he would, in conscience, have to register in some way his loathing for the system he was living under. With the months, and the events, that had since passed, his inner insistence that he could not remain silent had grown more urgent. But for him, as for everyone else who felt as he did, the central difficulty remained: What could anyone attempt against a colossus permanently poised to crush the first flicker of opposition?

Still, to do something was a necessity if one were to retain one's honor as a man and one's self-respect as a German. The two were, for Hans Scholl, opposite sides of the same coin. The National Socialist regime—the "system of the absolute state" was a phrase he used—outraged him both as a man and a German. His bent was literary, and he continually turned phrases and expressions over in his mind and stored them away for future use. For him Nazism was "this cancerous tumor" that had spread its pollution through the German people. He tried to find words extreme enough to describe the crimes of the Nazis: " . . . atrocities so appalling that they go beyond any limits hitherto known." Those were words and ideas he burned to shout aloud, to cast abroad, so that thousands would hear and be shaken by them. There must be some way of speaking out, he told himself, some way to rouse the Germans from the moral apathy—"that heavy, stupid coma of indifference"—into which they had sunk.

His dissidence was never the outgrowth of mere personal rancor. He had no sense of being put upon or being treated more unjustly than anybody else. In the blind lottery of wartime which decides who should be sent where and do what, Hans Scholl had drawn a fairly lucky number. As a student-soldier in Munich, his duties were not onerous and they left him free much of the time to do as he pleased. He was not required to live in barracks. An occasional inspection or roll call had to be attended, but for the latter it was often possible to get a friend to shout "*Hier!*" when one's name was called so one often didn't have to show up at all. There was a war on, to be sure, but since things were going famously in the East, and nothing was happening in the West, the demands for manpower at the front were not yet acute. The orders assigning the 2nd Student Medical Company to training in Munich remained in force. Now and again the training could be grimly practical. A notation in his daybook of this period tells of a transport of heavily wounded soldiers arriving from Russia. "For the next fourteen days there will be plenty of work to do . . ."

The ambiguity of his situation—part student, part soldier—was constantly borne in on him. He felt it as a paradox both painful and absurd that the state should be ordering him to heal while at the same time it was training thousands of others to wound and kill.

"Going from bed to bed to hold out one's hand to people in pain is deeply satisfying," he told his sister Inge. "It's the only time I'm really happy. But it's madness just the same. . . . If it weren't for this senseless war there would be no wounded to be cared for in the first place." But given that there was a war and that Hans Scholl was involved in it, he was more and more aware of his good fortune in having chosen to study medicine.

The Student Medical Companies, for one thing, were relatively free of NS fanatics. They included a good many young men who had gone into medicine because it got them off the parade ground and allowed them to continue studying for at least part of the time. To some it was frankly a way of avoiding combat. The political tone of a medical company was more free and easy than a conventional unit and the talk more uninhibited. There was less danger of falling afoul of the Secret Police, since the uniform was a barrier the Gestapo was bound to respect. The discipline and punishment of soldiers was a function reserved to the army alone. Membership in a medical company could, in fact, be made to serve as a cover, or shelter, where dissidents were able to make contact and associate with less fear of detection than in civilian society. It was among his fellow student-soldiers in Munich that Hans Scholl found companions willing, for the sake of conscience, to join him in his venture into opposition against a regime that had only one answer for those who dared resist: the blade at Stadelheim.

In appearance and style, the least likely candidate for the role of a subversive and the fate of a martyr was Alexander Schmorell. There was nothing grim or harsh about him. In fact, the nonchalance of his manner suggested that there was not much that he took seriously. He certainly did not take soldiering seriously, though he somehow managed to wear his shapeless noncom's uniform with a hint of elegance. He spoke with an odd accent which added to the impression that there was something cosmopolitan, if not exotic, about him. There was.

Alex Schmorell had been born in the Ural Mountains of a Russian mother, though he had been brought to Munich at the age of four by his German father, a doctor. He had grown up in the care of a Rus-

sian nurse who spoke no German and never let him forget his birthplace. He spoke Russian fluently and could recite Pushkin and Gogol and Dostoievski by the page.

Alex took up the study of medicine to please his father, a respected and affluent physician. What he really wanted to be was a sculptor and he had a gift for it. Before the army and the war interfered
with his career, he had produced a bust of Beethoven which was not
merely a good likeness but also captured something of the dark and
tormented spirit reflected in the features of the original. The Beethoven bust grew out of another of Alexander's passions, which was
music. He attended so many concerts that he was a familiar figure to
every cloakroom attendant in every concert hall in Munich.

Alex Schmorell was a year older than Hans and had also been in
the Hitler Youth. Unlike Hans, he had never had an enthusiasm for
the marching and singing and saluting; he had, in fact, found the
whole experience repellent. He despised the National Socialist idea
of you-are-nothing-the-state-is-everything and he loathed the political and social conformity which National Socialism demanded.
What he liked was to ride his horse through the Isar Valley and stop
at a chance farm to talk to the hands or banter with the milkmaid on
the way. He was attracted to vagabonds and gypsies to whom some
strain of kinship in his own nature responded.

After his *Abitur* he had, like Hans, volunteered for army service
to get it over with and get on with his sculpting. He was serving
with a horse-artillery unit (''to be able to ride, at least'') when war
broke out. His career again ran parallel to Hans' when he was assigned to a medical unit during the Battle of France after duty in
Austria and among the Sudeten Germans of Czechoslovakia. Even
more than Hans, he had seen National Socialism at work beyond the
borders of Germany and was repelled and shamed by what he saw.

Alex Schmorell, who liked to be called by his Russian nickname
''Shurik,'' was tall and athletic and would have been officer material if his heart had been in it, but he could hardly bear to wear a uniform. His style ran more to turtleneck sweaters and well-cut three-
button coats which, along with his habitual pipe, gave him rather
the look of a young English squire. More than once he got into trou-

ble with his superiors by wearing civilian clothes on the street when he was under orders not to, and more than once he had to call on his father and an influential uncle to get him out of scrapes resulting from his disregard of regulations.

With Alexander Schmorell this was not simply frivolity and self-indulgence. His aversion to military service and the war ran deeper than his surface attitude of insouciance indicated. When he was obligated to take the oath of induction he underwent an emotional crisis which nearly resulted in a physical breakdown. What most others accepted as routine caused a crisis of conscience in Alex Schmorell. The oath was of a kind no German soldier had been compelled to take before the advent of National Socialism. It called for absolute loyalty not to the constitution or the nation, but to a person: Adolf Hitler. Every member of the armed forces from top-ranking general to raw recruit was required to repeat: *"I swear before God this holy oath to give my unconditional obedience to Adolf Hitler,* Führer *of the German Reich and the German people, Supreme Commander of the* Wehrmacht, *and I pledge my word as a brave soldier to observe this oath always, even at the peril of my life."* Millions recited the words without hesitation or doubt, but some, officers and other ranks alike, were troubled at being made to bind themselves, on their honor and unconditionally, to a leader whose motives and actions were so often open to question—or to any leader. Alex Schmorell's misgivings in the matter were so compelling that he presented himself to his superior officer and acknowledged them. He said that he differed with the regime politically on many points and that the soldier's oath had gone against his conscience. He therefore requested to be released from duty.

His request was refused, and he never thereafter felt at home in his uniform or had any relish for his duties as a soldier. His protest to his superiors, and its rejections, had in effect cancelled the obligation expressed in the oath. His way of enduring a situation that repelled him was to take refuge in books and music, cultivate congenial companions, and indulge his sense of the absurd. And Munich was full of girls who responded readily to his lean good looks and his special mixture of style and unassuming good humor.

It was a style which appealed to Hans Scholl as well. That he should be drawn to so kindred a spirit in his own unit was inevitable, and a firm friendship developed between the two young student-soldiers. For an association which would have historical consequences, and in the end prove fatal to them both, the beginning was innocuous enough, almost routine. They were both preparing for their premedical examination at the time, and Alex invited Hans to come to his home in Harlaching, a residential section of Munich, and study with him in his father's house.

Dr. Erich Schmorell was not entirely pleased with the arrangement at first. He was wary of Hans, as almost everybody was wary of everyone else in Nazi Germany. Any stranger, every newcomer to an established circle, was automatically suspect until clearly shown to be otherwise. Questionable characters who might well be informers abounded and they assumed many guises. "How well do you know this boy?" Dr. Schmorell asked his son. "Who is he?"

Alex was able to reassure his father on the basis of his own observations and Hans' repute in the unit. Even so, it was only after both young men had passed the examination that Hans Scholl was admitted to activities of the Schmorell household more intimate than poring over medical books.

At the barracks to which he was assigned, Alex often engaged in political discussions with several other student-soldiers who shared his feeling about National Socialism and the army. This little group was loosely held together by their common convictions, which they aired only among themselves. Their idea of doing something against the National Socialist regime was to engage in a kind of one-on-one missionary endeavor, and even this was more speculative than actual. Each would attempt, whenever possible, to create dissidence by explaining to any potential convert the defects and drawbacks of the Nazi system. In this way, they thought, word would be spread from one man to another in an ever-widening ripple effect until a change in public opinion was achieved. One of these student-soldiers, Jürgen Wittenstein, remembered a joke current in the group. Perhaps in ten years, the jest went, a sign would be hung on the barracks door saying: THE RESISTANCE MOVEMENT WAS

LAUNCHED FROM HERE. (This was self-mocking fantasy at the
time but, in fact, Adolf Hitler's own army was the seed bed of the
most damaging resistance against him; the White Rose itself originated in the ranks of the *Wehrmacht*, exactly where the Nazis had
least reason to expect such a thing.)

Alex Schmorell was a leading spirit in those tentative and incon-
clusive discussions and was in touch with others of the same mind
outside the group. One such dissident was his closest friend, Christoph Hermann Probst, whom he one day introduced to Hans Scholl.
This set in motion a ripple effect of an unforeseen kind and one that
would have the gravest consequences for everyone involved.

Hans Scholl and Christoph Probst met at one of the periodic
gatherings known as "reading evenings" in the doctor's house. A
few friends would gather for what Alex called sessions of "spiritual
refreshment" which consisted of reading aloud from favorite
books—poetry, novels, philosophy—and protracted discussions of
the meaning and implications of what was read. Like the writing in
Windlicht, these evenings were defensive measures on the part of
people under spiritual siege, a way of manning the moral ramparts.
It did not damage the enemy directly but it helped sustain the morale
of the defenders.

At such gatherings, and in companionable encounters elsewhere,
Hans Scholl discovered in Christoph Probst a concord of ideas and
outlook with his own and a personality which offered a rare combination of depth and warmth. Hans was soon calling him "Christel" as his family and boyhood friends did. The two cemented their
friendship with shared enthusiasms for mountain climbing and ski-
ing, as well as for the same books and poems. It added to their relationship that they both had Swabia in their background.

To the authorities, when they laid hands on him, Christoph Probst
described himself as an "unpolitical person." This was quoted in
the indictment against him which then added a comment—"i.e., no
man at all!" For the Nazis the personality of Christoph Probst was
of a kind they could not fathom or cope with, but only destroy. His
opposition to National Socialism needed no basis in politics or soci-
ology or history or tradition. His motivations were moral.

Christel Probst was a large man, the tallest in the group of stu-dent-soldiers who were, almost without realizing it, forming a nu-cleus around Hans Scholl. He was gentle, almost shy, a quality which can seem incongruous, if not slightly absurd, in a big man but which inspires admiration and love when it proves to be genuine, as it was with Christel. One of his friends chose the word *"edel,"* no-ble, to describe the impression he made. It was a rare enough word for one young man to use about another, but it did not seem out of place when applied to Christel Probst. The same friend, Jürgen Wit-tenstein, noted the hint of melancholy that seemed inseparable from his friend's personality even when he was joining in the laughter of a jovial gathering, as he often did.

Probst's father was a scholar in oriental religions and Christel grew up taking books and learning for granted. His parents were di-vorced but remained on good terms with each other so that the bro-ken family had no traumatic effect on Christel or his sister Angelika. He was sent to private boarding schools, which were largely over-looked in the Nazi drive to take over public education. As a result Christel was spared the worst of the propaganda pressures to which young Germans were being subjected and he avoided membership in the Hitler Youth.

For Christel Probst medicine as a career was a more serious mat-ter than it was for Hans Scholl or Alex Schmorell. It was not some-thing he drifted into. Healing was, for him, a necessary expression of his feeling for his fellowman, a moral obligation. It grew out of the same sensitivity that had made everything about National So-cialism offensive to him from the start. He had never responded to any of the Nazi slogans or been affected by its emotional appeal. He had no early commitment to it to overcome, as Hans and Sophie Scholl had, and his moral aversion to it ran deeper than Alex Schmorell's. "I remember especially his holy outrage when he heard about the euthanasia program," his sister Angelika has said. "I myself did not at first grasp the full horror of the situation. Chris-tel made it clear to me. He showed me that it was not given to any human being, in any circumstance, to make judgments that are re-served to God alone. No one, he said, can know what goes on in the soul of a mentally afflicted person. No one can know what secret inner ripening can come from suffering and sorrow. Every individual's life is priceless. We are all dear to God.''

Even without the euthanasia program and the atrocities that followed it, National Socialism would have been totally unacceptable to Christoph Probst. His view of life had no place for the cold arrogance, the aggressive inhumanity, on which Nazism was based and which gave it its motivating force. No man capable of composing the following lines could ever, under any circumstances, have reconciled himself to the Germany of Adolf Hitler: "Love is the power of the world;" (he wrote in a letter to his stepbrother) "it engenders all life; it protects us; it leads to blessedness. . . . By contrast, see how far hate is bringing us and has brought us: destruction, blood and death, and nothing either lasting or good. And what has love engendered? Upon love cultures have been built: cathedrals have risen up. Love is the bond between all men. Love makes all happiness possible . . .''

The certainty and serenity of Christoph Probst's religious faith was all the more remarkable in that he had not been brought up to follow any specific faith nor had he joined any church. His father, steeped in all the religions of the world and undecided among them, allowed his children to choose their own faith, or none. They were never baptised. Christoph and Angelika accordingly followed their own inclinations and opted for the truth of the Scriptures. Roman Catholic doctrine made a strong appeal to them both but, wary of the church as an institution, they did not become formal Catholics.

When the war came, Christoph was stationed at Innsbruck, in the Austrian Tyrol, with a *Luftwaffe* medical unit. Munich was only about 65 kilometers to the north, which made possible frequent visits to join his former schoolmate Alex Schmorell and his friend Jürgen Wittenstein in talk, wine, and music. His new acquaintanceship with Hans Scholl made the trips to Munich even more rewarding. Though he was not the oldest in the group, he seemed to be. He was the only married one and he had married early, at twenty-one. The responsibility for a wife and two small boys in a world heavy with menace and uncertainty weighed on Christoph Probst, and it showed.

The world he had entered with his relationship to Hans Scholl was laden with more menace and uncertainty than he could have known.

The daily newspaper of the National Socialist Party, the *Völkischer Beobachter*, appeared on the streets of Munich with headlines that stopped passersby in their tracks on October 10, 1941. THE GREAT HOUR HAS STRUCK—THE CAMPAIGN IN THE EAST DECIDED! In the greatest battles ever fought the *Wehrmacht* had scored the greatest military victories ever known. The foremost Soviet marshals—Timoshenko, Voroshilov, Budyenny—had been beaten, crushed, routed. The last battle-worthy divisions of the Red army, so the newspapers said, were being surrounded and destroyed at Bryansk. The final drive on Moscow itself was under way with orders from Adolf Hitler that the city be "completely wiped from the earth." Another frontpage headline told the story another way: THE MILITARY END OF BOLSHEVISM.

The war was evidently all but over, and with the defeat of Russia, the *Führer* was proving yet again that he was indisputably the greatest national leader of his time, if not of all time. And he had done it, miraculously, without breaking the back of the German economy. Far from causing undue strain and deprivation, the war until now had meant a happy enhancement of the standard of living for most Germans. The spoils of victory could literally be eaten and worn— butter from Denmark, fur coats from Norway, silk stockings and champagne from France. And now there would be unlimited wheat from the Ukraine as well.

With the heady tang of victory in the air, the loot of a continent pouring in, and the 40,000 agents of the Secret State Police as grimly alert as ever, the time was highly inauspicious for anyone to think of stirring up internal opposition to the Third Reich of Adolf Hitler. But Hans Scholl's temperament was not so geared as to wait for the most opportune moment or governed by the kind of calculated prudence that congeals action. When Adolf Hitler was at the height of his puissance and prestige, Hans Scholl's resolve to work actively against the National Socialist state took form. It was then that he made a significant entry in his daybook: *"These are times*

that insist on decisions of the inmost kind, and how much better it
would be if, now and again, one would confront oneself and see
oneself as the answer instead of being merely the questioner indulg-
ing in a false high-mindedness by standing aside and keeping
aloof."

Almost without his being aware of it, his military and social activities in Munich were creating a circle of like-minded people
around him. The dissidents who would, in varying degrees of intensity, become involved in the action known as the "White Rose"
were being drawn to him, coalescing around him. He was peculiarly
gifted for the role he was assuming as even his Nazi accusers would
acknowledge. "In spite of his twenty-four years," one of the indictments accusing him of High Treason said, "he knew how to form
connections with all kinds of people with the greatest ease. He had a
large circle of acquaintances, to which older people also belonged."
Almost everyone, regardless of age or status, responded to his ready
warmth and vivacity and the quickness of a mind which made him
open to ideas and sensitive to fresh impressions. Some who met him
could remember for years afterwards the circumstances under which
it happened. Traute Lafrenz, who was young and sparkling, remembered. Carl Muth, a philosopher three times his age, did too.

For Hans Scholl and his friends the concert halls of Munich were
sanctuaries to which they could repair to escape the stultifying atmosphere of the police state and be temporarily cleansed of it. Like
going to church, attending concerts could also be a subtle form of
protest. To be musical or artistic or literary was to proclaim oneself
un-Nazi, or non-Nazi with a hint of anti-Nazi, since the true Hitlerite scorned everything intellectual or esthetic as effete and unmanly.
To cherish such things was a sign, a signal. In the concert hall one
could withdraw into a civilized enclave, unsullied and intact, amid
the encroachments of the brown barbarism. Besides being a musical
performance, a concert could take on overtones of a gathering of
Christians worshipping in the catacombs while the armed enemy
prowled the streets outside. Hans Scholl went to concerts for both
reasons—a natural love for music and a desire to come into contact
with people of his own kind and inclinations.

Traute Lafrenz remembered meeting him for the first time at the Odeon, a concert hall distinguished for its superb acoustics. She also remembered the program that night: Bach's *Brandenburg Concertos*. Alex Schmorell introduced them, and in this way the nexus forming around Hans was being selectively added to as new personalities were encountered and found acceptable. Traute Lafrenz would have been an asset and an ornament to any group, being both unusually bright and unusually attractive. There was nothing of the tamed and domesticated *Kinder, Küche, Kirche* ilk about her. Born in Hamburg, she had been studying medicine there and was now enrolled at the University of Munich for additional courses. In Hamburg she was part of a student group whose feelings about National Socialism were identical with those of Hans, Alex, and Christel Probst. She would shortly take over the function of liaison between the two groups as she shuttled back and forth between the university in Munich and her home in Hamburg.

Traute Lafrenz had what not many German girls, even the pretty ones, were blessed with: style. Like Alex Schmorell, she had a cosmopolitan air which contrasted vividly with the more provincial ways of the young Bavarians around her. But there was something hoydenish about her, too, a coltish vivacity inherited from a Viennese mother that made her an exhilarating companion and playmate. Hans Scholl found her so and they were soon going to concerts together, comparing lecture notes after class, and engaging in spirited discussions of the state of the world over wine in a favored restaurant called the Bodega. Before long they were visiting each other's rooms on easy and familiar terms, and their relationship developed into an intense love affair. A mutual loathing of the regime of Adolf Hitler, and a commitment to risk life itself to oppose it, did not preclude the burgeoning of the normal drives and passions of youth among the members of the White Rose circle.

Encounters which shaped and motivated Hans Scholl along the precarious path that his destiny had marked out for him were made in other ways . . .

The magazine *Hochland (Highland)* had just been suppressed after thirty years of publication, though it never so much as mentioned

Adolf Hitler's name in all that time. But according to their lights, the Nazis were right to ban the magazine. Its mere existence was a danger to them and what they stood for. The circulation never passed 12,000 but its every page, its every word almost, was a denial of the precepts on which National Socialism was based and a challenge to it. The austere articles in *Hochland* sought to examine and sustain the ideas and ideals which distinguish a community of civilized men from a pack of predators. What concerned *Hochland* most were themes which the Nazis valued least—religion, art, poetry, and their relationship to each other and to the texture of life. When the Nazis silenced him, the editor of *Hochland* had been a critic and shaper of German culture for forty years and his influence extended far beyond the numerical limits of his magazine's circulation.

The old editor, whose name was Carl Muth, lived on the outskirts of Munich in a little house surrounded by a modest garden and bulging with books, some of them written by him. He was a Catholic thinker of a high order and the absorption of his life was to reveal and foster the relationships between the esthetic and the spiritual. He saw the two as interlocked and inseparable. One of his most admired and widely discussed essays was called "Religion, Art, and Poetry." His ideas were often daring and unorthodox and it was said that he "hovered between sainthood and excommunication."

Though he lived alone, Carl Muth was seldom lonesome. Men of his own stamp came regularly to visit him to share their ideas while absorbing his. His neighbor Werner Bergengruen came often. He was a Catholic convert, a writer who had been investigated by the local headquarters of the National Socialist Party and found to be "politically unreliable." He was. He and Carl Muth spent long evenings together in troubled talk about the condition of Germany, about the "brown bolshevism" that was engulfing their land and the "Satanocracy" that was ruling it. Though Carl Muth, with his wispy white hair, his rimless glasses on a ribbon, his winged collar, and his neat goatee, had the classic look of a sage above the battle, he was capable of towering and intimidating rages when he discussed the Nazis or suffered their harassments.

One day in the summer of 1943 Carl Muth had an unexpected vis-

itor. Hans Scholl knocked at his door with a book he had been asked
to deliver. He was invited in and the two fell into one of those wary
and tentative conversations which preceded all new relationships in
Nazi Germany. But between the old scholar and the young soldier a
rapport was quickly established. Carl Muth was taken immediately
by the "inner glow" which others had also sensed in Hans and by
the engaging coupling of amiability and intensity in his manner.
Hans, for his part, knew of Carl Muth and his work and was impressed at being in the old scholar's presence. Carl Muth was soon
aware that his visitor was uncommonly well read and had a grasp of
ideas startling in a youth who had grown up under National Socialism and was wearing the uniform of a *Wehrmacht* sergeant. Hans
was invited back for more conversation, and a binding relationship
developed between the two; there was an element of father-son in it
but also a mutual affection and respect rarely found in persons so
widely separated by age and background. Muth conferred a kind of
accolade when he entrusted Hans Scholl with the rearrangement and
cataloguing of his voluminous but chaotic library.

Visiting the little house in the modest garden almost every day
through the following months turned out to be one of the most enriching experiences of Hans' life. Sorting out the books, he was able
to stop and read as he liked. All the great and formative works were
there, from Plato and Goethe in the past to contemporaries like Paul
Claudel, the French Catholic and mystic whose poems and plays
Hans particularly cherished. There would also be interruptions for
talk with the old scholar over cups of *ersatz* wartime coffee. A continual interchange of mental and moral nourishment took place
between the two. The old man found joy and refreshment in the
reassurance that there was indeed, as he had so fervently hoped, a
"secret Germany," a hidden community of the young, who would
act as custodians of the values to which he had devoted his life. The
association with Muth and others he encountered in that house provided Hans with intellectual weapons and moral armor for the ordeal that was coming.

Sometimes, of an evening, one of Carl Muth's friends and associates would come to read from a chronicle he was keeping on his

times. Eventually it would be published as *Journal in the Night* but not before it had been buried deep in the ground, to keep it from the Nazis, and then dug up after the war when it could be read without danger to either the author or reader. Theodor Haecker, the chronicler, was under *Redeverbot,* forbidden to publish or read in public. Hans Scholl first heard of the *Journal* at Carl Muth's where it was often discussed. He spread word of it and its author among his friends.

Haecker was then sixty-three. His square regular features and bow tie did not immediately suggest the scholar and philosopher he actually was. Besides being a translator and interpreter of Kierkegaard, he was an acute and original thinker on his own. As with Muth, there was a strong Catholic content in his philosophy and writing. On the eighth anniversary of the date of Hitler's coming to power, Haecker wrote in his journal: "We, as a nation, apostatized the 30th January, 1933. Since then, as a nation, we have been on the wrong road, on the wrong side. Yet even now there are few among us who suspect what it means: to be on the wrong road and the wrong side." He saw National Socialism as a religion opposed to Christianity and therefore an enemy of every Christian. His comments were often set in a scriptural context: "The National Socialist man must always have existed in the world. How otherwise could it be possible that the Bible continually warns against him?" The intensity of his feelings about the Nazis was caught in phrases he used to describe them: " . . . these inhuman beings sent as a plague upon Europe . . ."

The idea of a redeeming element that may save a wayward nation recurs in the *Journal:* "We shall need very many just people if there is to be anything left of us that can still bear a name before God and the world."

All this was part of the "spiritual resistance" that Hans Scholl was absorbing from minds he admired and respected. (If "resistance" is too strong a word to apply to unpublished opinion and private speech, then "nonacceptance" must serve; but even this had its virtue at a time when mental and physical terror enforced conformity and acquiescence everywhere and on all levels.) Hans' own belief that Germany was on the wrong road and on the wrong side was confirmed and strengthened. His feeling that just men acting together not only could redeem his nation but were obligated as Christians to do so hardened into conviction. All the elements—intellectual, moral, spiritual—that would support and justify the transition from nonacceptance into actual resistance were gathering strength within him. The questioner was ready to become the answerer as well. And a saying of Theodor Haecker's had sunk into his mind, and burned there: *"An idea achieves its full value and significance only when it is converted into reality by action."*

That was the time—the spring and summer of 1941—when the German genius for efficiency and organization, which had achieved so many successes on the battlefield, was put to another use behind the lines: the planning and management of mass murder. The "Final Solution," the program for the annihilation of Jewry, was being thrown into high gear in the conquered areas in the East. Methodically, one after the other, the extermination factories were blueprinted, built, staffed, and put into operation at Treblinka, Sobibor, Belzec, Lublin, Auschwitz, Belsen. The first of the 6 million earmarked for death were beginning to be fed into the gas chambers on the pattern of *Aktion t 4,* the euthanasia program, but on a vastly stepped-up scale. More efficient methods had been developed by management experts to handle the increased work load. Zyklon B gas, with a prussic acid base that was more deadly, and worked quicker, was now in use. It was manufactured under government contract by a Hamburg chemical concern. But before the mechanized and, so to speak, assembly-line methods could be brought to their highest efficiency, the program had to be carried out by more primitive means, such as old-fashioned shooting.

The Germans back home learned of the atrocities in the East in various ways, when they did hear of them. Rumors spread. Indiscreet letters from the occupied areas sometimes slipped through the censorship. Soldiers home on leave talked. Their stories were often not believed and were, in fact, difficult for anyone of normal human instincts to credit. Hans Scholl did not need to rely on rumor and hearsay for information about the atrocities he was about to expose in the leaflets of the White Rose. He learned about them from someone who had been there and knew.

"A young man appeared at the door of my studio one day that summer," a Munich architect named Manfred Eickemeyer recalled years later. "I had been told about him by a friend of mine who was also a friend of Carl Muth's. I was then on the lookout for young men with whom I could discuss what was going on and who might be able to do something about it.

"I invited the young man in. His name was Hans Scholl. We got along well from the start, and I invited him to come back several times. I told him in detail about what I had seen of the behavior of the Germans in Poland and Russia."

Eickemeyer spent much of his time in the East where he was involved in construction ventures. From his working base in Cracow he was able to travel around the occupied areas and observe what was happening in the wake of the German armies. He described to Hans Scholl the operations of the *SS-Einsatzgruppen*, the so-called Action Groups of the Nazi elite corps, whose specialty was the mass execution of civilians. An *Einsatz* troop was composed of some 3,000 men chosen for their fanaticism and ruthlessness. Their victims were Jews, partisans, commissars, and anyone at all who resisted the German occupation in any way.

The *SS* firing squads had begun their work with the "liquidation" (the technical term then in use) of the Polish intelligentsia, numbering some 3,500, because Hitler regarded them as "carriers of Polish nationalism." What began in Poland was carried on and intensified in Russia The procedure was to enter a town or village, round up all the Jews, seize their valuables, and order them to take off their outer garments. They were then marched or trucked to the execution site which was usually an anti-tank ditch or other large pit. Lined up at the edge of the pit, the Jews—men, women, children—were then machine-gunned by the Action Group in such a way that the victims fell into the ditch. Thus the necessity of digging graves was avoided. One execution troop alone, *Einsatzgruppe D*, was able, by using these highly professional procedures, to kill 90,000 civilians of both sexes and all ages in the space of a year. It was not easy work. Even the most merciless *SS* fanatics sometimes broke under the strain of repeated slaughter and became hopeless alcoholics or mental cases. The story was current in the East of how Heinrich Himmler, Chief of Gestapo, witnessed an *Einsatz* massacre in the Russian town of Minsk. He was so shaken by the spectacle that he had to avert his eyes and nearly fainted in full view of his men. But he did not put a stop to the killings. Instead, he praised the troops for obeying their orders in so exemplary a fashion and told them to carry on.

Eickemeyer also told Hans of the Poles and the Russians who were herded into the concentration camps as slave labor, and of the young girls in the occupied areas who were dispatched to *SS* bordellos to serve as prostitutes. Hans did not doubt what he heard. He himself had seen enough of the depredations of the Nazis as masters to know that Manfred Eickemeyer was telling him the truth. When the time came to enter into his conspiracy of conscience and act against the National Socialist state, Hans Scholl did not lack for motivation.

Afterwards, when he was asked what had compelled him to write and circulate the leaflets that cost him his life when he could have remained silent and safe like millions of others, he gave an answer that was devoid of eloquence but clearly traced the moral and emotional steps that led to his final commitment:

"After much agonized deliberation I became convinced that only one course was possible: to bring about a shortening of the war. Along with this was the consideration that for me the treatment by us Germans of the people in the occupied territories was an abomination. I could not imagine that after such methods of domination a peaceful reconstruction of Europe would be possible. Out of such considerations grew my antagonism for this state; and because, as a good citizen, I could not remain indifferent to the fate of my people, I decided to assert my convictions in deeds, not merely in thought. Thus I came to the idea of writing and producing leaflets."

This was the stripped-down, soldierly language he used with his interrogators when they probed for motives before sending him to Stadelheim and his death. It said nothing of the youthful passion that moved him and his comrades or of the purity of their motives which derived from sources—religious, cultural, literary—which Heinrich Himmler's agents could not be expected to fathom.

There was the memory of the verses he used to chant with his comrades in the *d.j.1.11* when he was younger, not then foreseeing the reality the chanted poetry would one day acquire. There were the lines that said: *"The time is coming when you'll be needed /See to it that you're prepared and ready . . ."* In the summer of 1941, Hans Scholl felt he was prepared and with his fellow dissident and friend Alex Schmorell he began to take the practical steps that would give readiness meaning. Implements would be needed, tools. A typewriter. Paper. A duplicating machine. A base where the work could be done. In Nazi Germany none of these necessities was easy to come by or could be acquired without arousing suspicion. Assembling them would require ingenuity and persistence. The problem of a working base, Hans thought, could be met through his new friendship with Manfred Eickemeyer. The architect was often absent in the East and his studio would be empty at such times. The studio was in an isolated spot and it had a basement.

Alex Schmorell was a tireless and resourceful collaborator, contributing not only time and energy but also the pocket money which was usually allotted to another concert or another date. If anything, he was even more impatient than Hans to make the transition from talk to action. "What are we waiting for?" he said more than once. "Until the war is over and everybody points to us and says we tolerated such a regime without protest?" That was a prospect which haunted them and gave added urgency to their actions. A concern for the opinion of the world and sheer embarrassment at the spectacle their country was making of itself determined them to send out a signal to let the world know that there were Germans who were ashamed and appalled at the figure Germany was cutting before mankind and history. Not only had National Socialism outraged them morally; it had grievously wounded their national pride.

While they were making their preparations, Hans Scholl and Alex Schmorell were obliged to continue their daily round of lectures and hospital duties as before. It was necessary to go underground not only to avoid detection by the authorities but to be certain that those nearest and dearest were also unaware of what they were doing. In a totalitarian state, knowledge could be as fatal as participation; the state punished those who knew as well as those who acted. The activist was thus obligated to deceive and mislead those to whom he might wish to be most open and whose support he most sorely needed. He had to live a life of multiple deceits out of the highest and purest motives. He had to lie and mislead in the interests of decency and integrity.

For Hans Scholl the problem was intensified by his closeness to his family, by the warmth and frankness that normally flowed back and forth between all members of it and especially between him and his sister Sophie.

And now Sophie was coming to Munich and they would be together every day.

Six

On her twenty-first birthday—May 9, 1942 the last birthday she would know—Sophie Scholl was on her way to Munich by train. On the baggage rack, beside her luggage, was a box with her birthday cake and a bottle of wine. Tucked behind her ear was a daisy, a splash of white and yellow against her dark brown hair. Her mood was festive. She felt as if she had just been liberated from a long bondage. The rumble of the train was music. It was taking her where, for so many dreary months, she had been longing to go.

After her six months in the Labor Service she had been obliged to spend another half year in the War Assistance program, a requirement imposed by the state if she hoped to realize her dream of enrolling at the University of Munich. For her War Assistance stint Sophie was shunted off to a little industrial town called Blumberg, near the Swiss border, an unattractive spot with an eyesore of a brick factory as its only distinction. Since Blumberg produced small nuts-and-bolts devices of use to a mechanized army, the place was integrated into the war effort. Sophie, along with some other girls in her situation, was sent there to help out. She was not assigned to the factory itself but to the local kindergarten where she was expected to keep watch over the young of Blumberg while their mothers worked in the factory and their fathers went off to war.

Aside from the pleasure she took at being with the children, the days passed slowly for Sophie Scholl. Finding no rewarding companionship in Blumberg, she felt isolated and abandoned, like a castaway on an unfamiliar shore. With every month of the war, the social climate grew more and more ugly in various ways, some minor but nevertheless oppressive. In the pay envelopes of the girls working in the factory, and in Sophie's too, printed notices were inserted to warn against involvement with the foreign workers and prisoners of war who were appearing in Germany in increasing numbers. These morose outlanders, male and female, were imported as slave labor for Germany's war effort and were visible evidence on the home front of Germany's callous exploitation of the people it had subjugated abroad. For Sophie the war was an aching unhappiness; being compelled to work for the state that was waging it became a continuing anguish. Her father had always told her and her brothers and sisters, "I want you to go through life upright and free." How was that possible when one had continually to bow under the pressure of a system that had abolished freedom? It made each day a grinding conflict of conscience and every hour a burden.

Sophie tried with every resource of her mind and spirit to keep alive her hope of surviving the war without becoming a slave to it, but the war impinged more and more directly on her life, clouding and warping it. Not long ago the Gestapo had come for her father. Three men had searched the house and then taken him away on the charge that he had openly expressed opinions unfavorable to National Socialism and its Leader. Mother Scholl had had to stand by in helpless hurt and bitterness as, once again, arbitrary authority laid hands on her family, violating her home and spreading the taint of its terror where she had established only love, comfort, and decency. Robert Scholl had been released after only a few days for the ironical reason that he was in the midst of a technical analysis which had to be completed for the Ulm Bureau of Finance. Mother Scholl knew, as Sophie also did, that the matter was not concluded. The three men would come back for Robert Scholl whenever the Secret Police might choose a more convenient time.

The war was continually making its encroachments on Sophie's family and eroding her social circle. Her younger brother Werner, nicknamed "Has," was in uniform on the Russian front. Her valued friend and favored correspondent, Fritz Hartnagel, was somewhere in the East, too. Ernst Reden, whose esprit of mind and personality had so taken the Scholl girls and enlivened their group, was also somewhere on the steppes. Otl Aicher was now in the army and his absence left another emptiness where closeness and warmth had been the rule. It was a torment to see those she loved and valued most disappear, one by one, into the maw of a war none of them approved of or willingly supported.

At Blumberg, in her isolation, she had withdrawn more and more into an inner immigration of her own and found some solace in it. Not far from her quarters in the grimy little town she discovered a chapel with an organ. She obtained permission to use it on free afternoons and evenings, and she spent hours alone in the empty church playing her favorite hymns and etudes on the wheezy but still functioning instrument. Another means of escape was the woods beyond the town where she could lie in a clearing and look at the sky, or watch the scampering squirrels, or even, in the green silence, catch sight of a grazing deer. These solitary outings proved for her again the wisdom of "knowing where to go when things go badly," of going to the grass and the trees. She could give herself up to the wind and the sky, noting that "the wind is allowing itself so many jokes that it would be stupid if one didn't laugh," and she did laugh. But the state of her world oppressed her and at night, in her diary, she would write passages that were thoughtful and somber beyond her years: "Many people think of our times as being the last before the end of the world. The evidence of horrors all around us makes this plausible. But isn't that an idea of only minor importance? Doesn't every human being, no matter which era he lives in, always have to reckon with being made accountable to God at any moment? Can I know whether I'll be alive tomorrow morning? A bomb could destroy us all tonight. And then my guilt before God would not be one bit less than if I perished with the earth and the stars together . . ." Those were heavy thoughts to cross the mind of one so young and so eager to pursue the promise of life, but they were not unusual for Sophie Scholl whose temperament could respond to the joking way of the wind but also give matters of time and eternity their due.

Now, however, in her crisply fresh white blouse, lovingly ironed for her the night before by her mother, and with the daisy behind her ear, she was not in a mood for brooding. The twin cupolas of the *Frauenkirche*, the Church of Our Lady, soaring high above the city like unlit beacons, were coming into sight which meant that not many kilometers were left of the 175 that separated Ulm from Munich. Once, when she was in the *BDM*, she and her entire group had hiked all that distance to see the Nazi shrines in the "Capital of the Movement." The hike had taken eight days. She had been only a girl then, and the shrines had been impressive, especially the "Eternal Watch." That was in the König Platz, in the center of the city, with *SS* guards standing perfectly motionless in their ominous black uniforms before imposing stone pillars that loomed over sixteen sarcophagi. She had to shudder then, and she shuddered now, at the sarcophagi. Inside were the corpses of the men who fell in the Hitler *Putsch*, his first attempt to seize power when he was still little more than a local rabble-rouser. The State Police had dispersed his Storm Troop columns with gunfire and thrown the *Führer*, as he was known even then, into jail. The fiasco of his Munich *Putsch* had delayed him hardly at all. He used his brief prison term to write *Mein Kampf* and then emerged to resume his drive toward power, this time with greater success.

On this visit Sophie Scholl would regard Nazi shrines in an entirely different light from that of the enthusiastic *BDM* girl she once was. Now she would go out of her way to avoid them, especially the Eternal Watch. People passing there were required to raise their arms in the Nazi salute, a gesture she had resolved never to use again. Hans would surely have far more agreeable places to show her in Munich which, even in the fourth year of the war, still had plenty of attractions and enticements to offer. After her six months in Blumberg, Munich would seem heavenly and she could hardly wait for the train to pull into the station. Her sister Inge, who had seen her off in Ulm, had noted the glowing impatience with which Sophie looked forward to the journey. "Her face had something endearingly childish about it," Inge remembered. "She looked at the world out of deep, dark eyes that were probing and warm at the same time. There was something of the sniffing curiosity of a young animal about her."

Hans was waiting for her in the station, as she knew he would be, and his reception was as warm as she had hoped. The old affection and excitement they always felt in each other's presence flared up again after the long separation. Any twinges of uncertainty she may have had about starting a new phase of her life in unfamiliar and possibly unsettling surroundings were quickly dispersed. Hans, big and competent, was there to rely on. It made her feel at home to hear him call her Sophia, the pet name he fancied for its lovely sound. "Come along, Sophia," he said. "I want you to meet my friends."

Hans had a room on the Franz Joseph Strasse, not far from the university. The May sunshine streamed in and the fragrant white of early blossoming jessamine brightened the room even more. Prints of French Impressionist paintings were pinned to the wall and books ranging from army medical texts to the sayings of Lao-tse were scattered about everywhere. That night there was a birthday party for Sophie who supplied its main ingredients herself—the cake her mother had baked for her and the bottle of wine she had brought along. She had heard much about Hans' friends—Alex Schmorell, Christel Probst, and a newcomer named Willi Graf—and they had heard much about her, which made the party seem more like a reunion than a first encounter between Sophie and the others.

It was characteristic of this gathering, and of the time and place, that the party game, proposed by Christel Probst, consisted in readings of obscure passages of poetry with the listeners challenged to identify the poets. When it came Hans' turn he reached into a portfolio and pulled out a typewritten page. "This one is going to baffle you," he said and began to read.

It was a poem of six eight-line verses that began by describing a robber who emerges from his lair in search of purses to steal. He soon finds better booty, a nation with the banner of its honor torn and its people made dull and stupid by want and spiritual emptiness. A master of deceit and malice, the predator turns prophet: "*Mount-*

ing the rubbish heap around him/ He spews his message on the world.'' Many follow him for personal gain and *''Where before one liar raged/ Thousands soon were thus engaged.''* The social order was overthrown. *''The masses lived in utter shame/ For foulest deeds they felt no blame.''* What once was only feared now comes true: *''The good are reduced to none, or few/ The wicked are a mighty crew!''* At the end the poem predicts that this nightmare period will pass with the overthrow of the tyrant, and one day his reign will be looked back upon, and talked about, like the Black Plague. Children will set fire to straw effigies on the heath in its memory—*''To burn joy from out of sorrow / And make light of ancient woe.''*

There was a long pause when Hans finished the poem. No one could place either the verses or the author. Every possible contemporary writer was suggested but none of the names was accepted by Hans. "Anyway," said Christel Probst, "those verses couldn't be more timely. They might have been written yesterday."

Alex Schmorell proposed that the poem be mimeographed and dropped over Germany from an airplane. "With a dedication to Adolf Hitler," he added.

"Or printed in the *Völkischer Beobachter*," Willi Graf suggested, ironically.

Since no name anyone could think of was accepted as the author, the consensus of the group settled on Hans himself. He rejected that suggestion, too. "Actually," he said, "the verses were written in 1878 and they don't refer to events in Germany at all, but to a political situation in Switzerland. The author is Gottfried Keller." This surprised everyone, since Keller was known to all of them for his stories and novels. It was somehow both heartening and significant that his poem so amazingly paralleled what had happened in Germany and that the outcome of his allegory could be taken as an assurance of what, in the end, would also happen in Germany.

There was a moon over Munich that night and it seduced the party away from political allegory and into the open. They took the bottle of wine and headed for the English Garden, Munich's oddly named but spacious and always inviting park. Hans brought his guitar along and Alex his balalaika. The wine was immersed in the Isar on a stout string, and while it was cooling, the group forgot where they were—in the Capital of Adolf Hitler's Movement—and who they were—captives of his National Socialist state and subject to its tyranny and terror. Under the May moon, by the softly gliding river in the green park fresh and sweet with spring, they played their music and sang their songs and drank the cool wine.

For Sophie Scholl, smiling and singing next to her brother in the moonlight, it was as happy a birthday as she had ever known, her twenty-second and her last. None of those around her would live long beyond the next May moon, either, except for the newcomer, Willi Graf. But he, too, was doomed. He would only have to wait longer than the others for the blade to fall at Stadelheim.

Sophie Scholl had come to Munich in time to register for the spring semester at the Ludwig-Maximilian University, known to the students as the "Uni." To do so she had to cross a square, part of the university area, that today is named for her and her brother and displays a sign announcing in white lettering on a blue background that this is GESCHWISTER [brother and sister] SCHOLL PLATZ. The legend would strike her as both incredible and absurd, and she would no doubt join Hans in hooting at it. Though her awareness of herself was constant and her imagination rich, she had no need for fantasies of future fame. A cool pragmatic streak in her temperament kept her always in touch with probability and down to earth. When she registered, it was not for courses in poetry and literature but for lectures in philosophy and biology. For Sophie Scholl in May of 1942, to be in Munich and at the Uni was dream enough.

The three-story, red-roofed buildings stretched along the broad and beautiful Ludwig Strasse and bordered on Munich's bohemia, the district of Schwabing. Aside from several rather modest triangles of grass and two undistinguished fountains, there was no area that could properly be called a campus. Rows of arched windows, Italianate in style, saved the lecture halls from looking too much like barracks, though some thought that, even so, they looked a good deal like cloisters. When the grass was green, the fountains splashing, and the bare un-ivied stone of the facade gleamed in the sun under the red roofs, the place was not unattractive.

When Sophie enrolled there, the University of Munich was the largest in the land but was not distinguished for much else. Like every other university in Germany, it had been purged and tainted by the process of *Gleichschaltung,* the enforced conformity that brought every public institution into line with the ideology of National Socialism. When Adolf Hitler came to power, the Minister of Culture of Bavaria had assembled all the professors of Munich and set the tone for the higher learning of the future. "From now on," said Hans Schemm, "it will not be your job to determine whether something is true or not, but only whether it is in the spirit of the National Socialist revolution."

Hans Schemm, who had once been dismissed as an elementary school teacher on morals charges, was also the principal speaker when the University of Munich participated in the book-burning organized by the Ministry of Public Enlightenment and Propaganda to celebrate National Socialism's break with the intellectual and spiritual past. Professors and students had marched together in a solemn torchlight procession, the scholars in their academic robes, from the university to the König Platz where a huge bonfire was blazing.

Ceremoniously, ritually, to the cheers and applause of the assembled academics, one book after the other was thrown into the fire, each one accompanied by cries of imprecation and abuse. "Down with decadence and moral perversion!" was the shout as the books of Heinrich Mann and Erich Kästner, a local satirist and storyteller, were hurled into the fire. "Literary treason against our soldiers!" was the verdict as flames licked at Erich Maria Remarque's *All Quiet on the Western Front.* Into the flames went Hans Scholl's favorite author, Stefan Zweig, and Albert Einstein, Sigmund Freud, Lion Feuchtwanger, and Bert Brecht, whose plays were first seen in Munich.

All over Germany other universities, once the admiration of the world for their scholastic excellence, were also burning books to signalize the "uprising of the German spirit" against the corruption of "un-German" literature and thought. No such spectacle had been seen anywhere in the world in modern times, but it was not an entirely new thing in Germany. More than a hundred years before, German students had gathered by night on a mountain in Thuringia and burnt other books for other reasons, prompting Heinrich Heine to write in his *Almansor* words that came horribly true in the later Germany that burnt his books as well: *"Dort, wo man Bücher verbrennt, verbrennt man auch am Ende Menschen"*—"Where they burn books they will also, in the end, burn people."

Now the book-burners were in charge of Germany's academic life in Munich, as elsewhere. The chancellor of the university was Professor Dr. Walther Wüst who also held the rank of colonel in the *SS* and was described in the Party press as "one of the most loyal and reliable followers of the *Führer.*" Professor Dr. Wüst was an acknowledged authority in the field then known as "Aryan Culture," meaning the supposed culture of an invented race of ancient supermen whose surpassing virtues and unsullied blood lines the followers of Adolf Hitler were assumed to have inherited. The chancellor of the University of Munich, who was formally addressed as *Eure Magnifizenz*—Your Magnificence—was a wholehearted supporter of the philosophy once expressed by Hitler in the saying: "The Aryan race is manifestly the bearer of all culture, the true representative of all humanity. . . . Take away the Nordic Germans and nothing remains but the dance of apes."

The student body, as Sophie Scholl quickly sensed, was also essentially Nazi in outlook and attitude, with admiration for the *Führer* and support for his policies rampant in classroom and corridor. All groups and activities were strictly supervised by the National Socialist Students Bund, an organization of young zealots who constantly monitored the actions and speech of students and professors alike. Activists of the Bund, some of them in brown shirts, acted as ideological police, always alert to catch and report any word or sign of defeatism, subversion, or irreverence for authority. Although German college students from the first outstripped the general population in their enthusiasm for National Socialism, the authorities were never able to overcome a rankling distrust of what might be going on in places where books were read, ideas discussed, and the working of the mind took precedence over the exercise of muscle. In the Nazi view, intellectuals were classified with Jews and, therefore, merited much the same treatment. With the coming of National Socialism, more than 1,200 university professors—mostly liberals and Jews—were dismissed, among them some of Germany's most brilliant scholars and several Nobel prize winners. With the outbreak of war, teachers unpopular with the Party were promptly drafted into the army.

The prevailing attitude toward books and learning was expressed in a widely applauded line in a play by the popular Nazi author, Hanns Johst: "Whenever I hear the word 'culture' I take the safety catch off my automatic." With the universities in the charge of *SS* colonels like Walther Wüst in Munich, the universities had almost ceased to be seats of learning and had virtually become branch offices of the Ministry of Propaganda.

But short of shutting, or burning, the schools down completely, not even the most fanatical system can wholly succeed in suppressing the passion to know, learn, and teach when it has permeated the atmosphere and seeped into the walls of what for generations has called itself a university, a society of masters and students. By picking one's way warily, as if negotiating a mine field, by choosing class and teacher cunningly, by skirting courses like "Racial Hygiene" and "Folk and Race" with which the curriculum was studded, it was possible, as Sophie Scholl discovered, to outwit the scholastic system imposed by the Nazis and make it disgorge benefits it meant to withhold.

The two disciplines she had chosen—philosophy and biology—turned out to be pockets of comparative latitude amid the rigid ideological constraints that prevailed elsewhere. She also found other such oases which had unaccountably survived deep into the Nazi era. A professor named Artur Kutscher read his class passages from the *Three-Penny Opera,* by the blacklisted Bertolt Brecht, and somehow survived. The chemistry department, presided over by Professor Heinrich Wieland, was known to the student underground as being indifferent to ideology, receptive to dissidents, and a haven for those suspected of the non-Aryan taint. There were even professors who dared to warn their students against the teaching of the "terrible simplifiers," by which they meant the ideologues of National Socialism.

One of the favorites of the dissident students was Professor Fritz-Joachim von Rintelen who lectured on the Greek spirit. It seemed a topic of remote relevance to contemporary Germany, but Professor von Rintelen was a master of veiled allusion and barbed reference by which he was able to use the Greek past to score points against the Nazi present. Students otherwise uninterested in Greek history swarmed into his lecture room to catch and decipher his allusions and repeat them afterwards. He would quote Goethe, whom not even the Nazis dared denigrate as an authority on everything: "Of all the peoples of the world, the Greeks have dreamed the dream of life most beautifully." Professor von Rintelen would pause and look long at the class and then out of the window. Clearly, no society could be more grossly different from the beautiful dream of the Greeks than National Socialism. Clearly, German society in its present phase was so far from the Greek dream as to be a nightmare.

Professor von Rintelen's allusions were not sufficiently veiled to escape the notice of the network of student informers. One day he failed to appear for his usual lecture. Nobody explained the professor's absence. No notice had been posted. The class, left to sit wondering what was wrong, became increasingly restless and suspicious. Before leaving, the students agreed to meet again for the next scheduled lecture in three days and meanwhile to try to find out what was happening.

One of Professor von Rintelen's more ardent admirers was Jürgen Wittenstein, the soldier-student comrade of Hans Scholl and Alex Schmorell. He kept a record of what happened when the class met again. "By then our suspicions were confirmed," he recalled. "The professor had been put under *Verbot*. But still we had been given no explanation and no official announcement was made. The authorities obviously hoped the class would simply disperse for good when it became clear that Professor von Rintelen was not going to return. The whole affair—the arbitrary dismissal of a popular and respected teacher without explanation—was supposed to be accepted without protest or comment. That was the way things were done then, but this time it didn't go quite as the authorities expected."

Wittenstein and a friend of his, a young painter, decided to take action. With a group of the professor's regular students, augmented by recruits from other lecture rooms, they marched together to the office of the chancellor to demand an explanation of Professor von Rintelen's absence from his classes. "At a time of despotism and blind obedience," Wittenstein's account says, "such a procedure was unheard of." It was so novel and unexpected that chancellor Dr. Wüst, the *SS* colonel, was taken wholly aback. He withdrew without replying to the students and locked himself behind his office door. "We whistled and stamped our feet," said Wittenstein, "but it did no good. He stayed barricaded behind his locked door."

Heartened that their show of strength had caused even the *SS* to retreat, the students determined to carry their protest further. "We decided to go to Professor von Rintelen's home and show our support for him. About fifty of us, boys and some girls too, formed up on Ludwig Strasse and marched off. Here was a student protest showing itself in broad daylight on the principal street of Munich! Nothing like that had been seen before in the Third Reich." But nothing came of it, either. Professor Fritz-Joachim von Rintelen and his dream of a society Greek in its beauty and sanity remained permanently banished.

The demonstration had not challenged the system or been overtly anti-Nazi. The authorities let it pass off as merely a college matter, nothing more than a nonpolitical spasm of student rowdyism, and did nothing. But not very far in the future there would be other students at the University of Munich to confront the Secret State Police with a more significant, and more explosive, situation.

Willi Graf was not particularly keen on studying medicine at the Uni. His interest lay elsewhere. He would have preferred to continue reading theology and philosophy at the University of Bonn as he had been doing until drafted into the army. After his experience with an artillery company in the East, he was grateful for the orders that sent him to Munich for further training as a medic. He had seen things in Poland and Russia that shook him to his soul. As a soldier in a combat zone he had expected to encounter wounds and death. He had been prepared for that. But he had not foreseen that he would be writing letters home with lines like: *"Some things have occurred in my area that have disturbed me deeply. . . . I can't begin to give you the details. . . . It is simply unthinkable that such things exist."* Or: *"The war here in the East leads to things so terrible I would never have thought them possible. . . . I wish I hadn't had to see what I have seen . . .''* He was not referring to combat but to what he had seen behind the lines.

Willi Graf was another one whose coming together with Hans Scholl was inevitable, and when they did meet Hans' remark to Alex Schmorell afterwards was: "He's one of us." And Willi did become one of them—to the end. He kept a diary, and already, before he knew the way that he would go, he had written in it: "Sometimes you can't just go where favoring winds send you. Sometimes one must take a direction which isn't that easy. You can't allow yourself to be continually blown about.'' With his meeting with Hans Scholl, Willi Graf's life took a new direction, though it would be some time before he was aware of it.

To allow himself to be blown about was never Willi Graf's style. As a boy of fifteen he resisted joining the Hitler Youth because something in him rebelled at being dragooned into an organization for which he had no sympathy. He regarded the Nazi insistence on lockstep conformity as an affront to his self-respect. He kept an address book of his neighborhood friends, and at the height of the Hitler Youth enthusiasm, he began crossing out names with the notation: "Joined HY." He could not be intimidated by the roving street gangs of young Hitlerites, and he gave as good as he got when attacked for his nonconformity.

Willi Graf's allegiance could not be coerced but when it was freely given it endured. He joined a group of young Catholics who called themselves "New Germany" and for the rest of his life his social and fraternal loyalties were bound up with his religious convictions, which were strong and deep. In the wave of arrests in 1938, when the Secret Police sought to break up all associations of the young except the Hitler Youth, Willi Graf spent three weeks in "investigative custody." As with Hans Scholl, the indignity of being jailed and imprisoned without legitimate cause hardened an already settled antagonism to the National Socialist system. Willi Graf never gave up his membership in "New Germany," though it remained under permanent ban by the State Police.

After the execution of Hans and Sophie Scholl, the Gestapo had a request for Willi Graf in his death cell. He was asked to write a brief autobiography. The authorities were curious to know the background and motives of a young German so thoroughly persuaded of the evil of a system they gloried in that he was moved to risk his life to oppose it. With a pencil stub, on long white sheets, Willi Graf wrote out his life story in ten-and-a-half pages of clear and unemotional prose. It is a document which, besides puzzling the minions of the Gestapo, might also give various modern schools of behavioral science some cause for wonder. Everything that is commonly assumed to go into the making of a rebel against authority—unhappy childhood, poverty, parental abuse, lack of love, frustration—was, by his own account, absent from Willi Graf's background. There was only one constant in his personality and its development: an innate and ineradicable decency.

"I spent my early life in the circle of my parents and sisters," Willi Graf with his stubby pencil in his death cell informed the Gestapo. "I never felt deprivation of any kind, since our family lived in rather good if moderate circumstances." His father was the manager of a wholesale wine enterprise in the Saarland and Willi described him as "correct and honorable" in both his private and business life, attributes which the father also required in his children. He could be strict but Willi mentions this with no trace of rancor; that was as it should be. "The relationship with my mother was extremely affectionate. She did everything for her children. Her concern for her family was her whole life."

School was easy for Willi and there was plenty of time for play, for violin lessons, for learning to use tools and exploring the secrets of a new device called radio. During his vacations he went on long hikes through the German countryside, sometimes wandering as far as Italy in one direction and Yugoslavia in another. Whatever he did and wherever he went as a youth he always felt himself "in the protection of a good and loving family."

So far Willi's story was so bland, proper, and conventional as to border on parody. A deeper note is sounded when his narrative speaks of "the great world of belief" which he entered early and never left. Political questions held no interest for him, he says, but problems of philosophy and belief increasingly did. The teachings of the Catholic church answered his need for assurance that there was a divine plan and purpose of life and that moral law governed mankind's seemingly bootless sojourn on the earth. For Willi Graf faith was no neatly packaged commodity which, once acquired, could be regarded as a safe and comfortable possession. "Belief is no simple thing," he once wrote to his sister. "It demands constant strain and struggle. It has to be mastered over and over again. To be a true Christian: exactly that is the most difficult thing of all, because we are never, ever, able to be true Christians—except perhaps in death . . ."

In his report to the Gestapo, Willi Graf mentioned, rather discreetly, his experience as a soldier in the East and how he came under the influence of Hans Scholl, all of which had a bearing on his fatal involvement in the subversive activities of the White Rose. But his death-cell statement leaves no doubt that his dissidence was a result of his settled judgment that National Socialism must be rejected because it had cut itself adrift from the anchorage of all order, stability, decency, and justice. "For us, the people of the Occident," he wrote, "Christianity is the tradition upon which we have built and carry on our spiritual and cultural life. . . . Without religion a state can have no permanence. All order comes from God, equally for the family, the people, or the state."

What the agents of the Secret Police in the reign of Adolf Hitler made of this testament is not on record.

Sophie Scholl and Willi Graf had come to Munich at about the same time. When she met him, she was impressed. He was big and broad-shouldered, but he had an easy and unaggressive way about him. His hair was blonde and his eyes strikingly blue and clear, and there was something almost bashful about his courteous manner and hesitant speech. Sophie liked what she heard when he did speak. "Everything he says sounds so genuine and reliable," she reported to her sister Inge. "You get the impression that he'd back whatever he said with his whole being." So Willi was accepted without reservation into the group that had coalesced around Hans Scholl.

The Scholls were the nucleus of the group, but Alex Schmorell was like another of their siblings and Christel Probst was also part of the inner circle on his frequent visits from Innsbruck. With time, Willi Graf was absorbed into the nucleus, though these gradations came about through no deliberate sorting out or conscious ranking, but because of circumstance and the character traits of the individuals involved. Traute Lafrenz, by virtue of her special personality and her relation to Hans, was prominent in all the group's acitvities, whether social or serious. Gisela Schertling, Sophie's friend from the labor service time, became another member when she began her courses in art history at the Uni. Inge Scholl, too, was present at the gatherings whenever her obligations in Ulm permitted her to visit her brother and sister in Munich, always a happy occasion for all three.

A number of like-minded members of the Student Medical Company were attracted to the group and became members of it in varying degrees of intimacy and permanence. Jürgen Wittenstein, a warm admirer of both Sophie and Hans, was one. Another was Hubert Furtwängler who often stood in for his comrades at roll calls in the barracks or on the parade grounds, sometimes shouting *"Hier!"* for three of them at a time—Hans, Alex, Willi—with appropriate voice changes for each.

There was no set criterion for entry into the group that crystallized around Hans and Sophie Scholl that summer in Munich, no fixed conditions on which admission or rejection depended. It was not an organization with rules and a membership list. Yet the group had a distinct identity, a definite personality, and it adhered to standards no less rigid for being undefined and unspoken. These standards involved intelligence, character, and especially political attitude— though, for the group, the three elements were interlocked and could not be separated, one following sequentially from the other.

The core members of the group became experts at sensing whether a newcomer was admissible or not in accordance with the German saying that "kindred souls greet each other from afar." Traute Lafrenz claimed she could tell after hearing a stranger speak two sentences, but this was an exaggeration which could be dangerous. The times being what they were, it was necessary to be absolutely sure since an error could lead to betrayal, arrest, and imprisonment if an unguarded remark or impermissible comment reached the wrong ears. An elaborate testing procedure, consisting of code words and phrases, was evolved to determine whether a person was *"einwandfrei"* or *"ein guter Mensch"*—code words themselves which meant "unobjectionable" or "all right politically." Conversations in the probing period were marked by arcane ploys of language and loaded references, all calculated to smoke out the true political bent of the person being tested while concealing one's own.

In this byplay, pauses and silences could be as significant as spoken words. If, in a general discussion, somebody expressed the opinion that Germany could not possibly lose the war, the speaker at once revealed himself as a convinced Nazi, as did those who so much as nodded agreement. Those who disagreed could not openly incriminate themselves by saying so but their lack of response to the remark was nevertheless an expression of opinion. By withholding assent in such situations, the like-minded identified themselves to each other. In a society where assent and submission were demanded of everyone, mere silence could be a form of dissent.

Members of the group had acute ears for what they called "sane talk," another code phrase which meant opinions with which they could agree. Describing an encounter with a new acquaintance, Willi Graf would write in his diary: *"Wir tasteten uns ab . . ."* —"We felt each other out." As the wary exchange continued, code words were offered and deciphered on both sides until, as they parted Willie could say: *"Wir verstehen uns"*—"We understand each other"—and another contact was made.

The term "Nazi" was originally a derogatory nickname, often spoken with a snigger of contempt. The Hitlerites themselves never used it, insisting on the full dignity of "National Socialist." Members of the group, of course, invariably said "Nazi." They shunned the use of *"Heil Hitler!"* as a greeting, though it rang out constantly all around them. They went out of their way to avoid giving the raised-arm salute, though this could easily attract unfavorable attention and comment. They collected and repeated anti-Nazi jokes for which the penalties could be severe, ranging from six weeks in jail to execution. Nothing enraged the Nazis more than ridicule.

They were called "whisper–jokes" and scores of them were in circulation, new ones being hatched to keep pace with every new development. They spread across the country by word of mouth with telegraphic speed and were repeated not only by the dissident but also by the merely disgruntled. With every other form of criticism cut off, the joke was the only means an ordinary citizen had of airing his resentments and frustrations. But listeners had to be chosen with great care and the telling was usually accompanied by the "German look" to be sure no informer was within earshot. One of the advantages of having friends one could absolutely trust, as in the Scholl group, was that whisper-jokes could then be freely exchanged and enjoyed without fear of betrayal.

Many of the lines were more bitter than funny. Once, the saying went, Germany was the land of *Dichter und Denker* (poets and thinkers) but now, under Hitler, it had become the land of *Richter und Henker* (judges and hangmen). The peculiarly German brand of jesting known as "gallows humor" figured largely in the whisper-jokes: "Enjoy the war. The peace is going to be terrible." The grosser personality defects of the leading Nazis—Goering's inordinate vanity, Goebbels' unbridled lechery, Hitler's egomania—were favored targets. No aspect of life in National Socialist Germany escaped:

> *"Bernard was arrested yesterday."*
> *"Bernard! Such a decent fellow! Why?"*
> *"That's why."*

Or:

> *Optimist: "We're going to lose the war."*
> *Pessimist: "Yes, but when . . . ?"*

And:

> *"What is the difference between Christianity and National Socialism?"*
> *"Simple. In Christianity one man died for everybody. In National Socialism everybody dies for one man."*

It was put forth as an ideal by the Ministry of Propaganda that every German should be honest, intelligent, and a National Socialist. The dissident wits pounced on this at once. "It can't be done," they said. "If a man is intelligent and a Nazi, he is not honest. If he is honest and a Nazi, he is not intelligent. And if he is intelligent and honest, he is not a Nazi.''

Almost nothing was too grave or terrible to make a joke about, which might be construed as callousness or frivolity, or both, by those who were not there. Though life was no laughing matter for unbelievers in the Third Reich, humor was, nevertheless, part of it and often a sanity-saving release, however momentary, from tension and terror. Sophie Scholl, for one, was eager to find something funny in even the grimmest situation and, as she said, "it has nothing to do with being superficial." Willi Graf, perhaps the most reserved and sober of the group, urged a friend on the brink of despair not to let the times overwhelm him. "After all," said Willi Graf, "we're young, and we can be glad of it."

They were young and they showed how glad they were of it by snatching what fun they could when they could. They met and talked and laughed in favored cafes and restaurants like the Bodega or the Lombardi, where the chianti was cheap but good and served in generous portions. Though they were never free of the sense of a menace closing in, of walking always where a trap might be sprung at any moment, of skirting ambush every day, their relish for life and for each other was never wholly extinguished. The pleasure they took in each other's company was one of the most sustaining and replenishing elements in their lives. They never felt so secure, stimulated, and alive as when they were together. Repeatedly, in Willie Graf's diary of this period, is the entry: ". . . it was already getting light when we broke up." Comradeship was not only a sustaining bond among them, but it represented something pure, shining, and certain in a world where almost nothing else was left untainted and uncorrupted.

They made a highly implausible band of rebels and subversives. All of them came from the same bourgeois background, all of them, in their own idiom, were *aus gutem Haus*, from a good family, and there was not a political radical among them. They were all well-mannered and properly brought up children of the middle class where conservatism and submission to authority were rooted attitudes, especially in the place that bred them, Germany. Yet they had chosen to reject the prevailing values of their society, to cut themselves off from the convictions and enthusiasms of their peers, to make themselves aliens in their own land, and to put their lives in jeopardy rather than accept the mores that a brutal despotism was determined to impose on them. They were oppressed and appalled by the feeling that the Nazi system was robbing them of heritage, that they were being plundered of their past and their future at the same time. They saw what they treasured most being steadily eroded by "a dirtying and weakening of all higher concepts," as one of their contemporaries called it. They were terrified that Spengler's chilling forecast might be coming true—the last violin lying broken on the ground and the last copy of the Mozart quartets thrown to the flames. Books, ideas, music, poetry, philosophy, religion meant incomparably more to them than any ideology of the right, left, or center. For them the advice of the critic and poet Friedrich Schlegel was a guideline: "Do not waste faith and love on the political world, but offer up your inmost being to the divine world of scholarship and art, in the sacred fire of eternal *Bildung* [development, growth]." It hardly seemed the appropriate equipment for the practice of sedition and revolt in the reign of Adolf Hitler, but where barbarism is rampant, to be civilized can be the extremest form of radicalism.

Though they were all students, or student-soldiers, none of their activities as a group centered on the university where the atmosphere was, for them, tense and uneasy. The dissident students were repelled by the Nazi temper of the student body and too many of the professors, and especially by the knowledge that an informer for the Student Bund was likely to be at one's elbow at any time. There was no social or fraternal life at the college except for Nazi-sponsored rallies and pep-talks which members of the group made a point of avoiding. They put the Uni behind them as soon as a lecture ended.

The group felt the need to gather frequently for talk, to exchange gossip and ideas, and to give each other the moral support which was one of the prime rewards of comradeship. They had constituted themselves a tiny island of dissent in an ocean of conformity. They were always, in effect, huddling together for comfort and support, feeling themselves alone and isolated for perversely holding to be-

"I want to feel the impact of the times directly in my own person," she said. "Sympathy for others becomes hollow if one feels no pain oneself." Sophie Scholl was fated to feel the ultimate pain of her time and place—execution for her convictions and beliefs at the hands of the National Socialist State.

She was not made for conspiracy and treason. "My heart continues to dream and clings to the promise of a good life," Sophie Scholl wrote in her diary. But in the Nazi nightmare she gave up the dream and promise, and life itself.

There was always something youthful and something mature about her, a mingling that gave her an aura of her own.

A squad leader of the Hitler Youth in his boyhood, Hans Scholl for a time represented the Nazi ideal of what a German youth should be. But he rejected National Socialism totally when he found that it warred against every ideal and concept which, for him, made existence tolerable and life worth living.

He looked more like an actor than an activist; there was nothing grim or surly about Hans Scholl. War and politics did not fill his life, even when he was risking it for his political and moral convictions.

"What are we going to show in the way of resistance when this terror is over?" Hans Scholl asked when the Hitler tyranny was at its height and the mass of his countrymen accepted it without protest. "We will have no answer when we are asked: 'What did you do about it?'" He and his companions of the White Rose saw to it that they would have an answer.

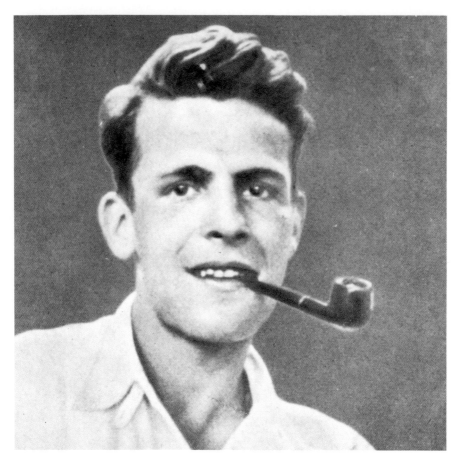

When the Nazis came to power, Christoph Probst "caught a whiff of hell" and opposed the New Order from the first.

Prof. Kurt Huber, making a common cause with the rebellious students, invoked Kant's categorical imperative before the People's Court to justify his opposition to the Nazi regime. He wrote the final, fatal leaflet—a manifesto to German students—and it cost him his life.

His style was light and life-loving and he had nothing of the fanatic about him, but Alex Schmorell was uncompromising in his opposition to National Socialism and what it was doing to his country. Some of the most passionate lines in the White Rose leaflets were his.

What interested Willi Graf was not revolution and social change but theology and the mystery of man's relationship to God. Yet Willi Graf could not endure living a life contrary to his innermost convictions as the Nazi dictatorship was forcing him to do. He joined the White Rose to give his opposition strength and focus. It cost him his life.

No judge in Hitler's Germany was more fanatical in using the courts to punish dissidence than Roland Freisler who sent the Scholls and their comrades of the White Rose to the guillotine. Roland Freisler died in an American bombing raid.

Koblenz Archives

"They fought against the giant conflagration with their bare hands and their faith." And the great conflagration consumed them: Hans and Sophie Scholl and their comrade Christoph Probst. Together in their noble treason to the Nazi tyranny, they died under the Nazi knife.

liefs which the overwhelming majority of their fellow Germans considered both wrongheaded and seditious. Self-made pariahs, they carried their secret convictions around with them like time bombs which at any moment could explode to public view and do them irreparable damage, destroying their careers, shattering and possibly ending their lives.

It was true that most of the men and women they admired, the writers and artists and thinkers, had given evidence that they, too, despised and opposed National Socialism. They had had to flee abroad or withdraw into inner immigration because they, like the members of the Scholl group, could not bend their souls to conform to the spiritual perversions imposed on Germany by Adolf Hitler. Yet it was unsettling that some of Germany's foremost intellectuals did bend—and not perforce but voluntarily, eagerly. Gottfried Benn, most brilliant of expressionist poets, whose strangely soaring lyrics had won him high acclaim and wide following, hailed Hitler and the Nazi movement as "heroic," a genuine and necessary revival of the German spirit. Martin Heidegger, one of the greatest living German philosophers, was a passionate adherent of National Socialism. On becoming rector of the University of Freiburg, he made a speech in which he said: "Not theses and ideas are the law of your being! The *Führer* himself, and he alone, is Germany's reality and law today and in the future." Could what the great poet and the great philosopher so unequivocally proclaimed be true? Millions of Germans thought it was. Such pronouncements from such sources caused many a doubter to revise his views and eased the way to conformity and acquiescence.

To the members of the Scholl group, the pro-Nazi pronouncements of such men as Benn and Heidegger were only additional examples of the *trahison des clercs*, the treason of the intellectuals, against values they were supposed to defend, and that too would be a theme of the White Rose leaflets. That towering members of Germany's cultural community could so wholeheartedly approve of Hitler and his movement spread confusion and dismay in the ranks of the intellectual young and made dissidence among them harder to justify and sustain. The members of the Scholl group needed all the moral support they could find and they found it chiefly in each other.

From the first, by common consent and without anything so formal as a vote, Hans Scholl was their leader. The role was tacitly bestowed on him by virtue of that quality in his personality which, in any group, made him the focus of attention. Alex Schmorell was usually at his side, his close collaborator. Between them they arranged for meetings and meeting places. While cafes and restaurants were agreeable enough for casual encounters, they were not satisfactory for more serious sessions. With vigilance relaxed by sociability, and tongues loosened by chianti, things might easily be said which could cause trouble if overheard at a neighboring table. The only safe places were where they could be alone and away from the threat of the informer, the ubiquitous *Spitzel* in the service of the police or the Party.

Sometimes they met in Hans' room for impromptu talk and discussion. For larger meetings they gathered at the Eickemeyer studio or the villa of Dr. Schmorell, an indulgent father who shared many of his son's views. These sessions were not conspiratorial in the sense that plots were hatched and violence fomented against the government. The theme of what-can-be-done? was explored over and over, but mostly in terms of fortifying the mind and spirit against the assaults of the brown barbarism which grew more virulent as the war progressed.

Often the group would meet with Theodor Haecker who came at Hans' behest. He would read to the students from his unpublished manuscripts, risking arrest and imprisonment to do so, since he was under continuing *Verbot*. From these sessions Hans and the others absorbed more of the ideas which would soon also be appearing as motifs in the White Rose leaflets, ideas whose impact derived from their moral and religious content and were devoid of political polemic. Always implicit in Theodor Haecker's message was the potentially explosive Biblical injunction that "we ought to obey God rather than men" and the Kantian dictum that when the state encroaches upon the individual's pursuit of morality, it is the Moral Law that must be obeyed and not the state.

In the more pragmatic gatherings at the Schmorell villa, it was Hans who led the discussion even when adults were present. Traute Lafrenz remembered his passionate advocacy of the idea that every possible measure should be taken to shorten the war. Once that was accomplished, other steps toward a renewal of a moral basis for government in Germany could be taken. Others would contribute their own ideas, Christel Probst rather oddly proposing that after the war a government patterned on the Austrian monarchy would be desirable. The future form of government after the fall of National Socialism was only dimly outlined at best, the immediate nightmare being too oppressive to allow for much speculation on what might lie beyond. Parliamentary democracy, having failed to prove itself in the Weimar Republic, was not urged with much zeal though some form of rule which would represent the will of the people was often stressed. Marxism, strangely, was not a frequent theme, pro or con.

Not all the talk was grimly serious. Sigismund von Radecki, a younger friend of Carl Muth, sometimes joined the group and spoke to it. Another Catholic convert, he was also an engineer, artist, essayist, and actor with a gift for treating serious topics with infusions of humor. He was a popular personality at the gatherings. Even in their pursuit of what Hans Scholl called *Läuterung* and Christel Probst termed *Klarheit*—clarification, clarity—the members of the group were never too solemn to let laughter break through.

For Sophie Scholl, sharing the activities of her brother's circle and attending the university were especially stimulating after the months of confinement in the labor service and the war assistance program. Not only was there a happy sense of release in being abroad in Munich with Hans and his friends, but she felt herself returned to the mainstream of life instead of being sealed off from it.

Now there were concerts and lectures to attend and congenial gatherings at the Bodega at noon and the Lombardi of an evening. Hans happily shared with her all his interests except the one which would have compromised her, and of this one he made no mention. She joined the sessions at the Schmorell villa where she was one of the most attentive listeners at the "reading evenings" and the discussions that followed. Hans took her to the suburb of Solln, to the little house with the modest garden, where he introduced her to Carl Muth. For Sophie, as for others who came to that place, "the world seemed to grow wider than before with every visit." She fell in love with the fragile old scholar. "I wanted to throw my arms around him to keep him from fading away entirely," she said.

At the university Sophie was spared the often awkward, and sometimes painful, ordeal of the newcomer who must grope to find a place and make contacts in a strange environment. Sophie was adopted at once by Traute Lafrenz whose easy self-confidence and knowledgeable ways were shields against the abrasions to which new arrivals are customarily exposed. Girls were comparatively rare at the university, the ratio being about one-to-ten; but Sophie, Traute, and Gisela Schertling made a self-contained trio which supplied its own needs in the way of sociability and like-mindedness. A little later the trio was expanded into a quartet when Katharina Schüddekopf was taken in. She was older that the others, having already studied in Berlin for her doctorate in philosophy. In spite of so sober and scholarly an ambition, Kate S. was a merry companion. She was small and attractive, with a pert sideways look and smile and a lameness in one leg that hampered her only slightly. She joined the group because, through the code and her own antennae, she soon discovered that its outlook was compatible with her own. Kate S., too, had been repelled by the "empty phrases" of National Socialist propaganda and by the thuglike boorishness of the brown-shirt mentality. Her admission to the group would, in the end, make her a victim of that mentality in a way she could not have suspected when she became the companion of Sophie Scholl and her friends at the university.

Others were drawn to Sophie Scholl at this time as well. To Jürgen Wittenstein she was "a rare mixture of enchanting youth with a ripeness that was deep and winning at the same time." Though she was not slight physically, being somewhat taller than average, there was that in her carriage and manner that made people think of her as fine-grained and delicate. She always seemed more mature than others in her age group. When Hans introduced her to Manfred Eickemeyer, the architect thought her "a quiet girl much concerned with religion." Her smile was radiant when it came, and those close to her saw it often. But for Sophie Scholl life was serious; it was not to be shrugged off, or skipped through, or laughed away.

More than once she had expressed her urge to be involved in her times, not to escape them but to experience them. "I want to share the suffering of these days," she once wrote, and added: "That is putting it too strongly, perhaps; I mean I want to be affected more directly. . . . Sympathy is often difficult and soon becomes hollow if one feels no pain oneself." For Sophie Scholl the war, its mere existence and continuance, was a constant ache of distress which she carried with her even in her lighter moments. It would not go away. Around her the signs of the war's intensification were multiplying; its ugliness spreading.

Now, on the streets of Munich, the Jews who still remained were forced to wear the symbol of David as a badge of humiliation and shame—"a hexagonal star, the size of a palm, bordered in black, made of yellow material, bearing the inscription '*Jude*' in black letters, affixed to the left side of their garments at the height of the breast," as the official decree required. In his *Journal in the Night*, from which Sophie heard him read, Theodor Haecker had written: "Is it not possible that the day will come when every German will be obliged to wear a swastika on the left side of his coat, the sign of the anti-Christ? . . . Today the Germans are crucifying Christ *as a people* for the second time. What is improbable about their undergoing similar consequences?"

The first bombs had recently fallen on Munich and air-raid shelters were being constructed all over the town. As the month of May ended, something truly shattering happened at Cologne: One thousand British bombers, the greatest number ever put into the air at once, had raided the city on the Rhine with catastrophic effect, a stunning reprisal for the many German air assaults on cities of England. Cologne was a foretaste, a sample, of what was in store for Germany which, until now, had been free of the wreckage of war while inflicting it without scruple on others.

The newspapers and the radio still trumpeted news of victories almost every day. Field Marshal Rommel had captured Tobruk from the British in North Africa. In Russia the *Wehrmacht* had seized Sevastopol and was advancing on a city on the Volga called Stalingrad (though some at home were wondering why the fighting in Russia was continuing unabated even though the imminent end of hostilities had been proclaimed months before).

Every new triumph, every additional demonstration of brute power as a national policy, only alienated Sophie Scholl further from her government and its leaders. For her it was increasingly evident that the more the rule of force expanded in the world, the less room would be left for the things which gave life meaning and value. Her own life became a steady pursuit of meanings and values which she sought to gather in and store up, as if to make as many of them as possible her own before the barbarians trampled them out of existence. In her questing she found an uncorrupted guide and mentor and she found him unexpectedly, almost paradoxically, in the purged and tainted university. He was her philosophy professor and his name would become as inseparably linked to the White Rose story as her own, though in age three decades stretched between them.

He was Kurt Huber.

Kurt Huber was not highly regarded in the academic circles of his time and was never appointed to a full chair, his highest rank being that of Assistant Professor or *Dozent*. When he applied for a permanent post at the University of Munich he was told by the official who passed on such matters: "We can only use professors who are also officer material." Kurt Huber decidedly was not. He was a cripple.

Infantile paralysis, if not multiple sclerosis, had left his right leg lame and it dragged behind him when he walked. His hands trembled and sometimes his head shook. It was a struggle for him to mount the rostrum for his lectures and he had difficulty getting his words out as he began speaking, the syllables seeming to get stuck or tangled in his mouth. Since he was uncomfortable to watch, the supposition would be that Professor Huber's lectures were sparsely attended, if at all.

They were crowded. Sophie Scholl made a point of arriving early to be sure of getting a seat and, infected by her enthusiasm, her whole group made something of a cult of the Huber class and of the professor himself. "Once he got into the swing of a lecture," Wittenstein remembered, "you quickly forgot your first impression of his physical handicap. You were carried away by the clarity and logic of his ideas and by the passion with which he expressed them. He built his structure of thought like an architect."

Kurt Huber won the applause of his students without making
things easy for them. He lectured on theodicy, the justification of
God's ways to man, the vindication of divine justice in the face of
the existence of evil. It was an abstruse and difficult subject at the
best of times, but a particularly complicated and sensitive one when
Sophie Scholl and her friends sat in his classroom as, in the world
outside, cruelty and madness clouded the lives of millions. What
Sophie and her friends were thirsting for was an acceptable explanation for the seeming insanity of the cosmos. It is a lasting tribute to
the pedagogical gifts of Kurt Huber that he was able to offer exposi-
tion and argument that held them, brought them back, and went far
to answer their need.

He did this largely through his elucidation of the philosophy of
Gottfried Wilhelm Leibniz to which he himself was devoted. Besides being a mathematical genius (inventor of the differential and
integral calculus), Leibniz was an advocate of the "pre-established
harmony of the universe." He argued, intricately and cogently, that
all things were arranged at creation to work together for ultimate
good, which implied the final elimination of evil. It was, at least, a
philosophy which Sophie Scholl and her friends could receive and
ponder with some hope that the abominations of their time were not
the last word on how the universe was ordered.

Students were drawn to Kurt Huber's lectures by his ability to
bring verve and spirit to subjects normally regarded as leaden. He
had the pale, intent look of the scholar obsessed by his subject but
his face could break into a smile of almost childlike gaiety. His
manner was stiffly proper as befitted a German professor of the old
school; his daughter, using the English word, saw him as a "gentle-
man *durch und durch*"—through and through—but a shy kind of
charm took the chill off all but the most formal encounters. He was
never above a joke where one was appropriate, even during the
heavier passages of his lectures, which were sprinkled with provocative insights and acute formulations. "There are some people," he
would say, "who write so badly that they can only write books."
Or: "How wide is the world of artistry in the simplest melody, and
how narrow is the subtlest analysis of it! One washes sand for gold
and lets the gold escape through the sieve of one's perceptions.

What remains is sand.'' In discussing the prolixity of many philosophers, he would remark: "Philosophical brevity is a moral obligation.'' When it came to philosophical truth as he saw it, Kurt Huber
would not compromise. Under the Nazis it was customary for teachers to ignore Jewish philosophers like Spinoza or dismiss them with
contempt. Kurt Huber did neither. He gave them their due and
sometimes in recommending their work to his students, he would
say with a smile: "Careful! They're Jewish, you know. Don't get
poisoned!''

He was a master of code language and sometimes caused a stir in
the lecture room by the daring of his comments which, though cam-
ouflaged, were grasped by most of his listeners. His lectures were
audited by the *Spitzel* of the Student Bund, as all lectures were, and
it is not clear why his were allowed to continue when von Rintelen's
were terminated. It is likely that the *Spitzel*, who were not unduly
bright, simply failed to catch hints of dissent when buried in a discourse on theodicy.

For Kurt Huber the imposition of Nazi dogma on German scholarship was a barely supportable burden and grief. He had been born
into a cultivated family where books and music were at the center of
daily life. Both parents were educators and encouraged his early
bent in that direction. His mother taught him the piano and his father
instructed him in harmony and counterpoint. He had perfect pitch.
The childhood illness that crippled his body left his mind whole. It
was an unusually lively and eager mind, capable of mastering technical information as readily as literary and philosophical subjects.
The physical affliction seemed only to have disciplined a character
innately strong. Studying under the most noted musicologists of his
time, he won his doctorate *summa cum laude* and not long afterwards qualified as a university lecturer.

Kurt Huber's work was distinguished by a fusion of the artistic
and scientific strains of his character. Along with his philosophical
studies he gave time to technical research and became an expert on
sound and acoustics. Combining the scholar and technician, he
made recordings of folk songs and folk music, a field in which he
became a recognized authority. In 1936 he represented Germany at
the International Congress on Folk Music in Barcelona. His was a

mind that immersed itself with scholarly zest in the music of peasants and mountain dwellers as well as in the philosophical profundities of Hegel, Schelling, and Fichte whom he also mastered. Though it paid him little and sometimes nothing, he took a German scholar's pride in the title of Professor Extraordinary of Musicology and Philosophy at the University of Munich.

His was the sort of academic integrity for which National Socialism had no use. Kurt Huber's clashes with the Nazi insistence on ideology over scholarship came early, were frequent, and all but ruined his career. His undoubted eminence in his field won him an appointment to the National Institute for Music Research in Berlin and he was put in charge of the folk song department there. It lasted little more than a year because Huber, stubbornly insistent on truth even when it warred with official propaganda, antagonized his Nazi superior who, among other dogmatic delusions, held that the major was the only scale natural for Teutonic peoples. Huber also refused to supply the local Student Bund with tunes suitable for what they called their "battle songs." He told them to make up their own; he wasn't about to give them any of his lovely folk songs for such a purpose. His appointment as department head was not renewed and he had to return to his subordinate and ill-paid post at the University of Munich.

He had to be circumspect even among his colleagues on the faculty, though sometimes emotion overcame caution and he expressed himself more forthrightly than was wise. When the first reports of atrocities filtered back from the East, his fellow professors dismissed them as rumor or kept their silence about them. Kurt Huber was shocked. If the reports were true, he said—and there was every evidence that they were—how could German professors, custodians of German culture and of the good name of Germany, be silent? How long could they go on facing their students without some display of manliness and responsibility? "But," said his wife afterwards, "he knew only too well that, under the system as it was then, any open protest was impossible and might accomplish nothing even if it were attempted. The Gestapo was always there, waiting to strike." So Kurt Huber kept his outrage within bounds until the time came when he could contain it no longer.

Under the system as it then was, the pressures exerted on professional people to join the National Socialist Workers Party, the Nazis, were accompanied by reprisals in their professional lives when they did not. As a nonmember, Professor Kurt Huber was sometimes reduced to penury through lack of academic appointments and career opportunities. At one point Clara, his tall, comely wife, had all of eight marks in her purse (then about two dollars). This sum represented the entire financial resources of the Huber family, consisting of the professor, his wife, his small daughter Birgit, and his smaller son Wolfgang, called "Wolfi." In her desperation, Clara Huber went to the nearest headquarters of the NSDAP and enrolled her husband as a member of the Party without his knowledge. For some time the family had been living on the professor's erratic income of some 300 marks a month. After he became a member of the party his income doubled, but remained meager and chancey even at that. His enrollment number was 8–282–981 which made it official, but he was not regarded as a genuine Nazi. He was suspected of being "in outspoken disagreement with certain aspects of the Party's cultural policy" and "hostile to any Party influence on his work in the folk song." An earlier report acknowledged his contributions as a scholar but gave him bad marks for never introducing into his lectures "even a breath of those questions which today ought to be in the center of discussions"—a Nazi way of saying that Professor Huber's lectures were free of Nazi rhetoric.

Kurt Huber tried to compensate for the damage which the ruling generation in Germany was doing to the cultural traditions he loved by associating with young people who, he sensed, had the spirit and inclination to resist the Nazi trend. Such students he regularly invited to his home where he treated them like distinguished guests and was inordinately pleased when family finances allowed Clara to spread an inviting table. The students in turn regarded him warmly as a guru whose gray hair signified ripeness and wisdom rather than merely age and pedantry, which in other professors put them off. Kurt Huber's feeling for students, and theirs for him, led to a radical, and finally fatal, alteration in the pattern of his life.

One evening in June of 1942 a Frau Dr. Mertens invited him to a gathering at her home. Frau Dr. Mertens had intellectual leanings and she saw herself as presiding over a salon rather than as a mere hostess at a party. Among the other guests were a prominent publisher named Heinrich Ellermann and Sigismund von Radecki, who was to read one of his pieces. The gathering also included a younger element composed of university students, mostly medical. Frau Mertens herself contributed to the elevated tone of the evening by reading "a little sketch" of her own composition on the theme of religious renewal.

It was not a success.

The students objected that the treatment of the theme was narrow and one-sided; but they particularly disapproved because, in their view, the little sketch was what they called *weltfremd*, remote from the world, irrevelant. This brought the conversation to more immediate matters and, with mounting dismay, the hostess saw her theme abandoned in favor of an animated political discussion of the sort which could later cause trouble for her and for everyone present. The recurrent topic of how "inner values" could be preserved and protected against the spiritual terror of National Socialism arose and became heated.

The publisher Ellermann contended that nothing could be accomplished by overt resistance but that the values under discussion could best be served by students who would cultivate and enrich them against the day when the Nazi cloud had passed. Another guest supported this view: "Nothing can be accomplished against such superior force." In the fervent and somewhat emotional tone of his lectures, Kurt Huber contradicted this. "Something *has* to be done," he said, "and the sooner the better." This view was supported by one of the medical students, a dark, intense young man whom the professor had noted previously that evening for his acute and sometimes oddly humorous remarks. (Once, to the question of what could be done, the young man had said ironically: "Let's rent an island in the Aegean Sea and give courses in world philosophy.") Now his comment was serious and direct. "Yes," he said in response to Huber's remark, "action *is* necessary. One can't hold back indefinitely."

The young man was Hans Scholl.

They made an oddly assorted pair, the vigorous young student and the crippled professor with the white of half a century in his hair; but each struck a chord in the other, and in intelligence and temperament they were much closer than age and physique would indicate. The professor was drawn by the vigor and intensity of the youth who, for his part, was impressed by having come into contact with a personality who had the authority of age but also the fire of an idealist. Before they parted they resolved to meet again, and next time not just by chance.

Kurt Huber became an accepted member of the Scholls' circle, learning to know the others in the group—Sophie, Alex Schmorell, Willi Graf, Traute Lafrenz. His intimacy with the group was further strengthened by the fact that he had been Kate Schüddekopf's faculty advisor for her doctorate studies. Participating in their meetings and discussions, he contributed the stabilizing influence of his maturity and experience. He won their admiration and respect and he rejoiced in it.

At the time he was not aware how deeply and dangerously Hans Scholl had already committed himself to active resistance, or that he, Kurt Huber, had already set his foot on the same path and would follow it all the way to its end.

Seven

For a composition that was frankly seditious and meant risking death for its authors, the first White Rose leaflet began sedately, almost pedantically:

Nothing is more unworthy of a cultured people than to allow itself, without resistance, to be "governed" by an irresponsible ruling clique motivated by the darkest instincts . . .

The leaflet, neatly typed double-space, went on for some 800 words in the vein of an analytical magazine article or a polemical essay rather than in the tempo of a flaming summons to the barricades. There were obligatory citations from classical German literature, including a long quotation from Schiller's "The Legislation of Lycurgus" in which the inhuman rigidity of the Spartan state was shown to be the cause of its downfall. The reader was left to draw his own parallel.

Though the language was often stilted and didactic, the intensity which inspired the leaflet in the first place showed through repeatedly in unequivocal phrases and paragraphs:

* * *

*. . . who can imagine the extent of the shame that will engulf us
and our children once the scales fall from our eyes and crimes monstrous beyond all measure are revealed?*

*. . . if the Germans, devoid of all individuality, have already been
reduced to a mindless cowardly herd, then, yes, they deserve to go
under . . .*

But, the leaflet argued, not all Germans were in so hopeless a
condition. By a *"slow, systematic, and treacherous "* process each
individual had been thrust into a *"spiritual prison"* but now, in a
desperate hour, everyone who felt himself a part of the *"Christian
culture of the West"* must defend himself *"against Fascism and every similar system of the absolute state . . . "* Let everyone now
offer passive resistance to *"the atheistic war machine before it is
too late and the last of our cities is reduced to rubble like Cologne
and the last of our youth perishes for the hubris of a maniac."*
The leaflet twice used a metaphor that would often recur in the
thinking and the language of the dissidents: the image of evil spirits,
demons, emerging from the pit to scourge mankind and subjugate
the earth. The conclusion drew on Goethe's "The Awakening of
Epimenides" both to evoke the metaphor poetically from the pen of
a master and to offer assurance that the beasts from the pit would not
prevail:

*He who has risen audaciously from the abyss
May conquer half the world
Through ruthlessness and cunning.
Yet to the abyss he must return.*

Then the voice of Hope is heard:

*And the beautiful word freedom
Is whispered and murmured
Until—how strange and new!—
We, on the steps of our temple,
Sing out with a fresh delight:
"Freedom! Freedom!"*

* * *

The leaflet did not end on this exalted note. A more mundane sentence was tagged on, soliciting help in spreading the leaflet's message:

We request that you copy this page with as many carbons as possible and pass it on!

For the first time in the history of the Third Reich, opposition to Adolf Hitler and his regime had broken through to the light of day and become visible, and this leaflet was only the first. Across the top of it was the heading: FLUG-BLÄTTER DER WEISSEN ROSE—LEAFLETS OF THE WHITE ROSE. The choice of a flower for a symbol, and especially a flower signifying purity and innocence, seemed oddly subdued and nonviolent for an underground organization. There would be much discussion about its meaning and the reason for the choice. The plural in the headline suggested that a series of similar leaflets was to be expected, and the second was not long in making its appearance.

The second leaflet, too, opened like an essay—*"It is impossible to discuss National Socialism rationally because there is nothing rational about it"*—before again castigating the German people for their apathy in the face of the crimes being committed in their name. After quoting from *Mein Kampf*, the essay stated that the book was written *"in the worst German I ever read,"* though to whom the *"I"* referred was not disclosed. The Hitler quotation read: *"It is unbelieveable to what extent one must deceive a people in order to rule it."*

In its innocence the leaflet suggested that the end of the Nazi despotism was near and that it was necessary for Germans of good will *"to find each other and spread information from person to person"* until everyone was persuaded of the need to fight the system, causing *"a wave of unrest"* to sweep the land. The leaflet then quoted a saying used by dissidents toward the end of the First World War: *"Better an end with terror than terror without end."*

The information Hans Scholl had obtained from the architect Eickemeyer and others about the atrocities in the East—the massacre of Jews, the outrages perpetrated on the occupied peoples—was reported in tones of revulsion and dismay: *"Here we see the most frightful crime against the dignity of man, a crime for which there is no parallel in all human history."* Why, the leaflet asks, were these horrors described again when they were so well known? Because it was necessary that everyone should be aware of his guilt in having tolerated a government which had committed such crimes.

> *The apathetic behavior of the Germans gave these low creatures the possibility to do the things they have done . . . The same attitude made it possible for this government to come to power in the first place! Everyone wants to exonerate himself from his share of the blame and then go back to sleep with a good conscience. But it cannot be done: everyone is* guilty! guilty! guilty!

This was the most sweeping indictment of the German people by a German to go on the record inside Germany, raising the question of collective guilt which the world would debate for many years afterwards. It took courage of the highest order, moral and physical, for young Germans to face the idea, to set it down in unambiguous phrases, and then spread it abroad as widely as they were capable of doing at the risk of their lives. The accusation of guilt, thrice repeated in italics—*schuldig! schuldig! schuldig!*— fairly shouted from the paper it was typed on.

The leaflet then made a concession. Perhaps before the war, it said, the German people were dazzled by the National Socialists who had not yet revealed their true nature. *"But now that they are recognized for what they truly are, it must be the first and highest duty—yes, the sacred duty—of every German to exterminate these beasts."*

As if reluctant to end on so violent a note, the leaflet returned to more moderate discourse and concluded with two quotations from Lao-tse, the founder of Taoism, whose philosophy taught the futility of violence and passion. Among the lines chosen from Lao-tse was one which said: *"A nation is a living organism; truly, it cannot be forced. Whoever attempts to force it, ruins it. And he who attempts to overpower it, loses it."*

And again there was the appeal to have the recipient of the leaflet duplicate it and pass it on.

Sophie Scholl had been in Munich about six weeks when the leaflets began to circulate, and at first she had as little knowledge of where they came from as anybody else. She read the first ones with a mixture of excitement and incredulity: at last somebody was saying something and doing something! There was a stirring beneath the surface in Munich— something never reported in the newspapers or mentioned on the radio or seldom even talked about—but she had already sensed it. Here was proof. These unpretentious but astonishingly forthright sheets of paper were signals—skyrockets, in fact—announcing that not only did anti-Nazi elements exist in Germany but they were, somewhere, actively at work. Sophie savored phrases from the leaflets that she herself could have written: *"Is it not true that every decent German is ashamed of his government?"* Sophie was, and so was everyone for whom she had respect. It was exhilarating to hold in her hand evidence that the feeling of shame and outrage so many felt but were forced to suppress was breaking into the open. But mingled with the exhilaration was apprehension. Whoever produced these leaflets, she knew, was in mortal danger. Still, Sophie Scholl could hardly wait to read the next one.

Jürgen Wittenstein, who was at the university at the time, remembered long afterwards the impression made by the first White Rose leaflets: "Astonishment" and "consternation" were the words he used. The typewritten sheets passed from hand to hand, causing tremors of excitement in their wake. Among the students, reactions varied from repressed approval to outrage and indignation, and on to bewilderment and disbelief. The bolder students snatched the leaflets from the hands of others, reading intently and skipping no word, until the sheet was in turn snatched away by someone else. Others hardly dared to glance at the typescript, as if from fear of contamination through the eyes. The less one had to do with such matters, the better. More than one student went directly to the Gestapo as soon as a leaflet came into his hands. It was always prudent to keep in the good books of the Secret Police. You could get into serious trouble for not reporting such a thing.

The leaflets were not concentrated in the university. They were, in fact, rather scarce there, though anyone interested could, by inquiring discreetly, obtain a copy to read. The pattern of distribution seemed to be erratic. In a secret report the Administration of Upper Bavaria, which included Munich, noted that "leaflets hostile to the state in the highest degree" were in circulation but that the authors of this subversive literature could not be determined. "The State Police in Munich has been alerted." Agents assigned to the case immediately saw that the leaflets were typewritten and then reproduced on a duplicating machine. No great numbers of them were discovered in any one area, and investigators learned that only people of a certain status seemed to have received them. The Gestapo was not even sure the leaflets originated in Munich, since they cropped up in surrounding towns and cities as well.

In all, four virulently anti-Nazi leaflets of unknown origin appeared in the course of eight or nine weeks that summer while the police, both criminal and political, continued a fruitless search for the perpetrators. All the leaflets carried the heading: THE WHITE ROSE.

One of the leaflets came in the mail to the house where Traute Lafrenz was rooming and it was passed around. Traute read it with breathless interest and an uneasy sense of recognition which increased with every line. "There was something about the style of it," she said later, "about the way the sentences were formed and about the quotations from Goethe and Lao-tse that had a familiar ring. It made me think the leaflet must be '*von uns*,' from our group. I wasn't sure at first, though, whether it was Hans who was responsible, or somebody else."

Traute Lafrenz scanned the following leaflets tensely, looking for further clues, and she found one that convinced her. It was a quotation from Ecclesiastes: "*So I returned and considered all the oppressions that are done under the sun . . . ,*" the first verses of the fourth chapter. She remembered that she had called this passage to Hans' attention some time before, and here it was in a White Rose leaflet! When next she saw him, she asked Hans if he was their author. He was not happy to hear the question.

"He was evasive," she remembered. "He replied that it was

never a good idea to try to discover who was responsible in such matters. That only endangered the person in question. In such cases the number of people involved must be kept very, very small. It would be better for me if I knew as little as possible.

"That's where the matter rested, but then I knew what the situation was and what my role in it would be. I did what I could to see that the leaflets circulated as widely as possible." On her next trip to Hamburg she took two of the leaflets with her to show to her dissident friends there.

Sophie Scholl made the discovery in a similar way but, as it turned out, with far graver consequences for herself. Nine months from her first knowledge of her brother's involvement in the White Rose enterprise, Sophie Scholl, like him, would be dead.

Not long after the appearance of the leaflets, Sophie dropped in to visit her brother in his room as she did almost every day. The room was empty, Hans being away at a lecture or busy in one of the clinics to which he was assigned. Sophie decided to wait for him and passed the time by looking again at the Impressionist prints fastened to the walls with thumbtacks and by paging idly through the books strewn around the room. On the cluttered desk was an old-fashioned volume from a set of classics. It was a collection of pieces by Schiller, and a bookmark was placed at the essay on "The Legislation of Lycurgus." In the margin was a light pencil mark along a passage, which Sophie began to read: "The state is never an end in itself. It is important only as a means by which humanity can achieve its goal, which is nothing other than the advancement of all of man's constructive capabilities . . . "

For Sophie, the shock of recognition she felt on reading this was mingled with a flutter of dread. The passage marked in Hans' book had appeared word for word in the first White Rose leaflet. It could not, she knew, be mere coincidence. Other ideas in the leaflet also coincided closely with what she had often heard from Hans in their many talks together and in the group discussions. And now she remembered what Hans had said when, in Ulm, the family had first received copies of the sermons of Bishop Galen: "*One ought to have a duplicating machine . . .* "

There was no doubt in Sophie's mind when she replaced the

bookmark and closed the volume of Schiller. Her brother Hans, she was sure, had crossed the line between passive and active resistance, which meant that he had voluntarily left the living space where he was comparatively safe and entered an area of deadly hazard. What he was doing was treason to the National Socialist state, and the penalty for treason was death. She could hardly bear to think of death in connection with her handsome, vital, laughing brother but now, she knew, he must be living in the shadow of it every hour of his days and nights. He had committed himself to active resistance against a state whose Leader had repeatedly warned that death would be the lot of any who dared to oppose him. Perhaps it would still be possible for her to stop him, to pull him back across the line that marked the territory where he was *vogelfrei*, an outlaw and fair game for the Third Reich's terror apparatus, which had been specifically designed to track down and exterminate scoffers, doubters, and resisters. If she was unable to pull her brother back, Sophie knew the alternative that was open to her and she knew she could unhesitatingly take it. If she could not deter him, she would join him.

It was not as easy for Hans to evade his sister's questions as it was to put off Traute Lafrenz. He had tried to keep Sophie in the dark, to keep her clear of the danger which his leaflet activity involved. It was not, of course, a matter of not trusting her or regarding her as unequal to the demands that would be made upon her. His exclusion of her now, where before he had included her in everything, was an expression of love and regard. He knew that if he should be arrested she would also be, automatically. He wanted her to be able to tell her interrogators with all the conviction of truth not only that she had no involvement in what he was doing, but no knowledge of it. Deceiving her was a gift of love to her.

But now she did know and now she insisted on becoming involved. For her it was unthinkable to draw aside and let her brother go his way without her. Until now her opposition to the regime had been a matter of attitude, of instinctive revulsion, an outgrowth of breeding and background. But it had been wholly passive and this she felt as a lack, a failing. In one of her letters she had written with contempt of people whose only reaction to the war was to survive it with a whole skin, disregarding honor and decency. It had become an article of faith for Sophie Scholl to involve herself in her time, to commit herself, holding back nothing. A little later she would express the depth of her commitment to the painter Wilhelm Geyer, a friend of hers and Hans' from Ulm, when she said to him: "So many are dying for this regime, it's only right that some should die against it!"

With the appearance of the White Rose leaflets and her discovery of her brother's responsibility for them, Sophie Scholl joined those who were willing to die against the regime of Adolf Hitler. She was prepared to act in the spirit of the declaration made by another member of the German resistance, the soldier Henning von Tresckow, who said: "The worth of a man is certain only if he is prepared to sacrifice his life for his convictions." Sophie Scholl would prove that the saying did not apply only to soldiers or only to men.

Hans Scholl and Alex Schmorell had begun their operation toward the end of May, each composing his own version of the first White Rose leaflet. They were two young men steeped in literature, excited by language, and respectful of learning, and they had a touching confidence in the power of the written word. They were sure that if an idea were well and strongly enough expressed, it could not fail to make its impact, especially when supported by quotations from sources which every educated reader was bound to respect. They set about the task of producing their seditious leaflets almost as if it were an assignment in creative writing on which they would be judged for style, form, and content. The leaflets were to be anonymous but the prose was to be of a quality that would be immediately recognized as coming from someone who had made his *Abitur* and had read all the right books.

This was not merely intellectual pretension, though there was an element of that in the first leaflets. Hans and Alex had decided to address themselves not to the general public but to persons selected for their roles in the cultural community, which National Socialism was in the process of destroying—university professors, school teachers, clergymen, people who could influence the opinions of others. Included in the first target group were a number of restaurant owners and innkeepers, on the theory that such men were always in contact with groups of people at places where the leaflets would be discussed and passed around.

The young men did not imagine that their leaflets would destroy Hitler and bring the regime to its knees. They were idealists; they were not fools. They knew, as one of their leaflets said, that military might alone would destroy Hitler. For them an immediate, visible result was not an important consideration. What was important was to launch a moral protest, to send out a cry of conscience. They wanted to make a start at eroding the faith of the German people in their leadership, to let their fellow dissidents know that they were not alone and that the monolith of public support for the regime was a propaganda myth. Among themselves, in their own expressions of purpose and intent, the word they most often used was *aufrütteln*— to shake up, to arouse. Kurt Huber, when his time came to speak out before his judges, expressed the motive of the White Rose in a sentence: *"To call out the truth as clearly and audibly as possible into the German night."*

There was another factor, aside from the content of the leaflets, which made them worth issuing from the viewpoint of the dissidents. The fact that they appeared at all was a blow at the structure of the absolute state. Their existence alone said that all was not well among the people, that beneath the façade of regimentation and conformity something was seething, something subversive was at work. If this much showed, more must be suspected. The Gestapo had no way of knowing whether a few hundred leaflets meant only a few hundred leaflets or were the surface symptoms of a threat to the whole structure.

There were difficulties about the logistics of the operation. Alex Schmorell, always resouceful and undaunted, found an obscure shop that dealt in secondhand office supplies whose proprietor was willing to sell him a used duplicating machine for twice what it was worth. Alex also contributed a typewriter. Together with Hans, and later with Sophie's help as well, the special paper for the duplicating machine and the stencils were also obtained through devious channels. The artist Wilhelm Geyer had to show them how to make the stencils, though he was not told what they were to be used for.

Hans and Alex received a monthly stipend of 235 marks apiece from the army for their medical studies, and Alex's father gave him additional pocket money. At the beginning they were able to subsidize their subversion out of their own pockets. When the two versions of the initial leaflet had been thoroughly argued back and forth with each author hotly defending his own phrases, quotations, and points, the synthesized final version was prepared by Hans. It was then typed out, stenciled, and run off the duplicating machine, ready for mailing. Telephone books and city directories supplied the addresses.

There is something of a mystery about how and why the title "White Rose" was chosen for the leaflets. When he was questioned by the Gestapo, Hans Scholl told his interrogaters that the name was picked because it was the title of a Spainsh novel he once read, but Hans misled the Gestapo whenever he could. No such Spanish novel has been found in German translation. The German author who signed himself B. Traven and lived in South America did write a novel called *Die Weisse Rose* whose story, laid in rural Mexico, tells of a ranch owner who fights a predatory oil company, which might be taken as a metaphor for the struggle between good and evil. The connection here is slim, if not entirely nonexistent, and there is no evidence that Hans Scholl ever read the book.

In Nazi Germany the edelweiss, another white flower, was sometimes used as a symbol of opposition among youth groups. Growing high in the Alps, the edelweiss could be taken as suggesting untouched and unspoiled purity (of outlook and motive), which a white rose would also bring to mind. A friend of Alex Schmorell's recalled that he once asked what her favorite flower was. She replied: "The white rose. It was the favorite flower of the last Czarina." Alex, with his relish for everything Russian, was delighted. "Yes!" he exclaimed. "The white rose is the symbol of beauty and purity." Purity and beauty being the ultimate opposites of National Socialism and its works, some such imagery was most probably in the minds of the two young men when they chose "White Rose" as the title of their first leaflets.

The third leaflet, like the preceding ones, opened on a rather studied note with some thoughtful lines on what a citizen had a right to expect from the state. It then, so to speak, lost its temper and called the present German government "*a mechanical political contrivance operated by criminals and drunkards.*" The unidentified "I" of the leaflet turned directly to the reader and asked: "*Why do you not rise up, why do you endure this . . . ? It is not only your right but your moral duty to overthrow this system.*" The Germans, said the leaflet, will deserve to be scattered across the face of the earth "*like dust before the wind*" if they do not, in this twelfth hour, summon up the courage that has so far failed them.

Should the reader have wondered what he could possibly do against the all-powerful system, the leaflet told him:

> *Sabotage in armament and war industry plants. Sabotage in gatherings, meetings, festivals, organizations, anything which supports National Socialism. Sabotage in all scientific and intellectual activities that promote the war effort. Sabotage in newspapers and publications which spread the brown perversions of truth. Don't give a penny to the street collectors for Party causes. . . . Don't contribute anything to the drives for scrap metal and clothing . . .*"

But the heart of this leaflet was in a paragraph which did not shrink from advocating the defeat of Germany in the most uncompromising terms:

> *. . . A victory for Fascist Germany in this war would have the most terrible and incalculable consequences. The chief concern of every German should not be the defeat of Bolshevism but rather, above all, the destruction of National Socialism. This must, beyond any doubt, be given first priority . . .*

The reader was promised that later leaflets would support the overriding truth of that statement.

This was a time when eleven guillotines were in operation in Germany. Every town and city had its Gestapo headquarters, and every Gestapo building had its cellar where dissidents were beaten and tortured as a matter of policy. In Berlin a man named Wilhelm Lehmann wrote "Hitler The Mass Murderer Must Be Murdered" on toilet walls. He was caught and his head was cut off. Under the all-inclusive rubric "for the security of the State" the Gestapo and its associated organs of repression were free to act with arbitrary violence against any citizen for any reason or none. The crime of sedition, of which Hans Scholl and Alexander Schmorell—and now Sophie Scholl, too—had made themselves guilty was the worst on the National Socialist roster of capital offenses. As the White Rose leaflets appeared, one after the other, the Munich Gestapo redoubled its efforts to discover their source. They found only indications that the leaflets were indeed produced in Munich and that they had been sent chiefly to people of some standing in the intellectual community, but no more. "Other evidence is still being sought," said one agent's report while the investigation proceeded.

Hans continued with his lectures and his work in the clinics and led his social life as before. Many who knew him then, even those aware of his political bent, had no idea that he was engaged in underground activity. Sophie, too, was known at the university for her sometimes unguarded comments, but no suspicion of illegal action fell on her either. That both were regarded as being vaguely anti-Nazi was, in fact, a kind of protection for them. It was not thought that anyone engaged in subversion would talk as the Scholls sometimes did and thereby attract attention to themselves. They would have kept their mouths shut. When, afterwards, the truth came to light, many who were close to Hans and believed they knew him well were astonished to learn that he had been active underground. A friend once showed him one of the White Rose leaflets. He read it carefully, as if seeing it for the first time, and then handed it back with some sharply critical remarks about its content.

Not everyone in his immediate circle was as astute as Traute Lafrenz in recognizing him in the style of the leaflets. When he transferred his affection and attentions from Traute to Gisela Schertling, a shift which caused some surprise in the group, Gisela made no connection between him and the leaflets though she was now considerably closer to him than before. When, later on, Gisela did find out that her lover was behind the leaflet operation, it happened by accident and not because he took her into his confidence. Even his sister Inge was kept in the dark, though she was close to him in every other way.

Inge Scholl sometimes participated in the "reading evenings" and the gatherings at which Theodor Haecker and Carl Muth gave their moral and intellectual guidance to the students in the Schmorell villa and the Eickemeyer studio. Her intelligence and warmth made her a favorite of them all. For love of her, for her own safety, she was never admitted to the secret that her own brother was the moving spirit behind the White Rose. She sensed, she had an intuition, that perhaps Hans and Sophie were playing a terribly dangerous game to which she was not privy. But with no evidence to go on, she played her own part in the game by not inquiring, by not pressing to know, though it caused her agonies of apprehension. "For all that time," she has said, "I was anxiety personified, knowing that Hans and Sophie were in some kind of danger but not knowing exactly what and not being able to do anything about it."

Once, while she was visiting Carl Muth, he reached into his pocket, took out his wallet, and carefully extracted a sheet of paper folded up several times. He showed it to her. It was the second White Rose leaflet which he had received in the mail. He handed it to her and she read it, holding her breath. She had never seen such a forthright and fiery attack on the regime in print before. She agreed with every word but her hand was shaking as she handed the leaflet back. She watched as the fragile old scholar folded the leaflet, slipped it back in his wallet, and put the wallet in his pocket.

"Do you carry it around with you?" Inge asked in surprise.

"Yes, always."

"But that can be dangerous. Why do you do it?"

"I'm an old man," Carl Muth replied. "If I should be struck down by a heart attack on the street, they would search my pockets and find the leaflet. And then somebody else would read it, too!"

Sophie, too, went about her college-girl routine in her usual quiet and unobtrusive way, listening to lectures, studying, writing in her diary, writing her letters. Sometimes she visited Professor Huber at his home where she struck Clara Huber as a typical female student of the kind who often came to consult her husband. Clara saw no sign of the rebel, the revolutionary, about Sophie Scholl. There was no indication that she, too, had crossed the dividing line that took her into outlaw territory where she, like her brother, was now *vogel-frei*, fair game for Hitler's huntsmen.

When the fourth leaflet came out, toward the middle of July, it conceded that in recent weeks Hitler had scored a number of new successes to which he could point— *"victories both in Russia and Africa."* But, the leaflet said, these victories were illusory and achieved at enormous cost while Hitler lied shamelessly to those who were paying the price. *"Every word that comes out of the mouth of Hitler is a lie . . . his mouth is the stinking pit of hell and his power is corrupt to the core."*

In this leaflet the integrity and idealism of the young dissidents emerged with a special glow. The White Rose had not waited to attack the Nazi system until it was staggering under the blows that were inflicted on it later, as the military plotters against Hitler did. Hitler's successes did not blur the vision of the student dissenters as those successes dazzled so many of their fellow Germans. The advance in Russia, the victories in North Africa, were only further proof of the demonic forces which Hitler had unleashed upon the world and which had to be opposed by any means available.

The apocalyptic theme of monsters emerging from the abyss was taken up again in the fourth leaflet. The fight against the Nazis was pictured as a struggle against satanic powers, against the minions of the anti-Christ himself. That, said the leaflet, was the metaphysical background without which the true nature of the war could not be understood. What was needed was a spiritual upsurge, a return to faith and religion. A long quotation from the mystic and poet who called himself Novalis supported the theme that *"only religion can reawaken Europe and restore Christianity to its earthly mission as patron and founder of world peace. "*

From its lofty peroration, in which the lessons of Augustine and Aquinas, of Carl Muth and Theodor Haecker were echoed, the leaflet returned to the brutal realities of the present: *"For Hitler and his followers there can be no punishment on this earth which will expiate their crimes. . . . An example must be made of them so that nobody will have the slightest inclination to attempt any such thing ever again."*

This leaflet took the pains to assure the reader that the White Rose was not in the pay of any foreign power and that no list existed of the people to whom the leaflets were being sent, all names being taken from the telephone books and directories. This was a needed guarantee at a time when anyone's name on such a list, if it existed, could have fatal consequences. And this was the leaflet which concluded with the vow:

"We Will Not Be Silent. We Are Your Bad Conscience. The White Rose Will Not Leave You In Peace!"

But after this, the leaflets ceased.

What the regime had not been able to do through its police organs—namely, shut off the production and distribution of the White Rose leaflets—it accomplished unwittingly through the army.

Orders came for the Student Medical Company in Munich to move to the Russian front.

Eight

The word *Blitzkrieg*, lightning war, had dropped out of the German vocabulary. Now it was never spoken except satirically, ruefully. The war in Russia which was supposed to be over in a matter of months was in its second year. It seemed no nearer its end than before despite the spate of victory announcements, which never seemed to end, either. The continuing thrust of the German armies into the Soviet Union had created an enormous suction in its wake; the deeper the penetration, the more it sucked fresh manpower from the rear into the maw in the East.

In Germany a grisly kind of bird-watching became widespread. The birds that were being watched in every neighborhood and on every street were the *Totenvögel*, the "Birds of Death." The name, the blackest kind of gallows humor, derived from the practice of having local Party officials inform a fallen soldier's next of kin that he had been killed in battle. In performing this function the Party officials wore a uniform with the spread-wing Nazi eagle on it. To the people they thus became birds of death, *Totenvögel*.

The toll of the war in the East had been stressed in the last White Rose leaflet with a passage that bordered on bathos but was justified by the sincerity of the sentiment: *"Who has counted the dead? Not*

Hitler. Not Goebbels. Thousands are falling in Russia every day. It is the time of harvest and the Reaper moves through the ripe crop with sweeping scythe. Grief and sorrow visit house after house in the homeland and there is no one there to dry the tears of the weeping mothers . . . "

Before the young crusaders of the White Rose themselves set out for the East, there was time for a farewell fling on July 22, 1942, the eve of their departure on the troop train. The day had been spent in packing and reporting for roll call and inspection at the barracks. Hans Scholl spread the word that there would be a party that evening and the whole group was invited. Manfred Eickemeyer's spacious studio was made available, and tea, cakes, wine, and brandy were provided in adequate amounts. (Beer was evidently not a favorite tipple of these young partygoers in the beer capital of the world.) Stools and hassocks were scattered liberally about the studio whose easy bohemian atmosphere was somewhat diminished by the heavy blackout curtains, a necessary precaution against the air raids.

About fifteen guests came and went in the course of the evening but the heart of the party was the half dozen closest to Hans Scholl—his sister Sophie, Alex Schmorell, Willi Graf, Christel Probst, Traute Lafrenz, Gisela Schertling, and Kate Schüddekopf. It was a gathering of young people, all in their early twenties, with the exception of the gray-haired professor. Hans had made a point of inviting Kurt Huber who made a point of coming; he welcomed any chance of meeting with his students socially and informally.

It was meant to be purely social, a going-away party for the student-soldiers—Hans, Alex, and Willi—with the usual banter, joking, drinking, and flirting to be expected at any gathering of a compatible group. Though the spirit was seldom grim, it was often serious. What was called "our situation"—Germany's and the group's—was discussed in pairs and clusters. Everyone there had seen at least one White Rose leaflet but most had no idea of their origin. Kurt Huber, too, had received one in the mail and he talked about it with Hans at the party, not knowing that it was Hans who had sent it to him.

The professor was tense and distraught that night. He viewed the

situation in Germany as alarmingly worse than when he had seen
Hans at the salon of Frau Dr. Mertens. The massive enemy air raids
on Cologne and Hamburg caused something like panic in Kurt Huber when he thought of the architectural treasures of his country
which were now threatened with destruction because of Hitler's
war: the cathedrals, the museums, the monuments which were the
visible emblems of the German spirit at its most exalted. To his anxiety for the protection and preservation of inner values against the
brown terror was now added the torment of seeing the physical manifestations of the culture he loved being reduced to rubble.

Again came the question that pressed on all of them continually:
What could be done, what was one to do? Alex Schmorell was for
increasing passive resistance (not revealing that he himself had already crossed the line from passive to active resistance). Kurt Huber
warned against any open demonstrations against the regime. "After
all," he said, "we are not factory workers. We cannot take to the
streets." Still, he advocated almost any measure to end or shorten
the war—illegal propaganda, sabotage, even assassination. He
spoke with such emotion, sometimes twisting his body to force out
the words, that Kate Schüddekopf was a little awed as she watched
and listened to him. The impression he made of a man passionately
concerned for his country stayed with her long afterwards. Hans
Scholl again agreed with the professor that more, much more,
would have to be done to oppose the system they all abhorred. Sophie, as was usual on these occasions, said little. She listened to
each speaker in turn, taking in what was said, considering it, weighing it. She was especially attentive to her brother, showing that she
agreed with him only by her attitude.

Kurt Huber left the party early. He asked Hans to be sure to write
him his impressions of Russia, and Hans promised he would. Christel Probst accompanied the professor to the streetcar that would take
him home. Probst, who was attached to a different unit, would not
be leaving with the others.

A late arrival at the party was young Hans Hirzel, who happened
to be in Munich on a visit from Ulm. He, too, had received a White
Rose leaflet anonymously in the mail; he immediately suspected that
it was Hans Scholl who had sent it to him. As the party was break-

ing up, Hans took young Hirzel aside and gave him 80 marks with instructions to see if he could buy a duplicating machine and keep it hidden until he, Hans Scholl, returned.

For Hans the studio party was a point of departure in more ways than one. The first phase of the White Rose undertaking was over, but he was already looking forward to a bolder and more hazardous assult on the system that one of his leaflets had called "an abortion from hell." The last of the leaflets had ended with the affirmation: "We will not be silent!" Hans Scholl did not intend to be.

Early the next morning, at 7 o'clock, the Student Medical Company was assembled in the Munich freight yard, standing by to board the troop train to the East. Somebody was there with a camera, snapshooting the soldiers as they chatted in pairs and clusters. In one group an anonymous medic is gesticulating as he talks, and Hans Scholl is smiling while he and Alex Schmorell and Willi Graf and Hubert Furtwängler listen.

They are all standing next to an open-work iron fence whose top reaches only a few inches over their heads. Peering down at them over the fence is Sophie, who is standing on something on the other side. She has evidently been there for some time. Her satchellike briefcase, probably filled with books, is hooked by its handles to one of the fence spikes. She is wearing a knitted sweater with broad stitches, and her dark hair is falling loosely to her shoulders.

Two candid shots of Sophie caught the two sides of her character as she perched there on the iron fence in the freight yard, looking down on her brother and her friends as they waited to go off to war. In one of the photographs her lifted arms are flung wide and there is a correspondingly wide smile on her face. It is a light and girlish gesture at a time which could not have been happy for her. In the other picture the mood has changed. She is holding on to the top spike of the fence rather tightly and looks down gravely, thoughtfully, at her brother and his comrades, all of them engrossed in their conversation and none of them looking at her. Sophie's smile is gone.

The train out of Munich followed roughly the same route toward Moscow that Napoleon's army had done, and Willi Graf's diary ticked off the stations on the eastward way: Warsaw, where they drank vodka "in little sips" at a pub when the train stopped and where they had time to walk through the city "surrounded by misery"; crossing the border into Lithuania, neat and orderly, untouched by war; passing through the university town of Kaunas by night and on into the Soviet Union proper. Then day after day across plains stretching to the horizon, straight eastward to Vyazma where, in the fall of 1941, the *Wehrmacht* had scored an enormous victory in what a German general called "a textbook battle."

Vyazma was in ruins.

They were entering the zone of the war without ending—"filth, misery, German march music," said Willi Graf's diary. Vyazma was a front assembly point. Their unit was assigned to the 252nd Division and they were posted at a place called Gzhatsk, hardly more than 80 miles from Moscow and due west of it. "The ruins of the tall houses rise up spookily in the moonlight," the faithful diary noted. "Russian artillery shoots into the town. You can see the muzzle flashes in the dark . . . " Gzhatsk was where the German drive on Moscow halted.

Now Hans Scholl and his comrades were where they could see at first hand the effect in human terms of the political system which the White Rose leaflets opposed. Here, in this war, the Nazis had canceled every restraint and restriction which the concept of chivalry had once, however inadequately, imposed on men facing each other in battle. This was where the most rabid dogmas of Adolf Hitler were accepted as valid guidelines by Prussian officers who once prided themselves on a code of professional conduct that was monastic in its severity. In the West, Field Marshal Fritz Erich von Manstein had fought more or less according to the code; but in Russia he issued an Order of the Day that said: "The soldier in the East is not merely a fighter according to the rules of war but also a protagonist of a merciless racial idea who must fully understand the necessity for hard but just punishment of Jewish sub-humanity."

Masked as a crusade against Communism, the war was designed to make Adolf Hitler the master of the land mass of central and eastern Europe which, he believed, would not only extend immeasureably the reach of German domination but give him, in geopolitical terms, control of the foreseeable future of mankind. As the

Heerenvolk, the master race of the West, the Germans were chosen by destiny to subdue the "Asiatic inferiors" of the East whose "bolshevistic chaos" was to be swept away and replaced by a new world order under the Greater German Reich. To realize this grandiose vision, nothing was too severe in the way of slaughter and repression. "This struggle," said Adolf Hitler, "is one of ideologies and racial differences and will have to be conducted with unprecedented, unmerciful, and unrelenting harshness."

In this atmosphere the young men of the White Rose felt themselves, more than ever, to be not only aliens but antagonists. Alex Schmorell was especially outraged at the spectacle of what the Germans were doing to the country to which he felt himself bound by the strongest emotional ties. His mother had been Russian; he himself had been born here; he spoke the language; his childhood imagination had been stirred by Russian folk and fairy tales. For him to be in Russia at all was a kind of homecoming, but the joy of it was cankered by his awareness of what he was wearing. The uniform of the German army marked him as an enemy, one of the foreign predators, when in fact he had come to the country with love in his heart.

Before he left Germany he had resolved that, should the situation arise, he would not shoot at any Russian. Nor would he shoot at a German. Being invincibly romantic, he had visions of somehow contributing to a reconciliation between Germans and Russians. He began by bringing his own comrades into contact with the people of Gzhatsk and the surrounding villages and farms. He took Hans and Willi and Hubert, and anyone else so inclined, to the home of workers and peasants, supplying the wine that eased the situation and acting as interpreter. He persuaded the peasants to sing their songs for the visitors in the enemy uniforms and he played German folk songs for them on his balalaika. The unending sweep of the steppes overwhelmed him, and the sky itself seemed to take on a special Russian coloration for him. Here, more than ever, he relished his Russian nickname, "Shurik."

He could not tolerate the brutish behavior of the German soldiers who believed that Slavs were, as the propaganda said, subhumans and that all civilization ceased at the eastern borders of Germany.

Once Alex came close to being court martialed when he physically interfered with a German guard who was beating a Russian prisoner bloody for some trifling offense.

Alex communicated his fervor for the country and its people to his comrades. Willi Graf was touched by Alex' passion, and in a letter to his sister Annaliese he caught something of the paradox of young German soldiers, who were supposed to be enemies of the Russians but who felt a bond of common humanity with them instead. "This land and its people first opened itself to me through Alex," Willi wrote. "We have often eaten and sung with the peasants and had them play their wonderful melodies for us. Sometimes one is able to forget for a while all the sad and terrible things happening around us. We have had wonderful afternoons and evenings with the Russians—while not far off the rifle and cannon fire was seldom silent and we waited for the call to care for the sick and wounded. Two worlds around us. . . . I know that you also must feel for the people who, like ours, must undergo the troubles and terrors of these times. I could tell you much more but do not want to trust it to a letter . . . "

Hans, too, told of drinking *Schnaps* and singing with new-found Russian friends in a letter he wrote to Professor Huber and which all four of the comrades signed. For Hans it was also a time of introspection and brooding. His mood was a mixture of melancholy and boredom intensified by an increasing revulsion against the war— "this most unimaginative of all human activities." Sitting in a bunker that shook and groaned as the Russian shells came screaming in, he wrote: "The war grips me only in the time between when a shell is fired and when it explodes." In the confines of the bunker he was reminded of his time in jail when he wrote the name of his girl in bread crumbs on the table. "I was really young in those days," he wrote now in his diary, being all of twenty-four.

Reading Dostoievski by candlelight—"Russia's greatest writer. I begin to understand him here"—he reflected on the culture of the Russians: Tolstoi, Gogol, Turgenev, Pushkin. He wrote scathing comments in his notebook on the idea that the Germans were defending civilization against the ignorant hordes of Asiatic Russia. He scorned the German notion that "culture consists of fingernail clippers and water closets'' and his indignation surged up again against the German intellectuals who put their brains and talents in the service of a monstrous cause. Pascal said that man was made to think but he, Hans Scholl, would make this a reproach against the German academicians who in a desperate time "devote themselves to evolving the newest refinements for the machine-gun while ignoring the primal questions of life: its meaning, its purpose."

As a medic functioning close to the front line, he was often in direct contact with the horrors that the newest refinements of mechanized warfare inflicted on those involved in it. "I have no music in me anymore," he wrote. "Now all I hear are groans and screams of people in torment . . . " Sometimes, looking across the Russian plains that seemed to stretch into infinity, he felt like leaving everything behind and simply beginning to walk—walking and walking to the East, farther and farther, to the Urals, across Siberia, to China, and beyond. He'd do it, he said, if he weren't a European and if this were not the wrong time to turn one's back on Europe.

Wide as Russia was, a coincidence of war stationed Hans' younger brother Werner, with a different unit, nearby. Hans was able to borrow a horse and ride a few miles to the west and visit with "Has," as the family called him. Never very voluble, "Has" had little to say when they met for the first time in many months deep in the foreign country they were invading. Hans found that he did not have much to communicate either. It occurred to him, as he afterwards noted in his daybook, that these were times when a new language would have to be invented to allow people to reach each other in situations so far out of the pattern of normal living. On a day in August he had occasion to visit Werner again and this time there was something to talk about.

Their father had been arrested by the Gestapo and sentenced to prison.

Hans got the news in a letter from his mother who asked that he and Werner each send a petition to the authorities requesting leniency for their father. She enclosed a petition of her own but she urged that similar pleas coming from two sons on the Russian front would carry far more weight. Werner took the news stoically, agreeing with Hans that they should both regard their father's arrest as a distinction, not a disgrace. As for Hans, he flatly refused to submit a request for favors from Nazi judges and jailers. "Not under any circumstances," he said. "I know what false pride is, but I also know what true pride is."

He learned the details of his father's arrest and imprisonment later. Robert Scholl, in his office in Ulm, employed a young woman as secretary whom he had befriended and treated with warmth and consideration, as he did everybody. The young woman returned his cordiality and he felt that their relationship was on an easy, almost familial, basis. But one day that summer she asked Robert Scholl what he thought of the war situation.

"The war!" he blurted. "It is already lost. This Hitler is God's scourge on mankind, and if the war doesn't end soon the Russians will be sitting in Berlin." His secretary looked at him and turned back to her work.

Two days later Robert Scholl was summoned by the Gestapo to appear before a Special Sessions Court in Stuttgart, the regional capital, for uttering sentiments damaging to the National Socialist regime.

The secretary who had acted as the *Spitzel,* the informer, was asked by a friend what she had against Robert Scholl. "Nothing," she said. "I liked him."

"Then why did you do it?"

Her answer gave a glimpse into the pressures and conflicts which the absolute state imposes on its citizens even in the ordinary situations of everyday life.

"I had to suppress my personal feelings," the secretary said. "I was fond of Herr Scholl and I was grateful to him, but when he said those things about the *Führer* and the war, I knew I couldn't let it pass."

The secretary's friend noted that she was far from happy about what her political conscience had impelled her to do.

Hans Scholl, in his bunker on the Russian front, sat on a wooden crate by candlelight and thought about his father in jail. He, Hans, knew what it meant to be unjustly deprived of freedom and confined to four walls and a barred window day after day and night after night, but he also knew that his father was physically and morally

strong and would survive his ordeal. There was for Hans a grim satisfaction in recalling a conversation with his father when Hitler invaded the Soviet Union more than a year before. "This means the
end of Nazi Germany," Robert Scholl said and Hans had agreed
with him.

As his tour of duty in Russia was drawing to a close in the early
fall of 1942, the situation at the fronts did not appear to be bearing
out the prediction. The *Wehrmacht* was deployed in force along the
Volga and had the industrial port and communications center of Stalingrad under heavy attack. The Germans had also captured Rostov
and overrun much of the Caucasus. In Egypt, Marshal Rommel's
spectacular *Afrika Korps* was still a formidable threat. Though the
day of the lightning war was past, the forward crunch of the German
armies continued.

For Hans Scholl and his friends the final outcome was not in
doubt. They were unshakably sure that Nazi Germany could not,
and must not, win. Though the great majority of German troops was
still fighting with traditional tenacity, there were signs and inklings
that if the White Rose leaflets had been distributed at the front, they
would not have met with total rejection. In Russia Hans and his
comrades found mounting evidence for their belief that they were
not alone. As the war wore on, telltale signs of disillusionment became increasingly apparent. The attitude of many soldiers toward
the Nazi leadership was caught in a joke which told of Hitler visiting
the front lines (which he never did) and asking a *Landser,* a German
infantryman, what his last wish would be should a Russian shell
land near him. "I would wish" says the soldier, "that my *Führer*
was standing beside me."

The report of an incident that occurred not long before some miles
to the south, at Orel, spread along the front. A company commander
named Michael Kitzelmann, who had come up through the ranks
and won the Iron Cross, had been arrested by the Field Police, court
martialed, and shot by a firing squad. Kitzelmann, another Swabian,
was executed for too freely expressing his opinion of the government, the Nazi Party, and the atrocities he had witnessed while serving in Poland and the Soviet Union. Once he was heard to say: "If
these criminals should win, then I would have no wish to live any

longer." The words might have been a quotation from a White Rose leaflet. And Michael Kitzelmann's story was not an isolated incident.

Though death was the ultimate penalty, it was not the only one for those who followed conscience and set themselves against a regime that would tolerate nothing less than absolute acquiescence. There were mental and emotional exactions which not even the most decided and unfaltering opponents of the system could escape. Hans Scholl could not. An entry in his Russian diary begins: "Wild, chaotic dreams fill my nights . . ."

In one of his dreams he symbolically separated himself from a large group of people with whom he had been walking in the mountains. He went his own way "without a sign or signal of any kind" to the others. He came to a deep valley where, though the sun glinted on the tree tops, there were dark shadows below. A silver river wound through the valley and the landscape had an unnatural coloration, like velvet that has been stroked the wrong way. He regarded this dreamily for a while and then suddenly noticed an improbably high railroad bridge over the valley. Without hesitation, he strode onto the bridge. He had a moment of dizziness as he looked briefly down, but he strode vigorously ahead. "Suddenly I knew: I would have to cross the bridge even if it cost me my life."

Then, with a lurch, the iron structure under his feet began to tilt forward until it hung vertically downward into the depths. All that remained for him to do to save himself was to climb down, which he did without hesitation since he was an experienced mountaineer. The bridge was now a kind of ladder which he descended rung by rung without much alarm. Only one thing bothered him. Some men were waiting at the bottom of the upright bridge. He knew they were waiting to take him in charge.

"There's no way out," he said to himself. As he reached the bottom he voluntarily gave himself into captivity.

Hans Scholl was already well on his way down the tilt of that fantastic bridge when the orders came sending him back to Munich. He had no thought of clambering back out of danger.

The Student Medical Company had been at the front less than four months but now, a recipient of the special indulgence with which the German army treated its student-soldiers, it was being sent home for more study and technical training. Not all the members of the company were pleased to be leaving. Russia, the land and its people, had gripped some of them strangely and strongly, without regard to ideologies or politics. When these young Germans talked among themselves about the place the word "Communism" was seldom mentioned; the talk was of the people, their songs, their way of life. "It is easy to make contact with them when one takes the trouble," Willi Graf noted in his diary. "One can learn much just by listening to them and watching how they move. . . . I feel at home among them and I'm greatly concerned about what will happen to them." Those were not the sentiments expected of a member of the master race describing his impressions of subhuman inferiors. For Alex Schmorell, sergeant in Adolf Hitler's conquering *Wehrmacht,* to be ordered back to Germany was a calamity. He announced he would return some day. He vowed that meanwhile he would never remove the mud of Russia from his boots.

Hans Scholl and Willi Graf took long walks through the countryside on their last days at Gzhatsk as a kind of farewell ritual of their own. They also indulged in a reckless gesture of defiance on the night before their departure when, in a local tavern, they sang anti-Nazi verses which outraged a group of Party officials who were visiting the area. The *Schnaps* had flowed freely, the mood was reckless, and besides, in a combat zone such as this, soldiers could get away with mocking mere Party members. This was army turf.

At the Vyazma assembly point, on the way back, the unit was marched to a delousing station but Hans and his comrades found the long wait too boring and drifted away to buy a samovar instead. It took almost all the money they had but it turned out to be what Willi called "a good friend" on the long ride in the cold, crowded cattle car that lay ahead. The samovar produced hot, savory black tea at regular intervals and did much to make the journey endurable. It was also a blessing that their particular cattle car held a number of fellow passengers who, according to the code, were entitled to be called *"gute Menschen"* and *"einwandfrei"*—good fellows with the right political attitudes.

For Hans Scholl the Russian experience had been both memorable and moving, but it had not involved any radical upheaval in his motives or beliefs. He had committed himself before coming to Russia. What he saw and experienced there only deepened his already rooted contempt and hostility for the National Socialist system. With his comrade Alex Schmorell he was already guilty of what a Nazi court would call high treason. The four White Rose leaflets had been described by the authorities as "in the highest degree hostile to the state" and yet the authorities had been unable to detect their source or catch the perpetrators. The leaflets were, among other things, a clear demonstration that the system *could* be attacked and damaged, and that retribution did not inevitably or necessarily follow. The system was not as invulnerable or invincible as it made such a show of being.

Now, as he and Alex had agreed in many a discussion, a broader, tougher, and more organized effort was required—a long stride beyond what had already been done. A network of reliable and courageous colleagues would have to be recruited. Hans Scholl was sure now, more than before, that the time was ripening when the slow, subsurface simmer of hatred and resentment of people against the brute barbarities of the Nazi regime would boil into open rage and revolt.

As the cattle car rattled and clanked across the Russian miles toward the West, he was convinced that the mission he had chosen for himself—"to make a breach in the wall of terror" that imprisoned his country—was not only practical and possible but a categorical imperative. It was, as the third White Rose leaflet had said, a moral duty.

There was always the risk, of course. But then he could be sent back into a combat zone at any time. The chance of losing one's life by enemy action was never remote from him or his comrades or even, with the mounting bombardment from the sky, from millions behind the lines. The attitude of Hans and the White Rose dissidents was reflected in the saying of one of them: "If you're going to risk your life in this war, why not against an injustice that cries to heaven?"

At Brest, on the Polish border, there was a long wait and an incident. Hans and his comrades saw a group of Russian prisoners being herded off to a nearby barbed-wire enclosure. The Russians, gaunt, filthy, and half-starved, were a picture of last-stage wretchedness. Hans, Alex, and Willi offered them their army-issue cigarets. This brought an explosion of curses from the Germans guarding the prisoners, and Hans and his friends retorted as hotly in kind. If the train had not begun to move just then, a melee might have ensued which could have resulted in severe disciplinary action against Hans and the others for fraternizing with the enemy.

It was not the first such episode.

Weeks before, Hans had seen a slender, sickly Jewish girl, with the yellow star of David on her left breast, wielding a heavy pick in a group of women working at repairing a road bed. The girl's face, once comely, was sallow and haggard, and pain looked out from her sunken eyes. Hans took his iron ration, a mixture of chocolate, dried fruit and nuts, from his pocket and gave it to her.

She threw it at his feet.

He picked it up, brushed it off, and plucked a wild flower from the railroad embankment. Then he laid the ration and flower at the girl's feet. "I only wanted to give you some pleasure," he said and walked away.

When he looked back, the ration had been picked up and the flower was in the girl's hair.

There was, too, the German private in Gzhatsk whom Hans had seen kicking a Russian prisoner. Pulling rank as a sergeant, Hans delivered a blistering tongue-lashing which sent the private, shaken but helpless to retort, slinking away. And somewhere in Russia there was an old Jew who was probably still bewildered by what happened to him when two German soldiers stopped him and asked him if he had tobacco for the empty pipe in his mouth. It had been a long time, he said, since he had stuffed and lighted that pipe. Hans and Alex emptied their pouches into the old Jew's pocket. As dedicated pipe smokers themselves, they knew what it could mean to be without tobacco. Once Hans and Alex had performed a grimmer service for a soldier who had fallen on the other side. In a field that had been fought over, they came upon the unburied corpse of a Russian whose head had been blown from the shoulders. The two young Germans dug a grave and put the body and head together in it. After the grave was closed, they found an arm nearby. When all parts of the dead Russian had at last been put underground, Hans and Alex fashioned a Russian cross and planted it at the head of the grave. *"Jetzt hat seine Seele Ruhe,"* said Hans. "Now his soul is at rest."

Among the massive oppressions the Germans were inflicting on millions of Slavs and Jews, these were slight and fleeting incidents, mere firefly glints of light in a time of overwhelming and impenetrable darkness. But they were manifestations of the unsleeping conscience that insists on asserting itself where decency and humanity are concerned, whether the matter is trifling or towering.

Nine

For Sophie Scholl, the train ride between Ulm and Munich always brought about a transformation of personality, one she rather enjoyed. "Those 150 kilometers," she once wrote, "change me so quickly that I'm amazed myself. Going one way, I change from an artless, carefree child to a self-assured adult. The other way reverses the process. But I only feel really safe and secure when I'm home where my father is always so pleased to have me and never understands why I leave, and my mother fusses over 1,000 little things around the house . . ."

There was nothing to hold her in Munich after the summer semester ended at the Uni and her brother and his friends left for the East. She came home. But it turned out to be a summer tense with developments which abolished the hope of a secure and agreeable interlude with her parents and sisters on Cathedral Square. The arrest of her father left the family shaken and her mother distraught. All the Scholls came under renewed suspicion with the jailing of Robert, and further searches and surveillance had to be reckoned with. Sophie made contact with Traute Lafrenz, and together they went to Hans' room in Munich and combed the place for anything—a note, a letter, an underlined passage in a book—that the Gestapo might

use as evidence. They did the same at Sophie's quarters in the Man-
del Strasse which she had kept for her return to the Uni in the fall.

The summer was further marred by the wartime regulation which
required Sophie, as a college student, to spend most of her vacation
working in a factory in Ulm as a contribution to the war effort.
Again she found herself in the galling position of being forced to
contribute daily to a cause which revolted her. She tried to compensate for her work in the factory by being pointedly helpful and con-
siderate to the Russian girls who had been sent there as part of the
Nazi system of importing slave labor from the occupied areas. Sophie and a few of her friends pooled their ration coupons for white
bread and other wartime scarcities and used them to supply the Russian girls who, for Sophie, were not aliens and enemies but sisters
with whom she was sharing a time of terror and distress.

That August, word came that Ernst Reden had been killed on the
eastern front. This was news doubly grievous to Sophie. She not
only held Ernst Reden dear as one of the most fascinating men she
had ever met, but she also felt his loss acutely on behalf of her sister
Inge whose relationship with Reden was much closer and warmer
and for whom the news was shattering. "Enough!" said Sophie in
something close to despair. "It's got to stop. Now I'm going to *do*
something." She was heard to vow that, one way or another, Ernst
Reden's death would be avenged.

The ugliness of the times was being brought home to her in more
personal, more immediate, ways with every month, every week, almost every day, that the National Socialist regime stayed in power.
The news of Ernst Reden's death came at a time when Nazi paranoia
had made a criminal of her father and destroyed the serenity of her
blameless mother; when her two brothers were stationed in a remote
war zone in the East; when Fritz Hartnagel, the friend for whom she
felt a special warmth and concern, was fighting at Stalingrad where
the news was growing more ominous every hour. Sophie Scholl's
wish to be caught up and involved in her times was being fulfilled
with a harshness that gave no promise of relenting. Her own conviction that the times must not be passively accepted, but opposed, was
being steeled and strengthened.

The times were such that not even her pleasure at the prospect of

Hans' return from the East was untarnished. "I ought to be over-joyed at being with him again, but there is something troubling my joy . . . ," she confided to her diary. She looked forward to the days they would be spending together in Munich, but the uncertainty that now hung like a shadow over her life, and everyone's, made planning for a happy tomorrow impossible. Now, she said, every new day came clouded. Doubt and suspicion had entered into almost every human relationship, and each uttered word had to be examined from every side to see whether it had double or hidden meanings. Now one had to exert all one's energy and attention on matters which, in a better time, would not be worth lifting a little finger for. "This," said Sophie, "depresses me day and night. It doesn't leave me for a moment . . ."

Nevertheless, there was joy in the house on Cathedral Square when, toward the middle of November, Hans returned from Russia and when, at about the same time, Father Scholl was released from jail after serving the comparatively mild term of four months for the crime of speaking his mind in an unguarded moment.

On his return from prison Robert Scholl was unsubdued. More than once Sophie heard him utter the key word of his philosophy with undiminished emphasis: *"Allen!"* His indomitable attitude toward the threats and pressures of his time was contagious. Sophie went back to Munich with her brother in the spirit of her father's favorite saying—*"Despite all the powers, despite everything, maintain yourself!"* In this uncowed outlooked there was a broad Swabian streak of Götz von Berlichingen as well. In view of what was coming, it was just as well that Robert Scholl had instilled those twin attitudes into his daughter Sophie and his son Hans.

As the winter of 1942 came on, Munich was feeling the impact of the war with a severity few had anticipated. To the inhabitants it seemed that enemy bombers were singling out the capital of Adolf Hitler's movement for special punishment, though industrial centers and seaports like Bremen and Düsseldorf were being bombed more heavily. Adolf Hitler took a perverse satisfaction in the difficulties of the city he professed to love so much. He felt that Munich's people, and Bavarians in general, were not paying sufficient attention to the war, were not putting their backs into it. To Goebbels he confided that he was not entirely unhappy the place was being bombed since the bombing would shake the people up and make them aware of the war in a way they could not easily ignore. He did not even mind, he said, that his own apartment had been damaged. There were those in Munich who were following the course of the war with an absorption hardly less intense than his own.

The White Rose group had not waited until the fortunes of the Nazis began to ebb before opposing them. Their commitment being moral, the group remained unaffected by political and military success or the lack of it. But the unprecedented and unvarying success of Adolf Hitler as a political and military leader was a major element in his unbroken hold on the masses who supported him. The corollary of this was that those who opposed him, inside Germany and beyond, thirsted for signs which might indicate that, at last, a reversal in his long run of luck was setting in, that finally the ancient principle of nemesis was beginning to operate. A Hitler without successes was an infinitely more vulnerable Hitler.

That November, when Hans Scholl returned to Munich, such signs seemed to be multiplying. The air raids, which the German people were promised would never happen, were happening with increasing frequency and ferocity. In North Africa the vaunted *Afrika Korps* of Field Marshal Erwin Rommel had been stopped at the gates of Cairo and was now in full retreat. In the greatest amphibious operation in the history of war, Anglo-American forces had landed in North Africa. In the East the Russians were mounting a massive counteroffensive at Stalingrad. The swastika had been hoisted over the Communist Party headquarters there, but the fiercest kind of house-to-house combat was still in progress. The city had not fallen. America, now fully geared for war, was producing armaments in mountainous quantities and the U-boats were unable to stop the flow of them across the Atlantic.

To Hans Scholl, the time seemed right and ripe for resuming the mission which his service in the East had interrupted—resuming it and expanding it beyond anything he had attempted before. Events, he felt, were increasingly on his side. Not only was he morally right but historically, as well. He would move into new areas of opposition.

Despite the worsening war situation, the student-soldiers were able to return to their curiously free and mostly unmilitary lifestyle with little change. They went to lectures at the university, including Professor Huber's, and assisted at army clinics and hospitals as before. Evenings were again open for concerts and gatherings of the group for its own purposes, social and otherwise. This resumption of the previous round provided its own kind of cover; nothing on the surface being altered, no unwelcome attention was attracted. Hans, Alex, and Willi were all members of the Bach Choral Society, and as Christmas approached, they attended rehearsals for the society's seasonal concert. Rehearsing Bach chorales is not an activity normally associated with young men bent on subversion.

Hans and Sophie were now living in two big rooms in a house at Franz Joseph Strasse 13 in Schwabing, within easy walking distance of the university. The landlady was conveniently absent most of the time, in the country where she fled to escape the air raids. Hans and Sophie could come and go more or less as they wished and receive visitors, without much fear of observation. The house, besides, was not far from the studio which would again be their base of operations.

Hans was driven by the idea, stressed in the last White Rose leaflet, that in National Socialism something irrational and unhuman was at work—"demons emerging from the dark"—which gave resistance to the Hitler regime a dimension both deeper and higher than mere political opposition. Marked in his New Testament was the passage in Ephesians which speaks of wrestling not "against flesh and blood, but against . . . the rulers of the darkness of this world, against spiritual wickedness in high places." He made it a principle that the irrational must be fought with rational means. Now the means at his disposal would have to be organized and expanded. New resources, new supporters, would be needed for his new effort, and he set about acquiring the one and recruiting the other. Hans Scholl became a traveling salesman of subversion.

A man named Eugen Grimminger, a friend of his father, was among the first to be solicited for moral support and financial backing in the cause of sedition. Hans and Alex traveled to Stuttgart to present their case. Something of the passion and persuasiveness with which it was presented can be judged from Herr Grimminger's response. He was a practical man in his fifties, a public accountant who had also been a civil servant, and was hardly a dreamy or erratic type but he had been shrewdly chosen as a prospect, nevertheless. As a friend of Robert Scholl's, it could be assumed from the start that his attitude was not far from dissidence. He was married to a woman who was, in the racist jargon of the Nazis, a *Volljüdin*, a full Jewess.

Still, the danger was there as it was in any such approach. What Hans and Alex had to say could not be discussed in a restaurant or office where it might be overheard, or even at home where such a meeting might lead to difficulties for the highly vulnerable Frau Grimminger. So the discussion took place while the three men walked the sidewalks of Stuttgart, with the most crucial talk confined to the loading platform of a transport company on the outskirts of town. There Herr Grimminger was told of the White Rose leaflets and of the plan Hans was now concentrating on.

He was going to organize resistance groups at the universities and link them together into a nationwide phalanx of resistance. Already, at the University of Munich, a group was active under the slogan of "Justice for All!" *(Gerechtigkeit für Alle!)* Similar groups existed at other universities. The vigor of Hans' language and the force of his arguments led Herr Grimminger to believe that more than the production of leaflets was being planned. He felt that something on the order of a putsch, a physical attempt to overthrow the government as a means of ending the war, was not far from Hans Scholl's mind and that he, Herr Grimminger, might have a role in a new government. This seemed less like sheer fantasy because Grimminger was in touch with certain industrial circles in Stuttgart where the possibility of a new government, with new personalities, was also being discussed. Afterwards, much later, Eugen Grimminger was to wonder at how readily he had succumbed to Hans Scholl's eloquence from which he drew the conclusion that matters were far more advanced in the student resistance movement at Munich than they actually were.

When Hans Scholl capped the discussion with a frank plea for money, Eugen Grimminger hesitated. He was practical enough to understand that the White Rose movement, of which he approved in principle, could not function solely on high ideals and noble aspirations. To be effective, he knew, it would need ready cash for basic materials and equipment like duplicating machines, ink, stencils, paper, postage stamps, envelopes. Without financial assistance, as Hans Scholl made abundantly clear, he and his comrades would not be able to keep their precarious operation going.

Herr Grimminger understood and was sympathetic. Yet for a respectable businessman to become involved in what was clearly a treasonable undertaking, one which could easily entangle him and his family in the gravest consequences, was a step he hesitated to take. The young men of the White Rose left Stuttgart empty-handed.

A few weeks later, after weighing the matter in the long hours of the night, Eugen Grimminger had a change of heart. He wrote out a check for the substantial sum of 500 marks and gave it to Hans Scholl. He asked for no receipt. There was no mention of repayment. It was a gift which testified both to the generosity and the idealism of Eugen Grimminger, obscure German accountant. It would cost him dear.

The architect Manfred Eickemeyer, who had already made his studio available to the group, contributed a handsome 200 marks even though he had not been keen on the White Rose leaflets, regarding them as too literary. He was prudent enough to make his donation in cash, which left no trace as the Grimminger check did. Willi Graf also contributed according to his means: 50 marks.

He did more.

At the behest of Hans Scholl and for the good of the cause, Willi Graf used his Christmas furlough to undertake a missionary journey. He visited Saarbrücken and Bonn and Cologne and other Rhineland towns as part of the effort to organize university groups into a unified pattern of resistance. His friends had warned him of the danger in what he was doing. To that Willi paid no attention, though it warred with his nature to slip from place to place under false pretense, to guard his speech and veil his purpose as if he were doing something shameful. He grappled constantly with the question of whether what he was doing was right and whether it was worth doing. Though he seemed to his friends a model of calm and self-control, Willi Graf was often inwardly ill at ease and unsure of himself for reasons he could not always decipher. "Sometimes," he wrote in his journal, "I am certain of the rightness of my course. Sometimes I doubt it. But I take it upon myself nevertheless, no matter how burdensome it may be." A friend with whom he spoke on his missionary travels wondered about him: "What were the circumstances that impelled a young man who grew up conventionally in a secure and happy home to go against the prevailing attitudes of his time at such terrible risk to himself?" The friend could only conclude: "He was one of those young people who have always found it impossible to remain indifferent in the face of injustice." He told his sister Annaliese that for him the most important thing was simply the preservation of "the world that shaped our culture and our life." So Willi Graf went his quiet and unspectacular way in search of converts to the cause.

He met with uneven success. At Bonn there were people who were sympathetic but not prepared to take any action, and some who were too engaged in their studies to think of anything else. But at the University of Freiburg he found that there was already a core of resistance which had made inroads even into the faculty. (Five of the professors there would later be arrested and imprisoned by the Gestapo.) He made contact with two brothers from the town he grew up in, Heinz and Willi Bollinger, and learned that both had become activists in their own spheres and in their own ways. Heinz, an assistant professor of philosophy, let Willi Graf know by the established methods of the code that he was in agreement with the aims of the White Rose. Then he went further. He believed that the ultimate goal of the resistance must be the assassination of Hitler if that was the only way the Nazi regime could be destroyed and the war ended. Willi Graf recalled that Hans had brought a Russian machine pistol back from the East.

Willi Bollinger was a medical officer attached to an army hospital in Saarbrücken and he was building a resistance group there. He was also acquiring a cache of weapons, mainly revolvers and machine pistols. On a later trip, Willi Graf would manage to pass a duplicating machine to Willi Bollinger, along with some leaflets for him to reproduce and circulate. This Bollinger brother proved to be an invaluable contact for the White Rose operation. He knew how to forge military passes, leave papers, and army railroad tickets.

Willi Graf functioned well and truly as a missionary spreading the gospel of dissidence, but he noticed that it was taking a toll of him. In his journal he recorded that when he paused in his travels for a relaxing game of chess, he couldn't keep his mind on the game and his play fell off— " . . . *ich bin nicht ganz bei der Sache.*" He wasn't with it. What he wished he could be doing was continuing his work on new forms of liturgy which he had begun with some other members of the illegal Catholic society to which he still belonged.

Back in Munich, he immersed himself in music as in a cleansing bath. There were, as always, plenty of concerts to choose from. He listened to the second "Leonora Overture" and Mozart's D-Major symphony, but another composer seemed more in accord with how he was then feeling. Bartok. "It is the monstrously rhythmic element that appeals to me," he wrote. "It won't let one rest."

For the others, too, it was a period of restlessness and tension, more a Bartok than a Mozart time. Something like an electric charge was running through the circle around Hans Scholl, making nerve ends quiver as if a crucial development of some kind, a decisive turn of events, was in the offing and had to be prepared for by the marshaling of all available sources. The mood was one of undefined emergency.

The replenished treasury was presided over by Sophie Scholl, who kept the books and meted out the cash as needed, but the acquisition of equipment and supplies for future operations was a continuing problem. Traute Lafrenz was commissioned to see what could be done about acquiring another, and bigger, duplicating machine. She was chosen for the mission because she had an uncle in the wholesale office supply business in Vienna. Traute made the trip by train and came away with nothing better than the promise of such a machine sometime in the spring, the war having curtailed the production of all sorts of civilian goods, including office supplies. Traute did what missionary work she could on the trip by filtering several White Rose leaflets into the University of Vienna through her Aunt Mimi who could be trusted and who had connections with the faculty and student body. Thus the White Rose message reached yet another seat of learning in the Third Reich.

Trim, attractive, and a little cheeky, Traute Lafrenz hardly suggested an agent of sedition as she went briskly about the business of being seditious. That winter she spent several weeks in her native Hamburg to study at a gynecological clinic, but she also strengthened her contacts with dissident elements among students and intellectuals there. The Hamburg movement consisted of a loosely connected group of about fifty which became known as the North German branch of the White Rose.

Traute brought with her several of the leaflets which were received with intense interest and approval. Hamburg was fertile ground—"Red Hamburg," long a stronghold of Social Democracy where Nazism had never won overwhelming acceptance from the largely working-class population. Among other symptoms of opposition, Hamburg boasted a club called the "Swingboys" whose members affected English nicknames and listened to illicit jazz whenever possible. The more serious dissidents—the students, intellectuals, some professors—met informally but frequently in two Hamburg book stores and selected coffee houses to discuss the perennial question: "What can we do?"

The Hamburg group, though larger than its Munich counterpart, was not as cohesive and focused and had not translated its attitudes into action. Its plans, however, were ambitious. There had been discussion of blowing up a railroad bridge, over which troop trains passed on their way to the front. Chemistry students in the group thought that nitroglycerin for such a stroke of sabotage could be obtained from laboratories to which they had access. There was also talk of putting tetanus germs in the Hamburg water supply and blowing up Gestapo headquarters.

Such projects, or most of them, originated with the leading spirit among the intellectual dissidents, a student named Hans Leipelt. He had served with a Motorized Infantry Regiment in France and Poland and had won the Tank Combat Medal and the Iron Cross II. Then he was dismissed from the army on the ground that his mother was half Jewish (though a practicing Christian). Hans Leipelt had the owlish, horn-rimmed look of a college grind who aims to become a professor, but his friends called him "Commissar" only partly in jest. His hatred of Nazism was fierce and burning. He became a close collaborator of the White Rose, and his commitment to its goals eventually brought him, too, to Stadelheim and the guillotine.

Traute Lafrenz was able to bring back satisfactory reports of the liaison which now existed between the dissident students of Hamburg and Munich, but Hans Scholl's vision of a whole network of resistance nests and strong-points went beyond student activities. He was bent on venturing into unexplored territory.

He was put into touch with wider elements of the anti-Hitler movement through a man named Falk Walter Harnack, who in civilian life was a director and producer at the National Theater in Weimar. Now he was a corporal in a reserve infantry company stationed in the industrial town of Chemnitz, not far from the Czech border. Through a Munich painter named Lilo Ramdohr, who was a friend of both Alex Schmorell's and Harnack's, a meeting was arranged in Chemnitz where Hans and Alex journeyed.

The meeting took place in a little hotel known to Harnack, the Saxony Court. It was a first meeting for all three but there was no need for the usual code words and preliminary feeling-out. "We all knew where we stood from the start," Falk Harnack said afterwards. Hans and Alex produced several of their leaflets and their contents were discussed and analyzed, with general agreement that in the future the tone to be taken would be more pragmatic and less literary, more realistic and less philosophical.

But Hans and Alex had not come all the way to Chemnitz to get another opinion on the style of their leaflets. What they wanted, they told Harnack, was to put the opposition of the students on a broader basis and thus give it added impact. They were eager to establish some kind of contact with the anti-Nazi opposition in Berlin where efforts were being made to bring together the various factions of the resistance—Communist, liberal, conservative-military—into a unified movement with a consensus on aims and action. Falk Harnack had the necessary connections, including contacts with high-ranking army officers whose plotting would one day result in the explosion of a bomb in Hitler's headquarters. Harnack promised to arrange a meeting between Hans Scholl and key conspirators in Berlin.

It was an extremely hazardous undertaking. Falk Harnack's own brother, Dr. Arvid Harnack, had recently been arrested and executed for his role in a conspiracy called the "Red Orchestra" in which military information of the highest importance was regularly transmitted to the Russians by a network of Communist sympathizers who had infiltrated the *Luftwaffe*, the German Air Force. Fifty men and women, including Arvid's American wife Mildred, whom he met at the University of Wisconsin, were executed in the Red Orchestra affair. The men were not granted the swift dispatch of the guillotine but, on Hitler's orders, were hung on meat hooks and slowly strangled to death. The courts had only sentenced the women to jail but Hitler insisted that they, too, be executed and they were.

The meeting of Hans, Alex, and Falk Harnack in Chemnitz was not the only one. Harnack twice came to Munich—partly to see his friend Lilo Ramdohr—and there were further discussions in which Professor Huber and Willi Graf also took part. There were acute differences of opinion between Professor Huber, whose outlook was in essence traditional and conservative, and Falk Harnack, whose orientation was to the left, as his brother's had been. There was no agreement on how the postwar government of Germany should be constituted, but there was unanimity that after the fall of Hitler all Nazi activists would be hunted down, arrested, prosecuted, and harshly punished. Only three political parties would be allowed—Marxist, Liberal, and Christian—in contrast to the dozens that had caused such political chaos during the Weimar Republic. But the immediate goal, to which all other considerations must give way, was the ending of the war as soon as possible and the downfall of National Socialism and its Leader.

Falk Harnack was the only participant in those tense and heated discussions who was still alive when at last Hitler perished and the war ended. Meanwhile, he kept his promise and arranged a meeting between the Berlin conspirators and Hans Scholl. The tryst never took place because the date set for it turned out to be the day on which Hans Scholl was executed. That, in its way, was symbolic of the fate of the German resistance movement as a whole. None of its plans and objectives—the worthy ones like the dubious—ever came to fruition. All its ways and doings were dogged by uncertainty, mischance, and malign misfortune. The welding of its scattered and contradictory elements into a cohesive movement that could strike with power and effect never materialized. Typical of the resistance in all its phases was the story of the bomb that on July 20, 1944, exploded in Hitler's headquarters. With admirable ingenuity and great daring, it was placed under the very map table over which Adolf Hitler was at that moment bending. It killed several of his aides and adjutants.

It did not kill the *Führer*.

On the Maximilian Platz in the heart of Munich, in the shadow of the twin domes of the Church of Our Lady, was a book store run by one Josef Söhngen, a favorite resort of Hans and Sophie Scholl. Söhngen, like many another book dealer, was a somewhat eccentric character and prided himself on it. He relished his own personality and his trade. "One of the most agreeable things about a bookshop," he often said, "is that people tend to relax and talk more easily in one. It's hard to be close-mouthed and hostile in the midst of stacks of books." Josef Söhngen talked rather freely himself, priding himself on knowing his own mind and speaking it. "Most of the people who came into my shop were aware of my opinions, especially how I felt about the Nazis and the concentration camps. My place naturally attracted young people like Hans and Sophie. They often came to buy books, and they often came just to visit and talk."

After Hans' return from Russia, the talk at the book shop took on a different tone. It was less relaxed and more intense. They used to discuss the poetry of Heinrich von Kleist or talk over religious questions like the mystery of the Trinity, subjects which Hans always

found of absorbing interest. Now he talked of the impression that
Russia—the land and the people, not the political system—had
made on him. He seemed more intense with something harder in the
look of his steady dark eyes. He had decided, he said, to give up the
study of medicine after the war. He would devote himself to politics, to public affairs, where the forming of the future lay. He spoke
to Söhngen of the coming time when National Socialism was swept
away and Germany would "resume its contact with the civilized
world." He speculated on what the political structure might, and
should, be. He thought a sane and workable system might be a United States of Europe under the leadership of England. Josef Söhngen
noticed in Hans the same quality that Harnack, too, had observed:
an inner drive and an eagerness for involvement that was held in
leash only with difficulty. He was lavish with his energy, expending
it freely from a supply that seemed inexhaustible but which had its
limits. Once he came to Söhngen's apartment above the book shop
at midnight, eased himself into a chair, and asked for a glass of
wine. "Let me sit here for a half hour and recover my balance," he
said. Then he was silent for a long time.

Söhngen knew that his young friend was engaged in subversive
activities. Hans had described, with the pride of authorship, the successes of the first leaflets. Now, he said, he was bent on expanding
his efforts in any direction that promised strength and support for his
anti-Nazi endeavors.

Josef Söhngen was in a position to help him there. He was in
touch with an art historian named Giovanni Stepanov who lived on
Capri and who had contact with the anti-Fascist movement in Mussolini's Italy. Söhngen sometimes arranged lecture engagements for
Stepanov in Munich and under cover of such occasions the two men
would exchange information on the progress of resistance in their
respective countries. Söhngen undertook the mission of bringing
Hans Scholl and Giovanni Stepanov together.

But mischance was again at work.

On Stepanov's next visit to Munich, Hans was away on a Christmas visit to Ulm. And when another meeting was arranged for February, difficulties with Stepanov's visa delayed matters unexpectedly. Before a date could be set, it was, again, too late. Like his dream

of forming an alliance with the conspirators in Berlin, Hans Scholl's hope of making common cause with the anti-Fascists of Italy came to nothing. But the book shop on Maximilian Platz, in the shadow of the Church of Our Lady, proved to be a source of aid and comfort to him in many ways before his course was run.

Like the man who never took off his overcoat because he would soon be moving on, Hans Scholl seemed at this time to be constantly on the move. He was restless at the university and contemptuous of it—"the same old faces, mostly stupid ones." He found that the pleasure he once took in writing was gone. He could not keep up his correspondence and wrote a friend whose letter had long gone unanswered that he could barely bring himself to mar a piece of paper by putting words on it. A blank white sheet had infinitely more appeal for him, not out of esthetic grounds but because "no lies have yet disfigured it, no threadbare phrases defaced it, while in an unused sheet of white paper there is a powerful potential . . ." He would wait until the pleasure he took in writing returned.

Nevertheless, the substance of another leaflet was growing in his mind. Events at the turn of the year encouraged it.

Throughout Europe the hope that had been all but extinguished began to glimmer. Nazi Germany now seemed less like some malign force of nature which no human agency could hold back or alter. It no longer seemed so certain that the Third Reich would live out the thousand years Adolf Hitler claimed for it. In North Africa and Russia the *Wehrmacht*, so long synonymous with victory and a stranger to defeat, was seen to be vulnerable to the blows of its enemies, East and West. Mutters of resentment in the occupied countries were gradually becoming more audible, here and there growing into snarls of defiance. In Germany the pulse of resistance was beating quicker. Theodor Haecker, keeping his nighttime journal in Munich, made an entry in January of 1943:

One can already hear the howls and whines of the demons more clearly in their dread-filled phrases. It is the last gasp of the crazed man who runs amok, just before the end. An official call to hate! The hate will certainly be found, all right, but it will not be the hate they intend, and want, today. It will be different . . .

* * *

The crazed man who was running amok was, in fact, far from his last gasp, but he was beginning to pant where before he had only bellowed. The difference was readily sensed by those who were waiting for any sign or symptom of a change.

That year the 470th anniversary of the founding of the university was being observed and the Nazi Party took the opportunity to combine the celebration with a heavy dose of discipline and morale-stiffening for the students who did not seem to be exhibiting the patriotic ardor expected from young Germans in the capital of the movement. Accordingly, all students were ordered to assemble on January 13 in the capacious hall of the German Museum of Technology, there being no auditorium big enough at the university.

The speaker was no less a personage than the *Gauleiter*, Paul Giesler. In addition to being the leader of the District of Munich and Upper Bavaria, known as the "Tradition" *Gau*, Paul Giesler was a Group Commander of Storm Troops and possessor of the Honor Badge in Gold for service rendered to the National Socialist German Workers Party. At forty-eight he was balding and had a beaked nose and a paunch but he saw himself as a paladin of the Party and a doughty defender of its ideology against heretics and scoffers. His speech was intended to whip the slack and recalcitrant students into line and imbue them with the spirit that had once set the Brown Shirts marching.

Several leaflets of the White Rose had been brought to the *Gauleiter's* attention by the Gestapo and though he had no evidence that they had been produced by students, he knew such sentiments were rife in the university. He prided himself on being what the Nazi press called him—"a man of the people"—and on the bluntness of his language, for which he was also known in Party circles. The rows of students in the hall before him, the attending professors and academic officials in their robes and decorations, did not in the least impress Paul Giesler.

Most of the students, women as well as men, were seated in the balcony. The auditorium floor was occupied by men in uniform, student-soldiers awaiting orders to the front or recently returned from it. Among them were a number of wounded veterans, some with

canes and crutches. On the platform, with the dignitaries, were local
and national leaders of the Bund, and *SS* guards were posted about
the hall. Leaning over the balcony rail in the front row were Traute
Lafrenz and Kate Schüddekopf who had come out of curiosity, not
out of respect for the occasion. In the audience, surreptitiously taking notes, was the dissident student from Hamburg, Hans Leipelt.

The *Gauleiter* paid scant attention to the occasion for the meeting. He launched instead into a tirade against students who, he said,
were using their studies as an excuse for draft-dodging and malin-
gering. He promised that there would be a drastic comb-out of all
those physically able either to go into the army or work in the war
plants. This was no time for pampering effete intellectuals who
might better be spending their time doing something useful for the
Fatherland. They all knew how the *Führer* felt about young men
who kept their noses in books while there was a war on. Then the
Gauleiter turned his attention to the female students.

"As for the girls," he said, "There is no reason why each of
them should not make an annual contribution to the Fatherland of a
child, preferably a son. Let all girl students with healthy bodies bear
children. That is an automatic process and, once started, continues
without requiring the least attention."

In his crudity, the *Gauleiter* thought that here he had struck a
popular vein, one that would bring appreciative chuckles from his
mixed audience. He proceeded to expand on it with a leering face-
tiousness that was a measure of how far he was from sensing the
temper of his listeners.

"Of course, a certain amount of cooperation is required in these
matters. If some of you girls lack sufficient charm to find a mate, I
will be glad to assign you one of my adjutants for whose ancestry I
can vouch. I can promise you a thoroughly enjoyable experience . . ."

In the balcony, Traute Lafrenz and Kate Schüddekopf sat back in
their seats and looked at each other in mingled outrage and disgust.
They were not alone in their reaction. There had already been some
scraping of shoes against the floor, a form of booing with the feet.
With the remarks addressed to the girl students, the noise of shuffling steadily intensified until it reached a crescendo that drowned

out the speaker entirely. Piercing whistles, the ultimate insult from
an audience, cut through the growing uproar in the auditorium. In
moments the observance of the 470th anniversary of the University of
Munich exploded into a tumultuous demonstration, an outburst of
rage and protest against a leadership whose coarseness and contempt for common decency were personified by the smirking figure
on the speaker's platform.

In the midst of the whistling and shuffling, women in the audience
got up to leave, though the ceremonies had not been concluded.
Male students also left their seats by the score, adding to the disor-
der and confusion. At the doors scuffles and fist fights broke out with
the SS men who tried to hold back the exodus. Dozens of indiscriminate arrests were made by the guards before the sheer mass of
the students swept them aside. The cripples in uniform were among
the most vociferous protesters, whistling and shouting and flourish-
ing their canes and crutches. Against them even the SS men were
helpless. What action could be taken against crippled veterans? In
the pandemonium, a young lieutenant wearing a high decoration for
valor was seen to leap on the platform, seize one of the Student
Bund leaders and begin pummeling him.

The students poured into the street and continued their demonstration there. Groups formed to chant in unison: "Free our comrades! Give us back our comrades!" Linking arms, male and female
students marched down Ludwig Strasse, shouting and singing, in
the only open display of political protest that the streets of Nazi Germany would ever know. Young, fervent and defiant, the demonstra-
tors did not disband until, on the orders of Paul Giesler, the Riot Police were called out. With flailing batons, they broke the marching
columns into segments, dispersing it and ending the demonstration.

There were repercussions.

A state of emergency was declared in Munich. For a time both
telephone service and radio were suspended. Heinrich Himmler,
chief of all the Security Services in the Third Reich, intervened
from battle headquarters somewhere in the East by teletype. He ordered his agents in Munich to ferret out the instigators of the demonstration who he thought were "wire-pullers from Catholic and conservative circles." He did not understand that the protest, being

wholly spontaneous, had no instigator—unless it was Paul Giesler. Himmler also commanded that police measures be discreet so as not to spread knowledge of the incident among the public and thus embarrass the regime further. No word of the demonstration appeared in the press, but news of it seeped across Germany anyway and set off lesser protests in Vienna, Frankfurt, and the Ruhr. The *Gauleiter's* speech made an impact far beyond anything he could have imagined when he was composing it.

Hans and Sophie had not heard it.

Adhering to their policy of passive resistance, they attended no Nazi functions of any kind for any reason. They were, of course, given full details of the speech and the uproar it set off, and for them the affair was electric with significance and hope. What happened at the German Museum, they were sure, was yet another sign that events were moving in the direction they wished for and expected. They took it as a spur to change over, again, from passive to active resistance.

Since his return from Russia, Hans had been associating with Professor Huber on increasingly familiar terms, not only attending his lectures but visiting him at his home, sometimes with Alex Schmorell and sometimes with Willi Graf (who made an appreciative note in his diary when Clara Huber served an especially tasty snack with a good cup of coffee, a rarity). At the end of December, Hans felt sufficiently secure with the professor to reveal that he was responsible for the White Rose leaflets. It was his way of accepting Kurt Huber into the circle without any reservations.

Kurt Huber was not at all sure that leaflets were a good idea. He thought they would have no appreciable effect on the public and that the danger of producing them outweighed any effect they might have. Paul Giesler's performance at the German Museum changed his mind. For Kurt Huber the *Gauleiter's* speech was an affront to the university and everything it stood for. He canvassed fellow members of the faculty for a statement of censure and protest. He got no response. "Not one of the professors or rectors dared to put himself on the side of the students," he reported. "It was then I decided to disassociate myself from the faculty, clearly and openly." He did not go directly to the chancellor, as he later explained in court, because the chancellor's views were too well known for Huber to hope for anything but rebuff in that quarter. The most he could do was to express his indignation at the start of his own lectures which now were drawing as many as 250 students at every session.

When Hans Scholl came to him for advice on the text of a new leaflet, Kurt Huber was ready to collaborate. Now he agreed that the leaflet was the only possible means of obtaining a hearing for views which urgently needed to be aired but which otherwise would have no outlet whatever. As for the legality of his actions, Kurt Huber had made up his mind on that score also. "In a state where the free expression of public opinion is throttled," he would tell the court that put him on trial for his life, "a dissident must necessarily turn to illegal methods." Kurt Huber had come to the point where the only way he could decently go led underground.

The professor began visiting Hans Scholl in his rooms in bohemian Schwabing which was behavior rather more unconventional than he was accustomed to. Sometimes Sophie was present when he called, but she withdrew to the other room when the discussions with her brother began. Professor Huber hardly noticed her except when the meetings were over and Sophie, playing hostess and observing the amenities, served an afternoon tea in the adjoining room. Kurt Huber did not know, and was not told, of Sophie Scholl's involvement in the leaflet operation and did not learn of it until after her arrest. This was in keeping with Hans' policy of shielding her from all unnecessary contact, even so reliable a one as Kurt Huber. The fewer who knew of her involvement, the better— for her and for the whole operation. At this time, Sophie was, in fact, helping her brother with the text of the new leaflet which would be the fifth in the series.

Two versions of it were shown to Kurt Huber for his comment and suggestions, one by Hans and one by Alex Schmorell. The procedure was a grim variation of the scholastic routine of students submitting their term papers to a professor in the hope of getting a passing mark: but here the common objective and the shared risk put everyone involved on the same level. The professor's views were weighed and respected but they were not always accepted as conclusive. Disputes over what should be said, and the manner of saying it, were frequent and heated. It was, after all, a life and death matter for each of them.

The leaflet was to have the title of A CALL TO ALL GERMANS!— *AUFRUF AN ALLE DEUTSCHE!*—and Alex Schmorell's treatment of the theme was flatly rejected by the professor. It had what he called "a communist ring." Staunchly conservative even in the midst of practicing sedition, Kurt Huber bridled at young Schmorell's pro-Russian passion which, if never ideologically orthodox, might be interpreted as support of the Soviet system. For Kurt Huber, one of the most deplorable tendencies of National Socialism was what he regarded as its increasing "bolshevisation," its aping of the Communists in their unrelenting assaults on religion and the trampling upon all manifestations of the free spirit in the interests of a doctrinaire materialism. This warred with everything Kurt Huber held dear as a Christian, a scholar, and a human being. He saw the totalitarianism of Adolf Hitler on the right merging with the totalitarianism of Josef Stalin on the left into one brutalized and inhuman system and he saw nothing to choose between.

Alex Schmorell's text failed to get a passing mark from the professor.

Hans' version of the leaflet did not pass unscathed, either, the professor exercising the right vested in him as a teacher to make corrections in style, to strike out phrases he disapproved of, and to clarify passages which seemed to him clouded. He afterwards admitted that, though Hans Scholl was receptive to suggestions and received them with respect, he tended to use his own judgment, and his own language, when composing the final version of his leaflet.

A change that Hans insisted on over Huber's objections marked a drastic alteration in the tone and style of the leaflet operation. The designation "White Rose" was dropped. Instead, the caption for the new series now read: LEAFLETS OF THE RESISTANCE MOVEMENT IN GERMANY—not "The German Resistance Movement." Hans had chosen the phrasing with care to indicate that this was not a German effort only but, rather, the German phase of a Europe-wide resistance against Hitler and his regime. It was a distinction which spoke of Hans Scholl's determination to expand his activity beyond Munich and its dissident students and link up with underground organizations everywhere, thus strengthening the overall efforts of the anti-Nazi movement and his own as well.

The fifth leaflet was harsher and more direct than its White Rose predecessors, and half as long. The essay mode of philosophical comment and classical quotation was dropped. The appeal was no longer narrowed to the intellectual community but was broad and unlimited. The blunt opening set the tone:

The war is approaching its inevitable end.

Then came a curt summary of the hopelessness of Germany's situation: its armies were being beaten back in the East while in the West the Allied invasion of Europe was being mounted. American armament production had not yet reached its peak but it already surpassed anything ever known before in history.

With mathematical certainty, Hitler is leading the German people into the abyss. He cannot win the war, only prolong it!

(The phrase "mathematical certainty" was a sardonic play on a phrase often used by Hitler himself when predicting success for his undertakings.)

Themes already stressed in the White Rose leaflets were repeated: the enormity of the Nazi crimes, the necessity for discarding indifference and taking action. *"A new war of liberation has begun! The better part of the people already fights on our side!"* To the official propaganda that Germany's fate was inseparably linked to that of National Socialism the leaflet replied: *"No pack of criminals can possibly achieve a German victory. Break with National Socialism while there's still time."*

In looking to the future, the fifth leaflet was more outspoken than any of its forerunners and took a boldly liberal line. Some form of *"reasonable socialism"* would free the working class from economic slavery. The *"misguided system"* of industrial autocracy would be abolished. *"Every nation, every individual, has a right to the good things of the world."*

The concept of imperial power, especially in the form of Prussian militarism, must be rooted out for all time. In a European federation based on the cooperation of all nations and peoples, Germany would take its place as a contributing member under a sound federal constitution of its own. The concluding paragraph of the leaflet had the ring of a passage from the United Nations Charter, two-and-a-half years before the Charter's existence:

> *Freedom of speech, freedom of religion, protection of the individual citizen against the arbitrary actions of authoritarian states—these are the foundations of the New Europe.*

And then:
"SUPPORT THE RESISTANCE MOVEMENT! CIRCULATE THE LEAFLETS!"

Ten

The Wittelsbach Palace, named for Germany's oldest dynasty, was a curious place to be headquarters of the Secret State Police in Munich and vicinity. The name and place were more suggestive of a royal and romantic past than of the terrors of a modern police state. Good King Ludwig I used to live there with the Irish dancing girl who called herself Lola Montez and whose carefree way with the royal exchequer cost him his throne. The unlikely story of the Wittelsbach Palace was only an aspect of the erratic history of the whole area. In one of the many political convulsions Bavarians have lived through, the palace once became the seat of a brief Soviet-style Republic which emerged during the revolutionary upheavals after the First World War. In an even more drastic wrench in history, the Nazis then followed the kings and the Communists as lords of the rather attractive English-Gothic edifice whose squat serenity and nearby Court Gardens, with their meticulously groomed lawns and flower beds, made an almost lunatic contrast to the ugly business being conducted inside.

One of the senior agents on the Gestapo staff quartered in the palace was Robert Mohr, a veteran of twenty-six years at his trade. He had been a policeman long before the coming of the Nazis and,

227

though a conscientious agent, he was not as deep-dyed in Gestapo fanaticism as many of his colleagues, a trait which would have some bearing on coming events. On a morning at the end of January, 1943, Robert Mohr's phone rang and a secretary's voice summoned him into the presence of the chief of the bureau, a man named Schaefer whose authority was sufficiently denoted by the thumping title he had achieved: *Oberregierungsrat* which, as nearly as it can be translated, meant Upper Administrative Official. Mohr noticed that on this morning his superior seemed agitated. Mohr also noticed that on his chief's desk was a small pile of oblong sheets with which the *Oberregierungsrat* intermittently fussed. He showed one to Robert Mohr.

It was an anti-Nazi leaflet. That, said Herr Schaefer, was Mohr's new assignment. He was told to drop everything else and begin an investigation of the source of the leaflets, which were turning up by the hundreds, by the thousands. They were being found all over the city, scattered in doorways and halls, in mail boxes, in parked cars, in apartment areaways, in movie-house lobbies, in telephone kiosks, on park benches, all over the place. And—*Donnerwetter!*— just read what those things are saying!

Already the leaflet was causing "the greatest disturbance and dismay in high circles," as Herr Schaefer put it, mentioning no names. Important officials in Party and state, he went on, his voice quivering, were insisting that this whole affair be looked into and cleaned up as soon as possible. Swift arrests were demanded and expected. Understood?

"Jawohl, Herr Oberregierungsrat!" said Robert Mohr and went to work.

He soon learned that the snowstorm of subversive leaflets in Munich was only the beginning. From all over southern Germany, and beyond, reports came in of a veritable *Blitz* of seditious handbills issued by some hitherto unknown organization that called itself the "Resistance Movement in Germany." No place of origin could be determined since the leaflets that went through the mails—and there were thousands of them—were postmarked from at least half a dozen different cities. Leaflets that turned up in Augsburg were postmarked Stuttgart but the leaflets in Stuttgart had been mailed from Vienna and so on.

The authorities were shaken. This was more serious than the spate of White Rose leaflets the previous summer, which had so abruptly ceased. This, perhaps, was a bold flexing of underground muscles, the beginning of what could be a "chain reaction," a phrase that was used in official circles. The timing of the leaflet attack seemed to have been chosen with cunning; it could hardly have come at a worse time.

With the grave setbacks at the fronts, especially in the Stalingrad sector where the outcome seemed more uncertain every day, the Propaganda Ministry had been straining to assure the world that the German people stood as firmly behind their leadership as ever. Only recently Dr. Goebbels himself had proclaimed that public support was the rock on which the Nazi war effort was based. "When a German soldier turns his face to the enemy," the Propaganda Minister had said, "he can be absolutely confident that the home front stands solidly behind him." Now, just when it could do the most damage, thousands of leaflets in half a dozen major cities were insisting that the German people were anything but unified in their support of the war and that inside the Third Reich voices were being raised that called for Germany's defeat and the downfall of the Hitler regime. The leaflets were a contradiction of everything the Propaganda Ministry was proclaiming. An anti-Nazi underground was active not only in the occupied countries but inside Germany itself.

How big was it? On the evidence of the leaflets it looked formidable. The number of them, their simultaneous appearance in widely separated cities, argued that an organization of considerable size was at work, one with capable leadership and considerable resources. The threat inherent in the leaflet action seemed serious enough to merit top priority on the crowded agenda of Agent Mohr and his colleagues. The atmosphere was tense in the Wittelsbach Palace.

Behind the leaflets there was, of course, no far-reaching conspiracy, no nationwide network of revolutionaries capable of bringing down the government as the Gestapo, in its more jittery moments, might have suspected. Behind the "Resistance Movement in Germany" were only the half dozen Munich students. They had contrived to make the Third Reich of Adolf Hitler take notice of their protest and feel the pressure of their commitment by pooling the only resources they had—idealism, courage, and ingenuity.

It was appropriate to their type and style that the base of their activity was an artist's studio. Its owner, the architect Manfred Eickemeyer, was busy with his affairs in occupied Poland, and Hans Scholl had again acquired use of the place and the key to it. This time, in addition, an excellent cover for the activity at the studio was provided by an exhibition of paintings, They were the work of Wilhelm Geyer, the family friend of the Scholls from Ulm, who specialized in painting on glass. Hans admired his work. He, Hans, and Sophie usually had breakfast together at the Bodega. Geyer was in no doubt of the political attitude of Hans and Sophie, but he was not initiated into the leaflet operation. Hans regarded Geyer's six children as responsibility enough without adding the strains and hazards of underground involvement to it.

The studio was ideally located for the use it was put to. It stood back from the street, isolated in a garden plot, and was convenient to where Hans and Sophie were living. Besides the main room, there was a smaller chamber and a cellar which was usually cluttered with picture frames, unused canvases, and the cast-off materials of a painter. Geyer's exhibit furnished a reason for the place to be open and active while its proprietor was away, when it would normally be dark and locked. Unlikely as a site for seditious activity, the studio was transformed into a kind of factory for the production of treasonous literature.

As before, Alex Schmorell managed to provide the equipment—a borrowed typewriter and another, larger, duplicating machine. Sophie and Traute Lafrenz were sent on procurement missions to stationery stores all over Munich to buy the special mimeograph paper the machine required, but never too much of it at any one store. Stacks of envelopes also had to be acquired, a batch here and a batch there. For Sophie and Traute these expeditions were adventures that turned commonplace shopping chores into conspiratorial actions, which were not performed grimly or furtively. Traute re-

membered the picture of Sophie stopping in a street to pat the neck
of a dray horse which had attracted her attention with a pathetic
whinny. "There, there, old boy," said Sophie, "everything'll be
all right." Then she strolled on to the next stationery store to buy
another box of envelopes with which to spread sedition across the
country.

The Gestapo estimated that the *"Aufruf!"* leaflet had been distributed on the scale of 8,000 to 10,000 copies. They had been labo-
riously ground out, one by one, on the hand-cranked duplicating
machine in the artist's studio in Schwabing. Night after night, hour
after hour, sheet after sheet was fed into the machine. The inked
cylinder with its neatly cut stencil was rotated by someone's aching
arm—Hans', Alex's, Sophie's, Willi's—and a lone typewritten
page fluttered out the other side and was added to the pile of its predecessors. The feeding and cranking and stacking had to be repeated
not ten thousand times, but several times ten thousand times, since
each leaflet consisted of several typewritten pages. Subversion as
practiced by the Munich students demanded more than idealism,
courage, and a sense of outrage. It also demanded the utmost in patience, endurance, and sheer drudgery.

There was always danger, always the possibility of discovery.
Where the meddler and the snoop proliferated, where tale-bearing
and informing were approved and applauded, hardly anybody's behavior was likely to go unobserved and unreported for very long.
They could never be entirely sure that they were not already suspected and being watched as they came and went. Even though the
studio was favorably situated for the use to which it was put, it was
not immune from possible intruders and trespassers. Leopold
Strasse, one of the town's key thoroughfares, was close enough to
be a source of concern. Often, while the duplicating machine was
working, enemy bombers rumbled through the dark overhead and
scattered their explosives in blind abundance on the city below. At
any time a near miss could blow away a studio wall, exposing everything. There was no hour without its tensions. Every day they
put behind them was a triumph of survival.

After a night's work, the apparatus and the leaflet pile were stored
in the cellar and covered with the litter there. When Hans had reason

to believe, as he sometimes did, that his operation was in danger, he would call the shop of Josef Söhngen and inquire whether a certain book was available. If all was clear at the book shop, his friend would reply that, yes, the book in question had come in and could be picked up at any time. Hans and Alex would then hide their equipment in Söhngen's basement until production could be resumed at the studio.

An even more daunting task had to be undertaken when, finally, the printing of the leaflet was done. They had to be distributed. In the White Rose phase it had sufficed to stuff the leaflets in mail boxes picked at random around the city of Munich. But to achieve the effect now aimed for would require a procedure far more complicated and chancey. The intent was to create the impression of a well-organized underground functioning in widely separated cities, to stage a show of coordinated opposition much beyond what the facts warranted and thus make the maximum impact on both the public and the authorities.

They decided to make few mailings, or none, in Munich so as to divert attention from the city as the base of operation. The scattering of leaflets around the streets and byways of the town would look like a merely local participation in the overall endeavor. Given their pathetically limited resources in manpower and money, the group was confronted with what seemed like a hopeless challenge. How to get the thousands of leaflets to the places they were intended for?

Hans had to deploy what forces he had like a guerrilla leader sending his irregulars on hit-and-run raids against a vastly superior foe. Having no heavy battalions, he would use his people as partisans or *francs-tireur,* operating on their own deep in enemy territory, armed only with their paper bombs, the leaflets. Afterwards a writer, with the writer's too ready resort to metaphor and hyperbole, would call them "a secret army of reason and humanity." Far from an army, they were barely a corporal's guard.

Out they went into the German night, the literal one and the figurative, their satchels and rucksacks stuffed with printed paper which might as well have been their own death warrants should the satchels and rucksacks be opened by hostile hands. They rode the crowded and irregular wartime trains and debarked in bleak and blacked-out railway stations. They trudged in the dark through silent and desolate streets, or past smoking rubble in the bone-chill of a wintry dawn after an air raid. And everywhere they walked with dread. No block afoot, no railroad mile, was ever free of threat or menace.

In Nazi Germany, in the fourth year of war, there was no such thing as free movement of unsanctioned travel. The state policed its citizens relentlessly as they moved from place to place, regarding them with indiscriminate suspicion, trusting nobody. The streets, the trams, the trains—especially the trains—were constantly patrolled, combed, sifted to winkle out the odd miscreant who may have made himself guilty of breaching one or more of the innumerable regulations with which the state had hedged the comings and goings of the people. There was a rich variety of police to enforce every last refinement of the applicable law: *Schupos*, the municipal police; *Kripos*, the criminal police; the wartime Home Guard, authorized vigilantes with police powers; Military Police, each branch of the armed forces fielding its own constabulary units; and always the invisible but omnipresent agents of the Gestapo.

It was ordeal enough for the blameless citizen, on his or her way to close a business deal or visit a grandma in a distant town, to run the gauntlet of the *Kontrolle*, the official apparatus of supervision over travelers. A whole packet of papers had to be produced repeatedly on demand: identification documents, travel permits, sometimes even the *Ahnenpass*, the certificate of Aryan ancestry. For a male of military age, like Hans, Alex, and Willi, the difficulties multiplied. In addition to all the other papers, the young male had to come supplied with documents relating to his draft status if he was in civilian clothes; if in uniform he had to produce his army pay book together with his leave papers and travel orders, all properly signed, countersigned, and rubber stamped. Even with everything in perfect order, it was no inconsiderable feat to pass through the meshwork of controls and checkpoints without incident.

For the young couriers with the perilous contraband in their satchels and rucksacks every mission was a walk across a minefield where every footfall was potentially fatal. The next station stop— what if there should be a sudden baggage search, something that occurred frequently and unpredictably? The police would not be looking for leaflets. They would be looking for rationed food without ration points, or smuggled goods, or black-market currency. What they might stumble on in certain satchels or rucksacks would be subversive leaflets, and that would end the walk across the minefield with a fatal detonation for somebody—for Hans, or Sophie, or Alex, or Willi, and probably for all of them.

They used a number of tricks and stratagems to thread their way through the pitfalls and booby traps that the enemy state had set for them. On boarding a train they would hoist the satchel or rucksack into the overhead baggage rack and then ride the rest of the journey in another car. If there was a search and the leaflets were discovered, the police would not know to whom they belonged. If there was no search, the satchel, or rucksack could be recovered at the destination. They had a selection of plausible if concocted stories on tap to explain why they were traveling ("Is this trip necessary?") and they always had all the required papers handy and in order, if also faked.

Even with every possible ruse and precaution, there was always the tremor of nerves and the dryness in the mouth at the sound of approaching jackboots and at every appraising stare from under the visor of an official cap. Every incident, no matter how trivial or commonplace, held the seeds of panic. On an unfamiliar street in a strange town, satchel in hand or rucksack strapped to shoulders— was the *Schupo* coming toward one just walking his beat or did he have something more sinister in mind? The stranger jostling one in a crowd—did he stare too long and too intently? Was it Gestapo? Was one being watched and followed every step of the way? There were no easy moments for the young couriers as they spread the word of resistance and rebellion among the people of Adolf Hitler's Germany.

Hans Scholl was a general who went into the field with his troops. Besides planning the strategy for the distribution of the leaflets, he acted as a courier himself. With about 150 copies of *"Aufruf!"* in his rucksack, he headed south into Austria, a touchy business which involved getting through the border guards coming and going. He mailed his leaflets at the post office in the Salzburg railroad station and returned to Munich without incident. He paid for the expedition out of his own pocket, rather than out of the group treasury.

So did Alex Schmorell on a longer mission which took him west with something like 1,000 leaflets in his bags and on his person. He mailed about 200 of them in the post boxes of Linz, a Nazi shrine hallowed by the boyhood years of Adolf Hitler. Moving on to Vienna, Alex posted several hundred more intended for that area, together with 400 addressed to residents of distant Frankfurt-am-Main. More went into the Salzburg mails on his journey back.

The *"Aufruf!"* leaflet penetrated as far north as Berlin, carried there by Jürgen Wittenstein. A dissident group of students already existed in the capital, headed by a young man named Hellmut Hartert who once roomed with Hans Scholl in Munich when they both studied medicine at the Uni. The Hartert group had their own duplicating apparatus and were able to reproduce the leaflets in limited numbers on their own. Single copies sometimes found devious pathways to unexpected destinations. An activist in the Berlin resistance named Helmuth von Moltke, bearer of an honored name in German military history, passed one of the Scholl leaflets to the Norwegian underground which translated it and circulated it. Other copies reached England by way of Sweden.

For his part, Willi Graf retraced the route of his exploratory Christmas journey but this time he was toting a square, clumsy-looking suitcase with him. Inside was a small hectograph machine and some copies of *"Aufruf!"* He would run off copies of the leaflet at stops in the Rhineland cities along the way. This time he was not merely a missionary but an itinerant production unit leaving a small flurry of printed subversion in his wake. Willi was not always a welcome visitor in his travels even though he picked his stops with care. Some who felt as he did had no stomach for expressing themselves in action and wished to have nothing to do with Willi and his leaflets. They were relieved to see him move on. But he was never betrayed to the police, though he had at least one close call with them. A line in his diary speaks of "getting past a snag at the travel control point in good shape."

In Saarbrücken he delivered his hectograph machine to Willi Bollinger who installed it in the business office of the hospital to which he was assigned—a duplicating machine in an office causes no comment—and he worked it after hours to reproduce the leaflet. He then mailed it to addresses in the area where he judged they would do the most good.

Willi Graf got back to Munich unscathed with his clumsy suitcase, now empty. He reported to his unit and recorded in his diary: "Roll call and inspection at the barracks. Imbecile speech by the company commander. . . . In the evening a very respectable cello concert."

In spreading the leaflets over the widest possible area, no one worked more coolly and efficiently than Sophie. Drawing on her circle of friends in Ulm, she organized a crew of young assistants and set up a distribution center there. She found an eager aide in Hans Hirzel who was already at work on a poster which displayed a swastika with the inscription: WHOEVER WEARS THIS SIGN IS AN ENEMY OF THE PEOPLE. He put this aside and, at Sophie's direction—(later an indictment would describe him as being "under the influence of the base Scholl female")—he recruited two of his classmates to help in the distribution of "*Aufruf!*" They found a convenient base of operations in the Martin Luther Church, of which Hans Hirzel's father was pastor. Sophie had brought about 2,000 leaflets to Ulm, and behind the church organ her three co-conspirators addressed envelopes with names from local telephone books and directories. They also folded the leaflets, stuffed them into envelopes, and sealed them. These were the three young dissidents—Hans Hirzel, Franz Müller, Heinrich Guter—who particularly appalled the authorities when it was discovered they were all members of the same class in the Ulm secondary school.

Using the device of leaving his satchel in one car and riding in another, Hirzel took several hundred of the stamped envelopes to Stuttgart by train. He got his sister Susanne to help stuff some of the leaflets into post boxes, though it is not certain that blonde young Suse, "a charming little creature," was aware of what she was doing.

Sophie herself was often under way from Ulm to both Stuttgart and Augsburg. Between the two places she poured more than 800 leaflets into the German postal system at different times. On one occasion she was unwittingly abetted by Gisela Schertling who held the post boxes open as Sophie fed batches of envelopes into them from a briefcase she was carrying. Gisela had no clear idea of what was in the envelopes. Though she was Hans' inamorata at the time, she had been kept as far in the dark as possible about the leaflet operation. What she ultimately knew she discovered by accident, when she came upon a rucksack stuffed with leaflets in a corner of Hans' room.

Indignation in official circles over the outburst of dissident literature was still simmering when a new outrage was reported to the Ministry of Justice in Berlin by the Chief Prosecutor's office in Munich. All over the city—on major streets and squares, in front of public buildings and theaters, at busy intersections, at Nazi shrines, in front of the university—slogans of the most offensive and impermissible kind had suddenly appeared. Painted in large letters that no passerby could miss, the slogans said:

DOWN WITH HITLER! . . . HITLER THE MASS MURDERER!

And over and over:

FREIHEIT! . . . FREIHEIT! . . . FREEDOM! . . . FREEDOM!

Next to every slogan was a swastika with an "X" crossing it out. The slogans were neatly stenciled in green paint—"peacetime" paint that was extremely hard to remove, as one exasperated official noted. "The perpetrators are unknown," said the report to the Justice Ministry.

Sophie Scholl found out who they were.

On an evening early in February she had laid out a little feast for Hans in their rooms. That day she had received a package from her mother, a loaf of her favorite homemade bread, a jar of marmalade, butter, apples, and cookies. It made an inviting spread and she could hardly wait for Hans to appear and share it with her.

She had a long wait.

The evening passed, and night wore on, and he didn't come. She got drowsy waiting and finally fell asleep, her spread untouched and untasted. It was nearly morning when she was awakened by Hans bursting into the room with Alex Schmorell and Willi Graf, who thumped a bottle of wine onto the table. They were all flushed and excited, and it took a while for them to calm down enough to be able to tell Sophie their story.

They had been roaming the dark and deserted city with brushes and paint confiscated from the studio, and with stencils which Alex had cut there. At every likely and conspicuous spot they had set to work, leaving behind one or more of their slogans and an Xed-out swastika. It was Alex' idea. He and Graf had done the painting while Hans stood watch. Hans was armed with a pistol in case they were surprised by a nocturnal police patrol. But everything had gone off without a hitch—another blow to the system, another successful nose-thumbing at the omnipotent state. Sophie was full of approval and applause and pleaded to be taken along next time. She could act as lookout, she said, while Hans helped with the painting.

She was out early the next morning to see for herself. The green graffiti had startled the town and shaken it. Everywhere the slogans appeared, crowds gathered to gape and talk, and the police were hard pressed to keep the streets and sidewalks clear and traffic moving. Scrub women were deployed in all directions to obliterate the shocking phrases from pavements and walls and cleanse the town of its eruption of political heresy in letters three feet high. As Sophie came to the entrance of the university, she saw two women, Russians, on their hands and knees scrubbing doggedly at letters that spelled out DOWN WITH HITLER! which they themselves could not read but which everyone passing by could. Sophie stopped to watch and after a moment she said to the scrubwomen: "Let it stand. It should be read. That's why it was put there."

That morning Hans, too, entered the university while the scrubbing was going on. Traute Lafrenz noticed him striding past the group around the slogan on the sidewalk with barely a pause or glance but with a small, mocking smile on his face. He walked slightly bent forward, and there was something about his attitude that frightened Traute Lafrenz. He seemed somehow obsessed, driven, she thought. From seeing his oddly superior smile, she wondered whether he wasn't being too self-confident, too sure of himself, in the terribly dangerous game he was playing. He seemed to be swept along by a kind of suppressed exhilaration.

The seven-city leaflet operation had gone off spectacularly well and, so far, with complete impunity. Now the graffiti exploit was stirring up the whole city and causing the Nazi system and its leaders additional embarrassment and alarm. Hans sensed the building of a momentum that confirmed a recent remark by Willi Graf: *"Der Stein kommt ins Rollen"*—"The ball has started rolling." And events of avalanche, of earthquake, proportions were adding to the feeling that, surely, at last, a turn in history was on its way.

On February 3, 1943, there came over the radio a "Special Announcement" which stunned, and almost paralyzed, the nation. It was preceded by the roll of muffled drums and a long silence. After it the funereal drums rolled again and the second movement of Beethoven's "Fifth Symphony" was played. The words that shook the nation were: *"The Battle of Stalingrad has ended. . . . The Sixth Army under the exemplary leadership of Field Marshal von Paulus has been overcome by the superiority of the enemy . . ."*

What this meant was that Germany had suffered the worst military disaster in its history and that some 300,000 of its finest troops had been lost at a distant city on the Volga where once a major victory had been promised. Privately, at a meeting with some of his Nazi Party leaders, Hitler himself called the defeat "a catastrophe of unheard-of magnitude." The German people did not know that their *Führer* had used those words, but they knew that that was what Stalingrad was.

Newspapers were bordered in black. Three days of national mourning were proclaimed. All places of amusement—concert halls, cinemas, cabarets—were shut down. Traffic all over the Reich came to a complete standstill for one minute on the first and last days of commemoration. Even as the survivors of the Stalingrad cauldron—gaunt, famished, freezing—were being herded off to the desolate prisoner-of-war camps in Siberia, Dr. Paul Joseph Goebbels was mustering all the resources of his Propaganda Ministry to put the best face possible on what his radio was calling "this tragic, heroic event."

Morale needed support.

The Birds of Death, the *Totenvögel*, were swarming everywhere. The newspapers were black with the little Iron Crosses that marked the notices of fallen soldiers—"my good and loving husband, *in tiefster Trauer*" ("in deepest sorrow"), "our dearly beloved son, *in stillem Schmerz*" ("in silent pain"). Inge Scholl remembered that at the time of Stalingrad the back pages of the newspapers "looked like cemeteries" with their rows of little black crosses, one after the other. So many wives and mothers were losing husbands and sons that a special clothing coupon was issued to allow them to buy mourning clothes.

With the disaster in the East came an intensification of the terror at home. All the clamps on German society were tightened. Once, when Adolf Hitler was clawing his way to power as a political agitator, he used a phrase that thrilled his followers and made his opponents gasp. "Heads will roll in the sand," he promised, when he came to power. The image was so horrifying and so vivid that it left a lasting impression, though no one took it literally. Like so much else he was saying at the time, the barbaric threat was regarded as just another example of his singularly repellent rhetoric. But the history of the Nazi era was the transformation of Adolf Hitler's rhetoric into reality.

Under the concussion of Stalingrad, heads rolled as never before. Victims were sent to the guillotine for offenses that formerly had warranted only the prison cell and sometimes for reasons so trivial they were hardly offenses at all. A businessman was beheaded because, in a conversation on a train, he was overheard to say that the war was going badly for Germany; a waiter was decapitated for "causing ridicule of the *Führer*"; the madam of a bordello lost her head for accepting foreign currency and failing to report it. Sometimes there were terse paragraphs in the papers that announced the death verdicts of the People's Courts, but for every publicized sentence a dozen went unreported. A friend of Robert Scholl's told of meeting a prison chaplain at a spa where the chaplain was recover-

ing from a nervous breakdown. On a single day he had accompanied
seven men to the guillotine and no day passed without its quota of
beheadings. The blade at Stadelheim broke down but its work was
not long interrupted. A substitute instrument was immediately sent
from Stuttgart.

Now there were refugees in the streets of Munich, German refugees. Sophie Scholl saw them in the crowded trams and overfilled
trains—mothers with drawn faces bent over pale, bewildered children, old people making their way, uncertain and unsteady, along
unfamiliar streets. They had fled the Rhineland and the cities of the
north where the mounting fury of the air war was radically disrupt-
ing the lives of millions of Germans. All the props and braces which
hold a community together and keep it in working order seemed to
be straining and creaking, as if ready to snap, under the remorseless
pounding from the sky which was steadily eroding public confidence as the bombers hit one city after the other. For many the twin
afflictions of wreckage and refugees, coupled now with the cata-
clysm at Stalingrad, were signs of disintegration and collapse,
omens of imminent defeat and dissolution.

This was a miscalculation that would be made repeatedly before
the war was over. It did not allow for the toughness and tenacity of
the system Hitler had built or for what a disciplined and resourceful
people can endure without breaking. But to the Munich students it
seemed that what was said in their White Rose leaflets was now tru-
er than when it was written. *"We are close to the end,"* the leaflets
had said. Events had surely brought closer the *"wave of unrest"*
that had been predicted months before. The urging of the second
leaflet that *"one last overpowering effort can shake off this system
once and for all"* rang more convincingly now than when it was
written.

Hans Scholl and Alex Schmorell saw the situation as ripe for a
manifesto that would use recent events to give fresh impetus to the
White Rose theme and raise the voice of resistance at a time when,
more than ever, it needed to be heard. Consulting with Kurt Huber,
they found him not only in favor of the project but ardent to participate in it. The professor was seething.

The news of Stalingrad had affected him not merely as a national calamity but, his wife Clara observed, "like a fearful personal misfortune." It seemed monstrous to him that not only had Hitler's arbitrary and inexpert strategy squandered 300,000 German lives but that the Nazi press was demeaning the dead and befouling the tragedy by exploiting it for political purposes. For Kurt Huber, all the grossness and cynicism of the National Socialist system was exemplified by Stalingrad. He was burning to give vent to his indignation.

Hans Scholl gave him the opportunity.

The new leaflet, it was agreed, would be written by Professor Huber himself, directed in style and theme to the university community, emphasizing ideas which were being discussed by the students themselves. The leaflet was also to be an answer to the *Gauleiter* and the speech that was still a rankling affront among the civilized students and professors. "My purpose," said Kurt Huber afterwards, "was to arouse the student community to a moral evaluation of the existing evils in our political life, not through an organization or any kind of violent action but through the unadorned word alone."

The next morning, before breakfast, Clara Huber found her husband working at his typewriter where he had evidently been occupied for hours. She saw what he was writing.

"Kurt!" she said. "How can you get yourself mixed up in such a thing! If you were ever caught with that!"

"Don't interfere," he said brusquely. "This doesn't concern you."

Whenever she inquired about his relationship to certain of his students with whom he sometimes conferred behind closed doors, his response was similarly curt. Her husband told her as little as possible, and often nothing at all, about such matters but she understood the reasons for his reticence. "Remember," he once said, "if anything should happen, you know nothing about anything." That was just true enough so that when, later, she too was interrogated by the Gestapo she was able to put on a convincing show of ignorance. She understood too well what danger there was in the paragraphs her husband was composing that morning.

"Students, men and women!" Kurt Huber had written. *"The*

eyes of Germany are upon us! The nation looks to us to break the National Socialist terror in 1943 through the power of the spirit as once before the Napoleonic terror was broken in 1813 . . . the dead of Stalingrad call to us!"

All through the leaflet the crisis of the times was related to youth; what youth had suffered under the Nazi regime, what youth could do:

> *"In the most fruitful years of our lives, Hitler Youth, Storm Troops, SS have tried to regiment, revolutionize, and narcotize us: 'Ideological education' was the name for this despicable method of smothering the budding independent thought of the young with a fog of empty phrases. . . . There can be only one rallying cry for us: Fight the Party."*

Already, said the leaflet, Munich students had risen up in protest against a *Gauleiter* who had offended their honor and besmirched the modesty of the female students with indecent jokes. *"That is a beginning in the struggle for our right to self-determination without which spiritual values cannot exist."*

What Kurt Huber saw around him, what he so passionately wished for, he projected on the nation at large. *"The people are seething, . . ."* he wrote in his leaflet. *"The day of reckoning has come . . ."*

He, too, misread events and the mood of the German masses for whom the nightmare of Stalingrad had not been enough to make them abandon what Dr. Goebbels called "the German dream." Following their *Führer*, they would pursue it long after Kurt Huber himself had become one of its casualties.

No one involved in the new leaflet seemed to have noted the irony, or oddity, of having a 51-year-old professor speak with the voice of, and in the name of, German youth, which illustrated how closely the dissident Munich students and their faculty mentor had come together in attitude and outlook. In the final stage of the leaflet's text, the teacher-student roles were reversed and it was Hans Scholl and Alex Schmorell who passed judgment on the work of the professor. They approved of his leaflet with one exception.

Kurt Huber, unswervingly conservative and patriotic even while committing a capital offense against the state, continued to admire the German army for its tradition, organization, and discipline. He considered it the one remaining counterweight to the domination of the Nazi Party and he expected that, in due time, the military would turn on Hitler and overthrow him. So in his draft of the leaflet, Kurt Huber included a paragraph in which German youth was urged to give its support to "our glorious *Wehrmacht.*"

For the students this clashed with the whole tenor of the leaflet and seemed totally unjustified. They saw the *Wehrmacht* as the instrument of the Prussian imperialism which in the Europe of the future would be banished forever. And as members of the *Wehrmacht* themselves, they saw it from a viewpoint radically different from the Professor's.

Hans Scholl struck the passage out of the leaflet.

An argument ensued as Kurt Huber defended his text to the last line and Hans and Alex remained adamant that the passage supporting the *Wehrmacht* was unacceptable. It was an indication of how fully Hans Scholl was in command of his operation that he could override the professor's authority and make his own view prevail. Kurt Huber left the meeting hurt and angry, virtually washing his hands of the leaflet as amended by the students.

That was the last time he saw Hans Scholl.

Eleven

One student on the fringe of the group afterwards spoke of Sophie Scholl's smile as "the happiest thing I remember from those dark days." In her trim fur cap and black coat she carried herself buoyantly at a time when the slouch of dejection and the droop of discouragement were more generally on view. "Our optimist," the student called her. It was Sophie's way—part of the code of *"Allen!"*—to show herself as dauntless and uncowed; but events, and her grasp of them, had darkened her inwardly.

That winter she wrote in her daybook of a kind of emotional paralysis that took possession of her. When she was alone, she said, a sadness would settle on her and deprive her of the will to function. "If I take a book in my hand it's as if somebody else were doing it, and I have no interest in it . . . a wretched condition." She thought that anything, even the worst physical pain, would be a thousand times preferable to what she called "this empty calm."

The mood was so alien to her character that only an overwhelming despondency induced by the state of her world, by what human beings were doing to each other and to themselves, can account for it. The trend and quality of her thoughts at this time are illuminated in other entries in her journal.

"Only out of life does life come. Or haven't they noticed that a dead mother never gives birth to a child?"

And:

"What they call the instinct for self-preservation is driving them straight toward self-destruction."

Sophie's spells of depression were never so deep and lasting as to rob her, for long, of her natural resilience and her determination to do whatever could be done to thwart and damage the system that was soiling her life, her country, and the world. Resistance was what gave point and purpose to her existence. The artist Wilhelm Geyer regularly had breakfast with Sophie and Hans and came to know both of them with the special intimacy possible only over morning coffee repeatedly shared. He sensed in Sophie Scholl a reined-in rage at injustice and cruelty of every kind, and an absolute fearlessness in her commitment to oppose them. As they sat over their rolls and ersatz coffee in the Bodega on these mornings in early February of 1943, the ultimate test of that commitment was not far off.

Sophie, as before, helped with the production of the newest leaflet, working through the night in the basement of the studio. She took her turn cranking the mimeograph machine which, on this run, ground out some 3,000 copies. They came in two versions because the stencil ripped and had to be done over and the second batch of leaflets was headed "FELLOW STUDENTS" instead of "GERMAN STUDENTS." In both versions Professor Huber's text was retained, with the reference to the *Wehrmacht* eliminated.

Sophie also helped Willi Graf with folding the leaflets and stuffing them into envelopes. The addresses were taken from a registry which Professor Huber had given Hans, which was why a number of people connected with the university, including the barrister Leo Samberger, came to find copies of the leaflet in their mail. In a moment of youthful impudence, one of the leaflets was addressed, and sent, to Karl Freiherr von Eberstein, the Police General of Munich.

As with the earlier leaflets, this one too was scattered about Munich by night. Slipping through the dark but familiar streets and spreading sedition as they went, the young students had the satisfac-

tion of seeing their DOWN-WITH-HITLER slogans still readable here
and there where the most vigorous scrubbing had failed to make
them illegible. In some places the police, unable to rub out the graffiti, had resorted to painting them over. It was heartening to Hans
and his comrades to see how literally and indelibly they had left
their mark on Munich. It buoyed them as they went about dropping
their sixth manifesto against the regime in parked cars and telephone
booths and anywhere else where it would be sure to be found in the
morning and, as they fervently hoped, passed along, opening eyes
and evoking responses in widening circles as it went from hand to
hand.

This guerrilla thrust at the all-powerful state, like the ones before
it, went off with impunity and added to the students' mood of self-
congratulations which sometimes bordered on cockiness, as when
the leaflet was prankishly sent to the police. But none of them was
ever entirely free of the weight of the choice he had made and its
possible consequences. They did not court death, but they were
risking it under conditions which called for the utmost in moral
stamina and inner certitude. All the pressures of tradition and patriotism—pressures under which the hardiest doubters and the most
settled cynics customarily crumble—were bearing on them to give
their allegiance and support to the Fatherland in time of war as millions of their peers were unhesitatingly doing. Not to do so was to
cut oneself off from the fellowship of one's compatriots and to take
one's stand in the lone and shadowed place society reserves for its
outcasts, its pariahs, its internal enemies. But they made the choice.
With an idealism known only to the undaunted and uncorrupted
young, they put conscience before conformity, and went their way.

After their sixth leaflet, not much of the way was left.

Friends began to notice a change in Hans Scholl. Traute Lafrenz
thought he was carrying himself badly and she sensed something
strained about him in contrast to the easy, self-assured manner she
associated with him. Jürgen Wittenstein also saw the alteration.
Hans might be hurrying along a street and pass an acquaintance
without greeting or recognizing him, a totally uncharacteristic act.

Something was, obviously pressing on his mind. To Gisela Schertling, his current sweetheart, he revealed what it was. He was being watched and he knew it.

The warning had come from several sources. The bookseller Söhngen was sure, afterwards, that Hans had a contact inside the Gestapo who kept him informed of the progress of the leaflet investigation and who alerted him when it seemed as if the Secret Police were about to close in. This was possible. The Gestapo, formidable as it was, had its chinks and soft spots. There were *Spitzel*-in-reverse who, for reasons of their own, sometimes leaked information from the inside to the outside. One way or another, the word came to Hans Scholl that he was being watched.

He considered flight. The Alpine passes that led to Switzerland were close by, and he was a seasoned mountaineer. It would be comparatively simple and sure to cross the border by night and apply for asylum in neutral Switzerland. The plan was possible, it was even plausible, but for Hans Scholl it had a flaw that made it unacceptable. A flight to Switzerland would be all the evidence the Gestapo needed that he was indeed guilty of subversion, and it would act accordingly. Its agents would fall like wolves on all of Hans Scholl's friends and associates. They would seize his family. The People's Courts and the KZs would loom for all of them. He could not possibly sit safe and secure in Switzerland while that was happening, knowing that his flight had brought it about. He dismissed the idea.

Though he knew that the Gestapo was on his trail, he did not know how much the Gestapo knew. Warnings were not necessarily fatal. Perhaps the Gestapo's watch on him was only a precautionary measure; the Secret Police, after all, kept watch on thousands who, in the end, were not arrested. Perhaps the Gestapo had bigger game in its sights and would not get around to his case until much later, and maybe not before the war was over. It was meancing, it was unnerving to live with the expectation of arrest at any moment, but the times were menacing and unnerving at best.

Hans Scholl refused to let the threat that hung over him freeze him into inaction. He had made plans and he went ahead with them.

He was thinking of the next leaflet and he turned to Christel Probst for ideas on what it ought to say.

Probst was still stationed with his *Luftwaffe* unit in Innsbruck and came to Munich only at irregular intervals. He had not been involved directly in the printing and distribution of the previous leaflets. Out of concern for his situation as the father of two young children, with a third expected shortly, the others spared Probst as much of the danger inherent in the operation as possible.

As the most prudent and settled member of the young activists, he was wholeheartedly in agreement with their aims but sometimes dubious of their methods. Hearing of the graffiti action afterwards, he sharply disapproved of it. The smearing of slogans on walls and pavements seemed to him both dangerous and childish, and he said so. He did respond to Hans' request for the outline of a new leaflet which would evaluate the situation in Germany in the wake of Stalingrad. Thoughtfully, deliberately, as he did everything, Christel Probst sat down one evening, took up a pen, and composed the paragraphs which were going to cost him his life.

He coined an epithet for the war lord who lost an army in the cauldron of Stalingrad: he called Adolf Hitler "a military charlatan." He urged immediate negotiations to bring about an end to the war that would be honorable to both sides. With the conflict over and the Nazi system eliminated, a better future would dawn under the guidance of world leaders like the president of the United States, Franklin D. Roosevelt—a reference which would particularly infuriate the judges of the People's Court when the case of Christoph Hermann Probst came before them. The leaflet ended with a plea for a return of peace, order and sanity to Germany and the world.

Christel Probst wrote his leaflet without telling his wife Herta. She felt as he did and her spirit was strong but she was frail and in the final stages of pregnancy. She was already a victim of the system her husband was now risking his life to oppose. Some years before both her brothers had to flee, "by night and fog" as the saying was, to elude the grasp of the Gestapo. Neither Herta nor her parents knew where they were or whether they were still alive. Herta Probst passionately hoped that her children would grow up in the kind of world her husband's leaflet was pleading for, but he spared her the knowledge of what he had done. Through a trusted intermediary, he sent the leaflet to Hans Scholl in Munich.

On the morning of February 18, 1943, Otl Aicher, home on leave from the Russian front, rang the bell at Franz Joseph Strasse 13. His visit was not entirely social. He brought greetings to Hans and Sophie Scholl from their family in Ulm, but he also had an urgent message to deliver. He was to repeat to Hans the three-word title of a book by Gerhard Ritter, a contemporary German historian. The title was: *Machtstaat und Utopie—Dictatorship and Utopia*. Otl Aicher did not know what the words signified but he was glad to perform the service of delivering them, being a close friend of the Scholls and the prospective husband of Inge.

Inge herself was not entirely clear about what the code title signified, either. In those times one did not pry unduly into such matters. The day before, the high-school student Hans Hirzel, who had some tangled and undefined contact with the Gestapo in Ulm, had come to the Scholl home and asked that the title of Dr. Ritter's book be conveyed to Hans as soon as possible. Hans would understand what it meant. Otl Aicher, who knew nothing about Hans' involvement in illicit leaflets, agreed to pass the words along when he went to Munich the next day.

There was no response to his ring or his knocking. Hans and Sophie had already left on a mission of their own. Perhaps if the coded warning of the title of the history book had reached them in time, their own history might have turned out differently.

They had left their rooms about 10 o'clock and set out for the university, which was not much of a walk from where they lived. Their way took them south along the wide Leopold Strasse, under the tall and symmetrical poplars which lined both sides of the boulevard. It was a Thursday and an unusually sunny and mild February day, an early foretaste of spring. To passersby Hans and Sophie must have looked like any other pair of attractive young collegians on their way to midmorning classes at the nearby Uni. It was not quite usual that the young man of the couple was carrying a suitcase which looked to be rather heavy.

It was packed full of leaflets.

Still under the poplars, they passed the undistinguished front of the Academy of Visual Arts on their right and came to the *Sieges-tor*, the Victory Arch. This commemorated the liberation of the land from Napoleon and also marked off Schwabing from the city proper, a sort of open gateway between the two. Just beyond the arch, with its flamboyant statue of a female Bavaria driving a chariot drawn by four lions, the university area began. Hans and Sophie crossed the square that one day would be called by their name, and passing the lone fountain splashing pleasantly in the morning sunshine, they went through one of the arches at the entrance of the university and entered the main hall.

Familiar with the routine of the place, they had gauged their arrival for a time when classes would be in session and nobody would be likely to be at large in the halls and corridors.But almost immediately they saw two people coming down the stairs from the second floor and hurrying toward the glass door through which they had just passed. They were Traute Lafrenz and Willi Graf.

They had left a class ten minutes early in order to be on time for their next lecture which was at a nerve clinic some distance away and had to be reached by streetcar. The four friends exchanged hurried greetings, Traute and Willi pausing only long enough for a "see-you-later" before rushing off and leaving Hans and Sophie alone in the empty marble hall.

In the trolley on the way to the nerve clinic, Traute Lafrenz felt uneasy—"*unheimlich,*" was the word she used. What were Hans and Sophie doing with a suitcase in the Uni at that hour when all the classes were in session and there was no reason for them to be there? It was puzzling and added to the oddity of Hans' recent behavior. Willi Graf shrugged when she mentioned it to him, but Traute noticed that he was restless during the class at the clinic. Usually, he dozed when Dr. Bumke was lecturing.

Traute Lafrenz and Willi Graf were right to be concerned. The whole White Rose circle, and everyone connected with it, was shaken by what happened at the university that day, though the event was less surprising to those in whom Hans Scholl had recently confided. Only two days before he had paid a visit to Josef Söhngen that made the book dealer fear for Hans' future.

Hans had given his friend a copy of the most recent leaflet and expressed his determination to use it in a special way. He had in mind a spectacular gesture of some sort, something more open and defiant than he had attempted up to now. Söhngen, alarmed at the tack Hans was taking, tried to dissuade him, urging that not boldness but increased caution was called for in view of the ominous political situation and the increased activity of the Secret Police. Hans dismissed the warning. For him the time for caution was past, he said. The Gestapo, already on his trail, might strike at any moment and he was determined to make one more show of resistance before arrest and imprisonment, and most likely death, rendered him permanently harmless and inactive. "What he afterwards did," said Josef Söhngen, "has sometimes been described as an act of youthful recklessness. I know that it was a final act of desperation." This was a judgment in which Inge Scholl, who had weighed all the elements in her brother's fate, would subsequently concur.

Hans Scholl had also disclosed his state of mind in a tense conversation with Falk Harnack on one of the latter's trips to Munich. The end of National Socialism was at hand, Hans argued. All signs pointed to it. Stalingrad and North Africa had turned even the military against Hitler. The Allied invasion was imminent. "What is needed now," Hans urged, "is an unmistakable sign or signal of some kind that will activate the dormant resistance of the German people." He seemed obsessed with the idea of sounding an alarm that would galvanize dissident elements into action. Through his conversations and in his journal the image of a fiery sign against the sky occurred over and over—a torch (*Fackel*) was to be lighted; a beacon (*Fanal*) was to blaze up; alarm fires (*Flammenzeichen*) were to be set burning.

The most recent of the leaflets had used the same metaphor, quoting a rousing line from a patriotic German poem: *"Up, Up, my people! The signal fires are flaming!"* Hans Scholl's friends were sure that he meant to set off a signal of his own even if the fire of it consumed him. Suppose the whole University of Munich could be made to explode into a blaze of rebellion . . .

Sophie Scholl concurred in all that her brother felt and said; not blindly or dumbly but because she had reached the same point of intensity and determination as he. She did not follow him; she walked unwavering at his side, well aware of where her steps might take her. There was, besides, a cool practicality about what she did that day. The leaflets in the suitcase were, after all, addressed to students. It would have been pointless and absurd to take the trouble and risk of producing them if they never reached their primary target. With her brother, Sophie was taking the calculated risk of making sure that the manifesto headed "FELLOW STUDENTS!" would, in fact, come to the attention of their fellow students.

In the empty hall of the university, they opened the suitcase and began taking out batches of the leaflets, which numbered about 1,700 in all. They went methodically up and down the corridors, depositing little stacks of paper at the doors of the lecture halls as they went. They left other piles on the stairs, on the windowsills, and all around the entrance hall which was almost as bright as the day outside from the sun that came streaming through the tall windows and a wide skylight. It was a curiously open and well-lighted place for the underground to be at work, but for Hans and Sophie Scholl it was the right place.

Together they put a little stack of leaflets on and around the two statues on either side of the broad staircase. These were reclining figures in togas or robes and in the academic setting they might have been taken for Aristotle and Plato. In fact, they represented two considerably lesser personalities of local origin: Ludwig I and the Prince Regent Luitpold. There were no identifying plaques on the statues and not many students had any idea who they were. Neither did Hans and Sophie but they paid their respects in their own way by putting generous stacks of their leaflet in the marble laps of Ludwig and Luitpold.

The suitcase was not yet empty and it would have been senseless to carry leaflets away with them. There were still some minutes left before the classroom doors were due to open with the ending of the morning lectures. By that time Hans and Sophie intended to be out on the street and away. On an impulse, they scooped up the remaining leaflets from the suitcase and bounded up the stairs to the high gallery that ran along three sides of the hall. From that height it was exhilarating—a true Götz von Berlichingen gesture—to fling leaflets by the handful into the air and watch them go fluttering, an indoor blizzard, down to the empty hall below.

As the last leaflets came floating down, the hall was no longer empty. Jakob Schmid had entered it.

Jakob Schmid was a porter and handyman. He was also a member of the Nazi Party and an off-hour Storm Trooper. The Gestapo had been in touch with him recently, instructing him to keep his eye out for any suspicious activity among the students, for any clue that might lead to the culprits who had been painting those subversive slogans on the sidewalks around the university and scattering leaflets all over the city. Jakob Schmid had been thoroughly briefed and programmed as a combination *Blockwart* and *Spitzel*. So when he saw pieces of paper showering down from the gallery he sensed immediately that something untoward and impermissible was a-foot.

Jacob Schmid went into action.

He locked the doors of the hall, went to the nearest phone and alerted the building superintendent, and then turned to the business of collaring whoever it was that had been throwing leaflets—he had picked one up; he knew what these pieces of paper were—from the gallery. By then the lecture-room doors had opened and students came pouring into the corridors and onto the stairs. But Jakob Schmid thought he knew who he was after. He lunged through the crowd at a dark young man carrying a suitcase and coming down the stairs with a slightly younger girl who stayed close to his side.

The doors being locked, nobody could get out and there was considerable milling about and confusion in the hall as Jakob Schmid hung on to the young man's arm in the press of students around him. The young man made no effort to get away and the girl remained at his side. *"Sie sind verhaftet!"* shouted Jakob Schmid, using the phrase prescribed for such occasions and meaning both of them, the boy and girl. "You are under arrest." If there was a ring of triumph in his voice it may have been in anticipation of the 3,000-mark reward he was going to receive from the *Gauleiter* and the promotion which the university would confer on him.

Hans and Sophie were taken to the office of Dr. Walther Wüst, chancellor of the university and colonel in the *SS*, who kept them under his baleful glare pending the arrival of the Gestapo which had been summoned as soon as Jakob Schmid's alarm was sounded. Meanwhile no one was allowed to leave the building and all activity at the university was suspended.

Robert Mohr headed the Secret Police contingent who came to take the suspects into custody. He was immediately impressed by what he called "the absolute calm" of the couple he was about to take in charge, "especially the girl." He asked for identification papers, which showed them to be legitimate students of the university. There was a small pile of leaflets on the chancellor's desk, Mohr noticed, but he spent no time examining them. He already knew them by heart.

As Hans Scholl was being taken away, he suddenly reached into his coat pocket, plucked a folded sheet of paper from it, and began tearing it into little pieces which he tried to throw out of a window. A Gestapo agent prevented this and retrieved all the scraps of paper from the corridor floor. Hans coolly explained that the paper had been thrust upon him by a student he didn't know and he had no idea what was written on it. The agent put all the torn scraps into an envelope and the envelope into his pocket.

Now both Hans and Sophie were handcuffed.

The entrance hall was crowded with students as they were led through it. Many had been searched and everyone had been ordered to turn in any of the leaflets they may have picked up in the corridor. Two Gestapo agents had methodically gathered up every leaflet that could be found and were packing them back into the suitcase, testing whether it could hold all of them. Outside a Gestapo car was waiting.

As Hans and Sophie were herded through the crowd, they kept their eyes straight ahead, looking neither to right or left. "They didn't want to give any sign of recognizing their friends," a student who was there reported. "They knew the Gestapo would suspect anyone who seemed to have any connection with them. They walked through us as if they had never seen any of us before."

The Gestapo car drove off and took Hans and Sophie to the Wittelsbach Palace. It was a short ride. In Hitler's Munich, the headquarters of the Secret State Police was barely a mile from the university.

The story got about, and was later repeated by serious historians, that Sophie Scholl was so fearfully abused by the Gestapo that she went to her execution with a broken leg. The Secret State Police were easily capable of this, and worse, but in fact Hans and Sophie Scholl were treated by their interrogators with a consideration which, under the circumstances, seems surprising, if not astonishing. The agents assigned to their case seemed hesitant at first to prove or press it. They did not know what to make of Hans and Sophie Scholl.

Here were two attractive, intelligent, polite young people, the girl a winsome and well-spoken college student, the boy manly, clean-cut, and a soldier, both of them obviously examples of the soundest and best sort of German breeding and background. And what were they supposed to be guilty of? The worst crimes a German *could* be guilty of. High treason. Urging the violent overthrow of the government. The destruction of National Socialism. The defeat of their own army in wartime. And, worst of all, the overthrow of the revered Leader of the German nation as a mass murderer and international outlaw. It seemed unbelievable and Robert Mohr, for one, was reluctant to believe it.

For most of the day of their arrest, on that Thursday, February 18, Robert Mohr was persuaded that Hans and Sophie Scholl were innocent and he was on the verge of letting them go. Case-hardened and suspicious as his years in the police trade had made him, he nevertheless found himself believing the story these young suspects were telling him. They had ready and plausible answers for everything.

Why were they at the university at that hour when they had no classes? Well, they had made a date the day before with one of their friends for that afternoon but had decided to go to Ulm instead.

They had stopped by to catch their friend coming from a lecture and announce their change of plans. But why were they carrying an empty suitcase? That was because they intended to pick up fresh laundry in Ulm and bring it back to Munich with them. As for being seized by Schmid, the porter: that was a mistake on Schmid's part. With so many students milling about the hall, the porter had got confused and pounced on the wrong individuals. After all, Schmid couldn't be sure who had thrown the leaflets from the gallery, he being below and looking up into the sun that was streaming through the skylight. Hans and Sophie, they said, had themselves wondered where the leaflets had come from. Sophie seems to have told her version of the story with uncanny conviction. She gave Robert Mohr the impression of being utterly believable—*"absolut glaubwürdig."* He saw little reason to hold her further. "I told Sophie Scholl that she and her brother would probably be on the evening train for Ulm after all," Robert Mohr said afterward.

But while the preliminary examination was going on at the Wittelsbach Palace, other agents were searching Hans' room on the Franz Joseph Strasse and evidence was being uncovered that abolished forever the possibility that Hans and Sophie Scholl would be allowed to proceed to the railway station with their empty suitcase to pick up their laundry in Ulm.

In Hans' room the Gestapo men found 8-*Pfennig* stamps, fresh from the post office, in numbers far larger than any young man would normally have use for. They were the same denomination as the ones on the envelopes in which the leaflets had been mailed. Some envelopes of the same kind as the leaflets were mailed in were also found. The most damaging evidence emerged from the shreds of paper Hans had tried to get rid of when he was being arrested at the university. Scrap by scrap, the fragments were pasted together in their original pattern and what resulted was the text of another leaflet which, among other subversive statements, called Adolf Hitler a "military charlatan" and urged the immediate end of the war, no matter what the cost to Germany.

Now the Gestapo, humiliated at having been fooled so long, and with such effect, by these mere students, these starry-eyed amateurs—how wounding to the pride of professionals!—went furiously about the business of regaining lost ground. Evidence which they had long been stumbling over without seeing was now uncovered in heaps. Working by their standard procedure of *"wer mit wem?"*—"who [associated] with whom?"—they soon established the links in the group around Hans Scholl, together with the names. Queried by Gestapo agents about her relationship to Hans, and Hans' relationship to others, Gisela Schertling became understandably rattled and confused. Intending no betrayal, she let slip names which should not, in the circumstances, have been mentioned. For her it only testified to Hans' good character to point out that he was a close friend of Professor Kurt Huber, but for the agents that was a *wer-mit-wem* clue which they followed up with mortal consequences to the professor.

Despite its occasional lapses, the Gestapo was doggedly expert at its work and, once on the scent, almost always ran its prey to earth. Inquiries in the neighborhood led them to the studio and to the contents of the cellar. The typewriter on which the leaflets were written was found, also the mimeograph machine with its special paper, its stencils, and its ink. In the cellar, too were the brushes and paint with which the anti-Hitler slogans had been painted on the walls and streets. Calling in to headquarters, the agents announced: "We've found the artists!" The hopelessly incriminating evidence accumulated quickly.

Confronted with it, Hans and Sophie reacted with a complete reversal of the stand they had previously been taking. Certain now that there was no way out for themselves, they changed without transition from insisting on their innocence and denying everything to admitting everything and denying nothing. It was a tactic meant to divert suspicion from others and attract it to themselves. If they could absorb all the guilt there was, none would be left to attach to Alex or Willi or Christel or Professor Huber or anyone else. In the storm the leaflets had created, Hans and Sophie offered themselves as lightning rods. Not once in the interminable hours of Gestapo interrogation to which they were now subjected did they vary from that course, though they were ceaselessly pressed to reveal new names, open up new avenues of investigation, and yield up fresh evidence for the prosecution. The pressures on them intensified hourly as the Munich branch of the Secret State Police received orders from Berlin to accumulate as much evidence as possible as quickly as possible. An immediate trial and conviction were being demanded for policy reasons by "the highest echelons" of the state. Heinrich Himmler himself was following the case closely. The atmosphere at the Wittelsbach Palace was consequently tense and feverish. The calmest people there were Hans and Sophie Scholl.

They were interrogated simultaneously but in separate rooms, never allowed to be together. At one point it became obvious to Robert Mohr that Sophie was worried about something besides the questions he was firing at her. Her mind seemed elsewhere, and he asked her why. "I've been told," said Sophie, hesitantly—she didn't want to hurt his feelings!—"that people who fall into the hands of the Gestapo are sometimes abused and beaten, and even tortured, to force confessions out of them . . ." She didn't think *him* capable of that. He had been treating her well, even with certain little attentions which, as he himself said, were "not exactly usual." But she was worried about her brother. What was happening to him?

Mohr got up and went to a door that led to an adjoining room and opened it. Through the opening Sophie could see Hans being interrogated by another agent in the same way that Mohr was questioning her. Her brother showed no sign of having been physically misused. She waved to him quickly before the door was closed again.

The agent assigned to Hans was Anton Mahler. He was also a seasoned hand at his business, but now he had encountered a type he was not prepared for. Hans Scholl came to his first interrogation with a certain eagerness, as if to a challenge which aroused his interest. His answers were ready and adroit. His mind seemed always clear and his emotions under control. As the questioning went on, Mahler decided that in Hans Scholl he had come upon the keenest and clearest intelligence in his experience. The heretical idea occurred to him, as he confided to his colleague on the case, that this was human material Germany could well use in the future—if only circumstances did not demand that he, Mahler, do his best to send the young man to his death.

Though Hans maintained coolness and control during the interrogations, he often returned to his cell shaken and exhausted. The possibility that a momentary lapse or an ill-chosen word might endanger one of his comrades preyed on him constantly and sometimes unnerved him. A mere *und* or an unconsidered *aber* was sometimes enough to cause Mahler to bore in remorselessly, gnawing at the word like a hungry dog at a bone, in the hope that a damaging fact, another name, an incriminating circumstance would come to light where Hans had intended obfuscation and evasion. Mahler's private opinion of Hans did not soften the cold professionalism with which the questioning was conducted. This, after all, was the Gestapo and "higher echelons" were looking over Anton Mahler's shoulder as he worked.

Hans' cell was kept lighted day and night, a sign that its occupant was a "death candidate" in the parlance of the prison. Lest he kill himself before the Gestapo had squeezed the last possible jot of evidence out of him, his razor was taken from him and he was given a cellmate to watch him. This was a Bavarian farm boy named Helmut Fietz who had been arrested when he was heard comparing Hitler unfavorably with the lesser livestock.

The precaution against suicide was unnecessary, since Hans' religious convictions precluded it, but he was glad to have Helmut Fietz in the cell with him. To Helmut he could confide his despair when Anton Mahler was pressing him dangerously— *"I don't know how I can avoid telling him what he's after. He's getting awfully close!"*—or express his triumph when, after all, he had held his own—*"It went wonderfully! They didn't learn a thing!"*

Helmut Fietz remembered Hans standing on a chair and pulling himself up by the bars of the little cell window and cocking his head back to get as wide a view as possible of the sky, drinking it in for long minutes at a time and no doubt dreaming of the same sky, ever so much wider, over the Swabian hills by the river Danube. At such times, young Fietz could hear his cellmate murmuring lines of poetry to himself.

They had given Sophie a cellmate, too, a girl named Else Gebel who was a political prisoner herself. Else made herself useful around the jail, doing clerical work mostly. No female Gestapo official being available, Else was assigned to relieve the new prisoner of her personal effects and search her. Through the prison grapevine, Else knew why Sophie Scholl was there, and while searching her, she whispered: "If you've got any leaflets on you, give them to me. I'll get rid of them. I'm a prisoner, too."

An immediate bond was established between the two young women and Else, like others before her, was captivated from the start by Sophie's unaffected sweetness and poise. Else noted that all through the humiliating business of being booked into prison, Sophie's attitude was composed, almost derisive. "They've made a mistake," Else Gebel told herself. This young woman with the unclouded look and the soft, girlish smile couldn't possibly be involved in anything so reckless and rash as treason against the state.

Else was confirmed in her impression that there was something special about the new inmate when Sophie was assigned to one of the "honor" cells which were usually reserved for Nazi Party bigwigs who got into trouble and which had bigger windows, bedsheets, a closet, and other touches denied to lesser prisoners. But Sophie was barely allowed to stretch herself gratefully on the bed for a moment or two when she was summoned to her first interrogation.

It went on for seventeen hours, and she returned to her cell at 8 A.M. on the morning of Friday the nineteenth, thoroughly exhausted but still composed. She reported to Else that, to her surprise, she had been served genuine "bean coffee" during the night, a rare treat at a time when an *ersatz* brew made from chicory had become the usual fare. She was allowed some sleep before the grind of interrogation began again. Like her brother, Sophie was at the stage of keeping herself under tense control to avoid incriminating any of her comrades while freely admitting, when not exaggerating, her own guilt. Though the constant questioning was less of an ordeal with Robert Mohr than it would have been with a more brutal Gestapo type, it was a torment nevertheless. No amount of consideration on the part of her interrogator could make Sophie forget for long that the lives of the people she loved most hung on her every answer and that in her own person the resistance movement itself was being called into question. Her only relief was to be returned to her cell where the warmth and concern of Else Gebel enveloped her. Else worried more intensely about Sophie's fate than did Sophie. There were long hours in the night when Else Gebel, kept awake by her dread of what was coming, could hear the regular, untroubled breathing of her cellmate who was fast asleep.

Sophie Scholl's composure broke only once while she was in the hands of the Gestapo and that was when Else brought her news of the arrest of another member of the group whose name the authorities had not yet announced. Willie Graf was already in jail, on the floor above, and Sophie had been able to smuggle him a cigaret on which she had written *Freiheit!—Freedom!* The new arrest, she thought, must be Alex Schmorell, gayest of companions, stanchest of comrades, and she was bitterly grieved. But then Else Gebel, with her access to the registry at the jail, found that it was Christoph Probst who had been seized. Sophie was desolate.

She had last seen Christel with his family in his little house in the Upper Bavarian mountains. She remembered him holding up his two-year-old son for her to admire while his own feeling for the child beamed from his eyes. There were three Probst children now, the most recent only four weeks old. Sophie never thought of Christel Probst apart from his family, from his wife, the children, and the sister in whom his existence was rooted. A man well aware of the possibilities open to him, he was content to draw the sustenance of his life from the simple virtues and the ancient verities. He belonged with wife and children regardless of the turbulence and upheaval in the world around him. For gentle, thoughtful, loving Christel Probst to be in a uniform, in a war, in a resistance movement at all was an egregious piece of miscasting by a blundering fate. It was only Christel's innate abhorrence of the system he lived under, and his instinctive commitment to social decency, that had brought him into the resistance to begin with. Only because of his probity and intelligence had he been asked to contribute his ideas, in writing, to the leaflet undertaking. He was in dire trouble because of his exceptional virtues.

The writing doomed him.

The Gestapo had little difficulty proving that the leaflet outline they had pasted together at the time of Hans Scholl's arrest was from the hand of Christoph Probst. They compared the writing on the outline with some innocuous letters he had written to Hans, and of course, the script was identical. The hand that wrote the leaflet also wrote the letters whose source was known. Probst's identity was established.

On the Saturday morning after the arrest of Hans and Sophie, Probst applied for his pay, as usual, to the company clerk of his *Luftwaffe* unit in Innsbruck. He was in a hurry to get away on weekend leave to visit Herta, who was still confined to a clinic in the aftermath of giving birth. But Sergeant Probst did not get his pay from the company clerk. He was told instead to report to the company commander, and he emerged from that confrontation white and shaken.

Two Gestapo agents were waiting for him, one of them with a suitcase. Probst was in uniform but now he was ordered to change into civilian clothes from the suitcase. Then they handcuffed him, bundled him into an unmarked automobile, and sped him toward Munich and the Wittelsbach Palace. It was significant, and ominous, that he was made to change into civilian clothes. Nazi law had abolished the authority of civil courts over members of the armed forces but now, in a hurried agreement between the High Command and the Reich Minister of Justice, this law was suspended and all members of the Scholl group in uniform were peremptorily separated from the army and put under the jurisdiction of the People's Court.

Sophie's dismay over the arrest of Christel Probst was tempered by the expectation that his sentence would have to be a relatively mild one, not more than a term of imprisonment. The leaflet he was charged with writing was only in outline form. It had not been reproduced and circulated. Nobody but Hans and Alex had read it. There was no proof that it would ever have been reproduced and circulated. Even if Christel were given a long prison sentence, the war might well be over before he served it out. Sophie was sure, as her brother also was, that the invasion of the continent of Europe by British and American armies was coming soon and this would mean the certain collapse of the Hitler regime and the end of the war. Sophie thought the invasion could not be more than eight weeks away.

That, again, was a miscalculation. The Allied invasion of Europe, what the world came to call D-Day, was not a mere eight weeks off as Sophie Scholl predicted to Else Gebel in their cell in the Wittelsbach Palace in February of 1943. It was, instead, almost sixteen months away and the end of the war itself was more than two years in the future. Even if the end had come as swiftly as Sophie hoped, she would not have been alive to see it.

She did not expect to be.

From the second day of their arrest, when the evidence against them was mounting, both Hans and Sophie knew they were doomed. Robert Mohr knew it, too, but Sophie had so won his regard that he offered her a way to save herself. "I tried with all the eloquence I could muster," he said afterwards. "I wanted to persuade her to make a formal statement saying that she did not agree with her brother's ideology, that she had gone along with him blindly without realizing the significance of what she was doing. This, I thought, might move the court to be less severe with her and perhaps hand down a prison term instead of the death sentence."

In his twenty-six years in police work, said Robert Mohr, he had never encountered anything quite like the case of Sophie Scholl. What he was offering her was, as he himself said, a "straw," but it was the kind of straw that people in imminent peril of their lives grasp for desperately, without hesitation. Sophie hardly allowed him to finish his proposal before she dismissed it. She had not been misled by her brother, she said. She had been fully aware of what she was doing. If her brother deserved the death penalty, so did she. She would make no such statement as Mohr suggested.

On another occasion Mohr took the missionary approach, seeking to show her that her attitude was wrong and that she was the victim of an immature and mistaken *Weltanschauung,* a confused way of looking at the world. She had not understood, he said, the underlying philosophy of National Socialism nor had she had the clarity of mind to appreciate the great things that Adolf Hitler had done for Germany. In view of the terrible plight in which she found herself, surely she must now see things in a different light and regret having taken the wrong path?

"Not at all," Sophie replied, without heat but unequivocally. "It is not I, but you, Herr Mohr, who have the wrong *Weltanschauung*. I would do the same again.''

Robert Mohr, agent of the Secret State Police in Nazi Germany, had done what he could within his limits, but he saw that here was a brand that would never be saved from the burning on his terms. He broke off the interrogation and sent Sophie back to her cell. There she found Else Gebel brewing tea and preparing a little feast of sausage, rolls, butter, cookies, and cigarets to which both warders and other prisoners had contributed. Sophie arranged to have some choice morsels of the spread conveyed to Hans on the floor above. The story of the Scholls and the fate that awaited them had filtered through the prison and feeling for them was strong among staff and inmates alike. Sophie was the pet of the place.

The gravity of her situation was brought home to her on Sunday afternoon when she was summoned from her cell to receive a copy of the formal indictment that had been drawn up against her. It was dated that day, February 21, and issued from the office of the Chief Prosecutor of the People's Court, Berlin. Named in the indictment were Hans Fritz Scholl (''no previous conviction''), Sophie Magdalena Scholl (''no previous conviction'') and Christoph Hermann Probst (''no previous conviction''). They were jointly accused of committing acts of High Treason with intent to
—alter the Constitution of the Reich by force;
  to render the *Wehrmacht* incapable of fulfilling its duty to protect the German Reich from its enemies;
—to influence the masses through the production and dissemination of subversive literature;
—to aid and abet foreign powers in time of war while damaging the fighting potential of the Reich;
—to paralyze the will of the German people in their determination to maintain their national integrity by military means.

It was a formidable bill of particulars, but if three lives had not been at stake, it would have seemed absurd, a parody of an indictment. In saner times it would have been inconceivable for one of the great nations of the world seriously to credit three of its young citizens with the ability to do such staggering damage to its institutions, its armed forces, and its morale through the distribution of a few thousand sheets from a hand-cranked mimeograph machine. Had the document not been also a death warrant, the accused might have been both amused and flattered to see the state attributing to them potentialities they would never have dreamed of claiming for themselves. They had not realized they were anywhere near as dangerous to the Greater German Reich as the Greater German Reich officially held them to be.

The indictment went on to trace, with a good deal of accuracy and detail, the background of the accused, the history of the leaflet operation beginning with the White Rose phase, and the particular offenses of Hans, Sophie, and Christoph. It made no distinction among them as to the degree of guilt. That Probst had not participated in the production and distribution of any of the leaflets, and had only written an outline for one which was never circulated, was not taken into account. The charges against him were as grave as for the others.

A curious paragraph in the indictment expressed uncertainty as to whether it was Hans or Sophie who first had the idea of producing the leaflets. This probably resulted from the combined efforts of Hans and Sophie to mislead and confuse their interrogators whenever they could, leaving them uncertain on a number of vital points. In a subsequent document, the prosecution linked brother and sister together on an equal basis with the assertion that ". . . *Hans and Sophie Scholl were the soul of the truly treasonous organization that gave aid and comfort to the enemy and sought to undermine our ability to make war."* In the end, the Nazi regime granted in full Sophie's demand that she be regarded, and treated, as her brother's equal in every respect.

What Sophie did and said in her three days in jail stayed in Else Gebel's memory and afterwards she wrote it all down.

Sophie brought the indictment back to her cell with her and read it through. Else Gebel noticed that her hands were trembling. Finished with the document, Sophie put it aside and gazed out of the special window of her "honor" cell in silence for a long time. Outside she could see people taking their Sunday strolls in their Sunday best. That February in Munich was unusually springlike, and a bright afternoon sun streamed into the cell. A little sigh escaped Sophie.

"What a glorious sunny day," she said more to herself than to Else. "And I have to go . . ."

Else said nothing and Sophie continued to muse aloud in the sunny cell which they both now knew was a death cell. "But so many men are dying every day on the battlefields, so many promising lives are being lost. . . . What does my death amount to as long as what we did served to stir up people and make them think? There will surely be a revolt among the students . . ."

Here Else had to restrain herself from interrupting, but she spoke only to herself: "Sophie, Sophie," she said, "you don't realize how cowardly the human herd can be." Else Gebel knew there would be no revolt.

But Sophie continued her reverie: "Or I could die of some sickness . . . millions do. . . . That way dying would be perfectly senseless, without any point, wouldn't it? This way, at least . . ."

What distressed her most, she said, was the thought of her mother.

"To lose two of us at once, and with another so far away in Russia! It will be terribly hard on her—harder than on either of us. . . . Father will be able to understand better why we did it . . ."

Else Gebel tried to offer a scrap of hope. Perhaps the court would, at the last minute, impose only a prison sentence. That sometimes happened. She had heard of such cases. But Else knew better.

From her always reliable sources in the prison, she knew that the trial for all three—Sophie, Hans, and Christoph—had been set for tomorrow, Monday, and that such a headlong rush to judgment boded no good. And Else had heard something else as well: the judge would be Roland Freisler. Everyone knew what that meant.

Sophie's reverie was over, and her hands were no longer trembling. There was a strong strain of the realist in her; she had schooled herself to face reality and accept it. She did not deceive herself with hope for a milder sentence and had no desire for one if it involved her alone. When a defense lawyer assigned by the court—the Nazi system made a point of draping its executions in legal trappings—visited her in her cell that evening, she jolted him with her coolness and candor.

Sophie made no pretense of innocence and she provided the lawyer with no material for a defense beyond her insistence that what she and her brother had done was right. But she did have some questions for him and they were not what he was expecting. She wanted to know whether Hans, as a soldier of the *Wehrmacht,* would have the privilege of a firing squad when the time came. After all, he had served at the front. The lawyer could only say he didn't know.

He was accustomed to seeing grown men quake and gibber at such conferences as this one and he was not prepared for the detachment and control with which the young woman before him, hardly more than a girl, asked her next question. Sophie Scholl wanted to know whether she would be hanged publicly or sent to the guillotine. Though she did not flinch at the question, the attorney did. He mumbled an evasive answer and withdrew in confusion.

The lights stayed on in the cell all that night. Else Gebel got no sleep at all. Sophie slept.

The next morning, the last she would know on earth, Sophie Scholl awoke about 7 o'clock and, sitting on the edge of the bed, she gave Else Gebel an animated account of a dream she'd had, one whose significance excited her. She had dreamed she was carrying a baby in a long white dress to a church for baptism. The way to the church was up a steep mountainside. "But," Sophie related, "it was a sunny day and I held the baby tightly in my arms and kept going toward the church.

"Then, without any warning, a crevasse opened at my feet, gradually gaping wider and wider. I had just enough presence of mind to place the baby on the other side of the crevasse, the safe side, before I plunged down into the abyss."

Sophie's eyes were shining but Else Gebel looked blank. She did not share Sophie's enthusiasm for this dream with its awful ending.

"Don't you see?" said Sophie. "The baby in the white dress is our idea. It will survive us and succeed despite all pitfalls and obstacles. We've been privileged to be forerunners, pathfinders, but we have to die before the idea comes to fruition." Again white was the symbol—the white rose, the white of a baby's dress—for the idea they were committed to, the idealism that would not wither even in the shadow of the guillotine.

That morning, a Monday, she saw Hans again for the first time since their arrest. The hours and days of remorseless interrogation had told on him and he looked pale and somehow shrunken. But, far from broken, he held himself steady and erect. Before leaving his cell he had taken a pencil and written on the whitewashed wall a message to all who would follow him there—and to himself: *"Allen Gewalten zum trotz, sich erhalten!"*

In their final hours in the Gestapo jail Robert Mohr came to them with a suggestion which, again, indicated a compassion oddly alien to his trade and affiliation. He advised them to write farewell letters. Afterwards, he said—meaning after the trial, at Stadelheim—there would probably not be time. It was an ominous reminder, if any were needed, that the trial would be only a grisly charade whose outcome was already decided and known in advance to all concerned.

Hans and Sophie wrote brief letters to their parents expressing gratitude for the goodness and love they had received and asking forgiveness for the pain and distress their actions had caused. They said they could not have acted otherwise and they were sure their parents would understand. They, Hans and Sophie, were sure that the future would justify them and that what was now condemned by many would one day be approved by all. Sophie wrote another letter to her sister Inge and asked that her love and last greetings be sent to Carl Muth. She also composed a farewell to Fritz Hartnagel, her warm friend and favorite correspondent who was somewhere in Russia.

None of the letters ever reached the people to whom they were written. Gestapo regulations insisted that all such communications be cleared through Reich Security Headquarters in Berlin. There the letters were ordered to be laid away in the files and under no circumstances delivered. It was feared that if they reached the public they could be used for propaganda against the regime. "We want no martyrs," said Berlin. The Third Reich of Adolf Hitler, though it defied half the world on the battlefield, lived in constant fear of the words and thoughts of its own children.

Christoph Probst, too, was allowed to write farewell letters. Through a quirk, or lapse, in Gestapo administration a letter to his

mother survived as it was written. It has a special poignance because he wrote the letter on the day of his arrest when he did not yet
know he was about to die. He assured his mother that life in jail was
not so bad. She was not to worry. He was being treated well. "I do
not know how things will turn out," he said, "I only know that
nothing is so difficult that it cannot be borne." He would tell her of
his deeper thoughts and feelings later, he said.

But his mother and his sister Angelika, to whom his devotion was
intense, were not allowed to possess the letters he wrote them later,
when he knew he was about to be executed. The two women were
only allowed to read them in the presence of a Gestapo agent who
then took them back. Christel's last phrases burned into their minds
and were written down immediately from memory. *"I thank you for
having given me life,"* he wrote to his mother. *"If I look at it rightly,
it was solely and singly a journey toward God. Do not be sad that I am
about to cross the last boundary. Soon I'll be closer to you all than I
ever was before. And one day I will prepare a glorious reception for
you!"* To his sister Angelika he wrote: *". . . I go to my death free of
all hate. . . . Never forget that life is nothing if it is not a continual
growing into love and a preparation for eternity. . . . Your Christel, always."*

At about 9 o'clock two Gestapo officials came for Sophie Scholl
and escorted her to an unmarked car waiting at the door of the jail.
They drove her the two kilometers to the Palace of Justice whose
forbidding Gothic facade was singularly suited to what went on behind it. Hans Scholl and Christoph Probst, both in handcuffs, followed in a separate automobile shortly afterward. All three were
made to wait in an anteroom for the spectators to take their places
and for Roland Freisler to mount the bench.

In one of his letters Christoph Probst had written "no man makes
his own fate; he can only accept it." In that mood he waited for the
proceedings to begin that would end the careers of all three of them.
Tallest of the group, Christoph also seemed oldest because of the
brooding melancholy that so often enveloped him. He was, in fact,
a year younger than Hans who was waiting with a typical touch of
impatience, as if the enforced inactivity was boring him.

Sophie seemed to be looking inward. The light frown familiar to all who knew her crinkled her brow, indicating not worry and distress but musing thought. Here the three of them were about to be tried and sure to be condemned. What would happen to the others? Willi Graf. For unexplained reasons he was not mentioned in the indictment and had been left behind in custody, also without explanation. Alex Schmorell. He had not been arrested, Sophie knew; he had somehow escaped so far. Where was he and what would happen to him? As for Professor Huber, she could only speculate and hope.

Meanwhile, all three—Sophie and Hans and Christel—waited in the anteroom for the next stage of their journey toward Stadelheim to begin . . .

The jail they had just left seemed unnaturally still and empty to Else Gebel after their departure. All life and animation seemed to have been drained from the place. *"Ausgestorben"* was the word Else used to herself—"quiet as the grave." Having finished her clerical chores for the morning, she went to the cell she had been sharing with Sophie to put things in order for its next occupant. She knew Sophie would not be back.

Sophie's bed, she noticed, was tidy except for a typescript which had been tossed on it. Looking closer, Else saw that it was the indictment. Sophie had left it behind, face down. She had written something on the back of it, a single word.

The word was *Freiheit!*

Twelve

Not all the spectators who, on invitation, crowded room 216 of the Assize Court in Munich on the Monday morning of February 22, 1943, knew why the trial was being held with such urgency. The accused had been taken into custody only last Thursday. Even the gravest political cases were sometimes delayed for weeks and even months, but these three young defendants were being brought to judgment, with a haste that could only be called hectic, on the fourth day after their arrest.

There was a reason for the urgency, as the better informed among the spectators knew. It was a reflection of the tension that had gripped the Nazi authorities in the wake of Stalingrad and the revelation that a nest of subversion not only existed in the capital of the movement but had spread its message of dissidence to cities throughout the Reich. If there was indeed a growing revolt among university students—and among students in uniform at that!—it had better be halted with exemplary speed. The only way to react to a budding resistance movement was to visit the vengeance of the system upon it swiftly and terribly, as a warning to any others who might be inclined to take the same path. In a totalitarian state the thing to do with a white rose was to crush it under the heel.

The system was represented in the courtroom in full panoply—
"from *Blockwart* to heroes of the Knight's Cross," as one observer
noted—when Roland Freisler in his billowing scarlet robe took his
seat on the bench and called the People's Court to order at 10
o'clock. On either side of him sat several subsidiary judges, including an *SS* Major General named Breitbart and a Group Leader of
Storm Troops named Köglmaier. Their function was not legal but
atmospheric. They were there to emphasize that in this place not
justice but power prevailed, a situation which the uniformed audience also proclaimed. To this display of puissance on the bench and
in the auditorium, the accused trio made a strikingly puny contrast.

Hans and Sophie Scholl with Christoph Probst, each flanked by
two policemen, sat in the dock with their backs to a window. They
were to the left of the bench behind which hung a portrait of Adolf
Hitler. Though they sat erect and unbowed, all three were pale and
drawn after the long strain of interrogation in a Gestapo jail. It must
have occurred to more than one spectator, even in that audience, to
ask: Was it possible—could it be—that these young persons, one of
them hardly more than a schoolgirl, were a serious threat in the existence of the Greater German Reich which had brought 400 million
people under its sway and dominated the continent of Europe from
the Baltic to the Mediterranean? It was, in its way, one of history's
most impressive tributes to the power of the spirit and the word that
the mighty National Socialist system should think so.

Roland Freisler thought so.

He conducted the trial as if the future of the Reich were indeed at
stake. He roared denunciations of the accused as if he were not the
judge but the prosecutor. He behaved alternately like an actor rant-
ing through an overwritten role in an implausible melodrama and a
Grand Inquisitor calling down eternal damnation on the heads of the
three irredeemable heretics before him. Even in that audience there
were some who cringed inwardly. Leo Samberger, the young barrister from the university, squirmed with shame for German law and
German justice as he stood in the doorway of the courtroom watching the performance of Roland Freisler, Chief Justice of the People's Court of the Greater German Reich.

There was no trial in any acceptable meaning of the term. Evidence was produced—the leaflets, the duplicating machine, the stencils, the brushes and paint of the graffiti action. Jakob Schmid, warmly congratulated on all sides for his capture of the culprits, was on hand as a witness if needed. So were Robert Mohr and Anton Mahler. But no witnesses were called, since the defendants had admitted everything. The proceedings consisted almost entirely of Roland Freisler's denunciation and abuse, punctuated from time to time by half-hearted offerings from the court-appointed defense attorneys, one of whom summed up his case with the observation, "I can only say *fiat justitia*. Let justice be done." By which he meant: Let the accused get what they deserve.

Only the few statements permitted to the accused redeemed the proceedings from being totally what Hans Scholl called them when he entered the courtroom: *"Affentheater,"* sheer buffoonery, an ape theater. When everything said by judge and lawyers in room 216 that morning was long forgotten, Sophie Scholl's retort to Roland Freisler was remembered and repeated: *"Somebody, after all, had to make a start. What we wrote and said is also believed by many others. They just don't dare to express themselves as we did."* At another point she shocked the bench and much of the audience by saying what they least wanted to hear: *"You know the war is lost. Why don't you have the courage to face it?"*

Toward the end, each of the three was allowed to make a statement in his own behalf. This was customary and even the People's Court adhered to some of the established procedures to keep up its pretense of legality. Sophie, evidently convinced that nothing she could say would have any effect in such a setting, stood silent. In his earnest and undramatic way, Christoph Probst tried to explain to the court that he had acted in the best interest of his country by trying to bring the bloodletting to an end and save Germany from further Stalingrads. He was shouted down by the bench and parts of the audience and could not continue. He then pleaded that his life be spared on account of his three children and a wife who, as he spoke, was sick in a clinic with childbed fever.

This was met with stony indifference from the judges and Hans attempted to intervene with support for his comrade's case, pointing

out that Probst had contributed virtually nothing to the leaflet operation. Freisler cut him off with a snarl, saying: "If you have nothing
to bring forward for yourself, be so good as to keep quiet."

Like his sister, Hans disdained to plead in his own behalf. None
of the three retracted anything.

The sentence of the court was about to be read when a sudden
commotion drew everybody's attention to the door of the auditorium. A man and a woman, both middle-aged, were pressing their
way into the room over the protests of the guards. There was a
scuffle. Voices were raised. The proceedings came to a halt. The
couple forcing their way in were Robert and Magdalene Scholl who
had come to be at the side of their children and offer them what
comfort and support they could.

Friends of Hans and Sophie had telephoned the news of their arrest to Ulm immediately on Friday, and an agonizing weekend of
anxiety and frustration followed for Robert and Magdalene. They
were told that visits to the jail were not allowed on Saturdays and
Sundays and the hours passed in uncertainty and despair. Their
younger son Werner had unexpectedly come home on leave from
Russia and that, at least, was a prop at a black and trying time. They
were all on an early train to Munich on Monday morning.

Otl Aicher was at the railroad station to meet them and he was
frantic. The trial was already well under way, he told them, and
they would have to hurry to get there before it was over. This was an
additional shock. Robert and Magdalene had no warning that their
children were to be put on trial with such headlong haste. They
knew now that only the worst could be expected. They hastened to
the Palace of Justice in panic.

Once in the courtroom they found no empty seats and stood there,
wild with anxiety, not knowing what to do. Magdalene turning to a
court attendant and asked: "Will they have to die?"

The attendant nodded.

For the only time in her life, Magdalene Scholl lost control of her
nerves and collapsed. She had to be helped out into the hall by the
attendant. When she recovered she sought to return to the courtroom
but was stopped at the door by a uniformed guard. "But I'm the
mother of two of the accused," Magdalene Scholl told him.

"Aha, the mother!" said the guard. "You should have brought them up better."

In the courtroom Robert Scholl had pressed forward to the table where Hans' defense attorney was sitting. "Tell the President of the Court," said Robert Scholl, "that I am here to defend my children."

The attorney, unexpectedly, did so. He went to the bench and Robert could see him whispering to Roland Freisler, who had been scowling through the few unruly moments that the entrance of the Scholls had caused. Now he could be seen sweeping his arm in a gesture that was more like a blow as he listened to the attorney. He barked an order to the guards and Robert Scholl was seized and forcibly escorted from the courtroom. As he went, the whole auditorium heard him shout: "One day there will be another kind of justice!" And before the door closed behind him he added: "They will go down in history!"

Outside in the hall Leo Samberger, moved and shaken by what he had seen and heard, approached Robert and Magdalene Scholl and offered to prepare for them a petition of leniency to be presented to the Office of the State Prosecutor, the only legal resource left. The Scholls accepted the offer gratefully, knowing that Samberger was endangering himself by making the offer. It was a humane and selfless gesture, but a fruitless one.

Meanwhile, the brief interruption over, Roland Freisler proceeded with the business he had been summoned from Berlin to carry out. He pronounced the death sentence on Hans Fritz Scholl, on Sophie Scholl, and on Christoph Hermann Probst for committing acts of High Treason and attempting to destroy the National Socialist way of life.

All three were manacled and led away by uniformed police. As they were leaving the courtroom, Hans was heard to say: "Today they're hanging us. Tomorrow it will be their turn."

In the corridor Werner Scholl, fresh from the front and in the uniform of the German army, made his way to the three condemned prisoners and pressed the hand of each of them in turn. As he did so, Hans could see that tears were welling up into his eyes. "Stay strong,'' Hans Scholl said to his young brother. "Make no concessions!''

It was the set intention of Paul Giesler, the *Gauleiter*, to have all three of them hanged in public. He had already commissioned a master carpenter to start building the gallows. His only question was whether it would make a more effective spectacle to stage the hanging before a mass audience in the central square of the city, the Marienplatz, or at the university. He was inclined to favor the university as the more appropriate site, under the circumstance.

The matter was taken out of his hands by higher authority. Heinrich Himmler wanted no martyrs. He also feared a possibly explosive reaction—at home and abroad—to such a naked display of Nazi barbarism. The thing would have to be done quietly, attracting as little notice as possible.

The three of them were taken to Stadelheim.

Before the National Socialists came to power, the place had been unremarkable and undistinguished, even as prisons go. Marring an otherwise agreeable suburban neighborhood, Stadelheim occupied a block of walled-in buildings on the south fringe of the city. Before the Nazi miasma enveloped it, the place served routinely as a punishment facility for lesser criminals—vagabonds, petty thieves, prostitutes, and similar types—who served terms of several weeks or months and were then returned to society to continue as before.

From time to time Stadelheim had housed local characters of some color and distinction, such as the Bavarian tale-teller and satirist Ludwig Thoma who was arrested for being more satirical than the law allowed under the Kaiser, or the bearded bohemian Kurt Eisner who put aside his duties as a drama critic to start a quasi-Marxist revolution after the First World War. A less quaint inmate, who spent all of four weeks there, was Adolf Hitler. He was then a beerhall agitator hardly known beyond the limits of the city. He was sentenced for his first act of public terrorism which consisted of breaking up a rival's political meeting and chasing the speaker off the platform and into the streets. He survived his mild stay at Stadelheim to see the place become the execution site for hundreds of his opponents.

In February of 1943 the Protestant chaplain of the prison was the Reverend Karl Alt who had other duties as well, the Stadelheim district being only one of the three which composed his parish. When, at about one o'clock on the twenty-second, he received an urgent call to come to the prison he dreaded to respond to it. He knew what such calls usually meant. A gentle man who, like his father before him, had grown up in the tradition of Social Democracy, Karl Alt was no supporter of Nazism. As a man of God he was morally obligated to provide what spiritual comfort he could to those caught in the mills of Nazi justice at Stadelheim. He paused to fortify himself with prayer before leaving to deal with whatever awaited him at the prison.

Hans and Sophie Scholl, with their friend Christoph Probst, were already there. Unexpectedly, against all probability, Robert and Magdalene were also there. Ejected from the courtroom, Robert had not been cowed and had not abandoned his determination to see his children. With his wife, he made his way to Stadelheim and there insisted on his right of visitation as a parent. Though the authorities at Stadelheim were powerless to alter the judgment of the People's Court, they had a limited leeway in their own domain. They were neither Gestapo nor *SS* types but civil servants who had been in the penal system before the Nazis (and would outlast them). When Hans and Sophie and Christoph were delivered to them, all three were given numbers in the prison records as routine procedure required—Probst was #524, Hans #525, Sophie #526—but the administration at Stadelheim was not entirely dehumanized. Father and Mother Scholl were not turned away at the gates.

Hans was first to be brought into the visiting room and what he said and how he looked was burned into his parents' memories forever. Afterwards, at home, they described every detail to their daughter Inge who wrote it all down for the record she was keeping.

He was wearing the shapeless striped denim of a convict. His face was pale and tight, "as if after the strain of a battle," his father thought. But his eyes were clear and steady and he showed no sign of dejection or despair. He thanked his parents again for the love and warmth they had given him and he asked them to convey his affection and regard to a number of friends, whom he named. Here, for a moment, tears threatened and he turned away to spare his parents the pain of seeing them. Facing them again, his shoulders were back and he smiled. "I have no hate for anyone anymore," he said. "I have put all that behind me . . ." He reached over the barrier which separated him from his parents and shook hands with each of them.

His face glowed with love for them as he was taken away. They saw that his carriage was steady and his step, as always, was light.

Then a woman prison guard brought in Sophie.

She was wearing her everyday clothes, a rather bulky crocheted jacket and a blue skirt, and she was smiling. Her mother tentatively offered her some candy, which Hans had declined.

"Gladly," said Sophie, taking it. "After all, I haven't had any lunch!"

She, too, looked somehow smaller, as if drawn together, but her face was clear and her smile was fresh and unforced, with something in it that her parents read as triumph.

"Sophie, Sophie," her mother murmured, as if to herself. "To think you'll never be coming through the door again!" Sophie's smile was gentle.

"Ah, Mother," she said. "Those few little years . . ."

Sophie Scholl looked at her parents and was strong in her pride and certainty. "We took everything upon ourselves," she said. "What we did will cause waves."

Her mother spoke again: "Sophie," she said softly, "Remember Jesus."

"Yes," replied Sophie earnestly, almost commandingly, "but you, too."

She left them, her parents, Robert and Magdalene Scholl, with her face still lit by the smile they loved so well and would never see again. She was perfectly composed as she was led away. Robert Mohr, who had come out to the prison on business of his own, saw her in her cell immediately afterwards, and she was crying.

It was the first time Robert Mohr had seen her in tears, and she apologized. "I have just said good-bye to my parents," she said.

"You understand . . ." She had not cried before her parents. For them she had smiled.

Robert and Magdalene Scholl left Stadelheim that afternoon believing that there was still time left to them for last-ditch appeals and last-straw pleas for clemency. They thought some hope, however slim and desperate, might still remain. They knew that the condemned were often held at Stadelheim for six or eight weeks and sometimes longer. They did not know that even before they boarded the train that would take them back to Ulm, their children would be dead.

There were no relatives with Christoph Probst as his end approached. His wife, confined in her hospital bed, did not know he had been tried and condemned to death, and did not learn of it until after he was dead. No other member of his family knew what was happening to him, or why. He was at Stadelheim awaiting execution because of a vagary of fate, because of a side-effect of a destiny intended for others. As such, what was happening to him was particularly hard to bear and to fit into his philosophy that "everything has meaning and nothing in this world happens by chance." How could what was happening to him be reconciled with his belief that "all things are related to the struggle for good"? Yet not even Stadelheim was able to destroy in Christoph Probst the conviction that there was a divine order and that he was part of it.

His faith had long been deep and firmly anchored, but he had never committed himself to any single form of faith. He had never been baptized, though his inclination and study had for years bent him strongly toward Catholicism. Now, from his cell, he asked to see a priest and his request was granted. A Father Speer, the Roman Catholic chaplain, came to talk and pray with him, and Christoph Probst was admitted into the church *in articulo mortis*, at the point of death. At an improvised altar made from a small table, kneeling on the concrete floor of the jail, Christoph Probst received his First Communion, which was also his last. "Now," he said, "my death will be easy and joyful."

When Karl Alt arrived at the prison, he entered the cell of Hans Scholl uncertainly and, as he said, "with beating heart." How could he prepare this young man and his sister, neither of whom he had ever seen before, for the ultimate ordeal which was now only minutes away? What could he say to them? Unsure which Bible passage, if any, would be suitable and have the desired effect, Pastor Alt was relieved, and surprised, when after a brief exchange of greetings, Hans Scholl proposed that together they read a Psalm he had already chosen. It was the ninetieth.

Lord, thou hast been our dwelling place
in all generations.
Before the mountains were brought forth,
or ever thou hadst formed the earth and
the world, even from everlasting to everlasting,
thou art God . . .

Here were words that lifted the mind and spirit immeasurably far above the human concerns of the instant, reducing them to insignificance in the perspective of eternity and the unending majesty of God. There were also verses in the Psalm which Hans had chosen— or so it seemed to Karl Alt—not for himself only but for his people also:

Return, O Lord, how long? and let it repent
thee concerning thy servants. , , . Make us
glad according to the days wherein thou hast
afflicted us, and all the years wherein we
have seen evil . . .

Then Hans proposed the passage he had cherished, and carried with him, ever since his boyhood: *"Though I speak with the tongue of men and of angels and have not charity . . ."* Together he and Pastor Alt spoke the verses from the thirteenth chapter of First Corinthians which in German are called the High Song of Christian love, the love that *"beareth all things, believeth all things, hopeth all things, endureth all things."* And there was the verse which must have had its special meaning for Hans: *"For now we see through a glass, darkly; but then face to face . . ."*

Before administering the Eucharist, Karl Alt spoke a brief sermon for Hans Scholl for whom he now felt a closeness and warmth from which all faltering and uncertainty had vanished. He quoted the Bible verse which says that no man has greater love than he who lays down his life for his friends and, said Karl Alt, that was what Hans Scholl had done in urging his countrymen to cease the insane bloodletting which was bringing disaster on them all. There was One, said Karl Alt, who had laid down His life for all mankind and had been executed as a criminal. But His sacrifice had opened the gates of heaven for everyone and proved that death had no power to kill the soul, which was all that mattered in eternity. To die with love and faith in one's heart, Karl Alt told Hans Scholl, was to die a good death, even under the knife of an executioner.

Then Pastor Alt administered the *Heilige Abendmahl,* the Lord's Supper, to Hans Scholl and they parted. In her nearby cell, the prayers, the sermon, and the sacrament were repeated for Sophie Scholl—"a girl," said Karl Alt afterwards, "as sweet as she was brave."

There was little time left now.

The bureaucratic formalities were over; the last rites had been administered; the executioner had arrived and his instrument was being made ready. The three of them had been in the prison for less than two hours but the special aura they brought with them had permeated the place and affected the guards, the wardens, and even the inmates. Candidates for death were no novelty at Stadelheim. They came from all levels of society and in all gradations of character. They had no distinguishing attributes. But these three were recognized at once as being of a different type, a different strain.

Observers at Stadelheim, from the director of the prison, a Dr. Koch, down to the turnkeys marveled at what someone afterwards called their *Seelenkraft,* their strength of soul. Physical courage they had. No one had ever seen them cringe or quaver. All three had, besides, what could only be called a spiritual poise. It came from a source deep within and observers felt it with something like awe without being able to define or explain it. In tacit recognition of what they were, as an unspoken tribute to them, the prison administration took the risk of breaking the usually inviolable rules of

procedure and allowed the three of them out of their cells to smoke a
last cigaret together and exchange last farewells . . .

About forty meters from the main cell block was a much smaller
building which, from its look, might have been a garage or a small
storehouse of some kind. It was rather high for being just one storey
and it had no sign or other indication to reveal its character. It was
the domain of Johann Reichhart, the executioner, and it housed the
guillotine.

Hermann Goering had re-introduced beheading into the German
penal system in 1933 when the Nazis came to power. It suited the
Reich Marshal's taste for the brutal and the barbaric. He would have
preferred a headsman with an axe, but the instrument actually in use
was essentially the same apparatus that was used with such appalling effect in the French Revolution. No major mechanical improve-
ments had been made since, none being necessary. From the first,
the guillotine had worked with nearly flawless efficiency. People
knowledgeable in such matters called it "a benevolent horror" because, whatever else might be said of it, the guillotine when skillful-
ly handled did what it was made to do very, very quickly.

Johann Reichhart, a man of middle height in a high hat and bow
tie, was practiced in his profession. So conscientious a technician
was Johann Reichhart that he had contrived innovations for his
gruesome trade which, it must be granted, benefited those who came
into his hands. Because of his improved procedures, Johann Reichhart had cut seconds from the time needed to accomplish his task.
The saving of seconds was no small boon to those condemned to enter the domain of Johann Reichhart.

Sophie Scholl was the first to go.

She was chosen to be first out of the consideration which everyone, including the Stadelheim officials, felt for her. In the whole ordeal, nothing could have been harder to bear than the waiting.

Manacled, with assistant executioners on either side of her, she
walked the forty meters to the unmarked building with an unwavering dignity which those who were watching could hardly believe.
One who saw her go used a colloquial German phrase, a homely idi-

om, to describe how Sophie Scholl went to her death. The meaning of the phrase was: "Without turning a hair, without flinching." She entered Johann Reichhart's domain carrying herself, as was said of her once before, like an Old Testament maiden.

In the main building, a dull muffled thud could be heard. It was 1700 hours, or 5 o'clock, of February 22, 1943.

Christoph Probst was next.

Over their last cigaret together, he had said to Hans and Sophie. "Well, in only a few minutes we shall be seeing each other again. In eternity."

Now, on his way to the unmarked building, he was heard to say, with a kind of wonder in his voice: "I did not know dying could be so easy."

Hans Scholl was last.

Like his sister Sophie, like his friend Christel, he went with steady tread, a lightness in his stride. There was, too, something of exaltation in his face, as if he were walking toward a place where a revelation awaited him. " . . . *now . . . through a glass, darkly; but then face to face . . .*"

He did not hesitate as he approached Johann Reichhart's doorway, but before he passed through it he called out loudly, for anyone within earshot to hear: *"Es lebe die Freiheit!"*

"Long live freedom!"

Now the three of them were gone, but the blade at Stadelheim had not finished its work. The cutting down of the White Rose was only half done.

Thirteen

The bombers of the Royal Air Force were over Munich again on the night of February 24 and thousands of men, women, and children were again huddled in air-raid shelters and cellars while bombs called "blockbusters" shook the earth and smashed buildings overhead. In the cellar of an apartment house on the Hapsburg Platz, in Schwabing, a group of women slumped dejectedly on benches along the walls. There was little talk. The air raids came often now but there was no getting used to the fright and exhaustion that came with them. To flee to the cellar night after night and cower there was to lead the life of rats, and while the blockbusters were exploding above, there was nothing one could do but try to hold on to one's nerves and strain one's ears to catch the wail of the all-clear siren which would announce that the raid was over.

Suddenly the door of the cellar was flung open and a tall young man, who looked haggard and worn to the point of desperation, peered into the dim-lit shelter. He scanned the faces of the women one after the other. Startled, they stared back, and one of them gave a start as she made out his features.

"Shurik!" she said.

He spoke to her.

"Marie Luise, " he said. "Please come out for a moment. I must talk to you."

The woman looked at him with something like dismay in her eyes. Instead of answering, she turned to her neighbor on the bench and they whispered excitedly back and forth. The whispering spread among the women, from bench to bench.

Alex Schmorell stood motionless in the doorway, waiting.

When Marie Luise did not respond to his plea and the whispering continued, he knew that he might as well stop running . . .

He had been running ever since he heard of the arrest of Hans and Sophie. He knew that the police—both the Gestapo and the criminal police—would be looking for him. He could not go home. He could not even call. A Gestapo agent was already planted in the waiting room of his father, the doctor. The phone was being monitored. He could not, of course, report to his unit and by now he would be marked AWOL. All he could do was run.

With the help of Lilo Ramdohr (women had always been kind), he altered the identification papers of a Russian worker and substituted them for his own. Then he headed for Innsbruck where he telephoned another woman, a Ukrainian this time, and asked her to meet him there. She was close to the man in charge of a camp for foreign workers and it was Alex' idea to get into the compound and lose himself among the Russians there. His knowledge of the language would stand him in good stead and the police might never find him. When his Ukrainian lady friend missed a train and failed to meet him, he had to move on.

At a sanatorium in the mountains, at a place called Elmau, was a Russian coachman with whom Alex was also acquainted. The coachman took him in for several days but somebody reported to the police that a suspicious stranger was lurking about the place, and Alex had to leave when local constables came to check. The coachman gave him a blanket and some supplies and Alex attempted to find a refuge deeper in the mountains. But here, too, his luck ran out. Severe snowstorms stopped him and turned him back.

He was now without money and supplies and at a loss where to turn and what to do. He could appeal to none of his usual friends, all of whom were more or less connected with the White Rose and thus sure to be under observation if not under arrest. Running the muster of friends and acquaintances through his mind, he came to the memory of Marie Luise. A while ago, he had spent many a pleasant hour with her in her Schwabing apartment and she had no connection with the White Rose or, as far as he knew, any political activity at all. Marie Luise would be safe.

Alex Schmorell turned back to Munich.

For days the whole city had been aware that he was a fugitive from the police. There were "Man Wanted" posters all over the town and the newspapers were running his picture and stories on the manhunt, under the headline: CRIMINAL SOUGHT/1000-MARK REWARD. The stories gave his complete description: *". . . between 1.82 and 1.85 meters tall, slender, dark blond hair, blue-gray eyes, prominent ears, erect carriage. Speaks High German with a Bavarian accent. When last seen he was wearing a gray-green sports hat and windbreaker, light gray trousers, and worn brown shoes."*

The public was urged to join the manhunt. Information phoned to Police Headquarters, or the nearest neighborhood precinct, would be kept in confidence. The 1000-mark reward would go to the private citizen whose information might lead to the arrest of Alexander Schmorell, former medical student, age 25.

There were few persons in Munich who did not know what Alexander Schmorell looked like and that the Gestapo was in hot pursuit of him. The women in the cellar on the Hapsburg Platz knew. When he opened the door of their shelter, the shock of recognition was great and they panicked.

By appearing among them, Alex Schmorell was involving them in police matters. The terror inspired by the Gestapo was such that everyone in the cellar instinctively cringed away from him as a marked man whose very presence might incriminate them. The whispering that went around the benches was all a warning to Marie Luise: "Don't have anything to do with him!" "Don't go outside with him!" "Call the superintendent!"

Marie Luise herself was pregnant and she panicked with the others. Alex, whom she still called "Shurik," the nickname by which his dearest friends knew him, waited in the hallway of the cellar while the whispering went on, but he knew what the outcome would

be. He waited hopelessly, not moving, almost as if paralyzed, while
the women called Herr Hauff, the building superintendent. Herr
Hauff knew his duty and did it. He called the Gestapo.

The all-clear siren had hardly died away before a black Gestapo
car was speeding toward Hapsburg Platz to take Alex Schmorell
away to the Wittelsbach Palace.

When the interrogation began—and it began at once—Alex
Schmorell did not know that Hans and Sophie were dead. In accordance with the pact they had all agreed on, he freely admitted everything the Gestapo charged him with, his intent being to attract as
much police attention to himself as possible as a means of diverting
it from his comrades. He did not realize that he was laying himself
open needlessly, since nothing he said now could benefit Hans and
Sophie. He admitted more than he needed to. Caution and circum-
spection were not predominant in Alex Schmorell's character.

They linked him to the typewriters, on which the White Rose and
Resistance Movement leaflets were written, and to the duplicating
machines. His role in the operations, second only to that of Hans
Scholl, was established by relays of interrogators, sometimes two or
more at a time, under blinding lights in classic third-degree style
which fell just short of actual torture. Falk Harnack, himself under
arrest and interrogation, remembered passing Alex in a corridor and
exchanging silent greetings with him. "He was still erect and handsome," said Harnack, " and his special style was still in evidence."

The Gestapo dragnet was now bringing in one suspect after the
other—Hans and Susanne Hirzel from Ulm; Grimminger from
Stuttgart; Bollinger from Freiburg; and people like Helmut Bauer
and Franz Müller and Heinrich Guter who had been marginally involved (addressing envelopes, obtaining stamps) or who, knowing
of the operation, had failed to report it. Gisela Schertling and Traute
Lafrenz and Katharina Schüddekopf, the young Ph.D. candidate,
were also caught up in the Gestapo sweep. Sometimes, as with
Fraülein Schüddekopf, they were arrested by mail. The Gestapo
sent a letter directing Katharina to report at Wittelsbach Palace and,
putting on her best blouse for the occasion, she did and was ushered
into a cell.

Gestapo activity had been so accelerated that prison space became a problem and suspects were distributed in various detention cells around the city. In the two months that elapsed between the arrest of Kurt Huber and his trial, he was for a time shunted into a cell with common criminals, a cruelly demeaning experience for a man as proper and fastidious as he. The news that his wife and sister were also arrested was kept from him; in the few notes she was permitted to write him, Clara Huber was ordered to pretend she was still a free woman. Birgit Huber, also under Gestapo supervision, was instructed to tell anyone who inquired that her parents were away on a trip.

For Kurt Huber, to be arrested, accused, and jailed was a special torment. He was immediately stripped of his status as a university professor and civil servant, which cut off his only income, canceled his pension, and left his wife and children destitute. When he was not being interrogated, he worked in his cell on articles dealing with his speciality, folk music and the folk song, and on his book on the philosopher Leibniz. He was frantic to use the time left to him to provide for his family and to leave behind something to honor his name and memory. He would have been immensely gratified to know that one day there would be a Professor Huber Platz in the vicinity of his beloved university, but nothing could have seemed less likely as his trial for High Treason approached.

Kurt Huber was under no illusion about what the outcome of his trial would be. When the prison chaplain suggested that perhaps, in view of his achievements as a scholar who had done credit to German learning at home and abroad, the Nazi authorities might consider a pardon or at least leniency, Kurt Huber shook his head grimly: "You don't know that gang," he said. The night before the People's Court reconvened in Munich for the second trial of the White Rose seditionists, Kurt Huber wrote a letter to Clara: *"If I should have to suffer death in this fight for freedom, than I ask all of you to be happy and rejoice for one who has found his way home to the final freedom of the spirit. Then the sacrifice of life will have made me totally free . . ."*

On the morning of April 19, 1943, a green police van went through the streets of Munich picking up the accused in the White

Rose affair from their detention cells. There were fourteen men and women inside when the van, its roundup completed, headed for the Palace of Justice.

It was the first time all the defendants were together and for some it was the first time they had ever met. There was a small crack in one side of the van and Falk Harnack squinted out of it to catch glimpses of street scenes in a bright sunshine. "Beautiful Munich . . . !" he muttered to himself.

The Palace of Justice was guarded by a cordon of police, and limousines were pulling up to discharge Nazi dignitaries, among them General Field Marshal Erhard Milch, second in command of the *Luftwaffe,* and the Lord Mayor of Munich. The authorities were bent on making an even more impressive show of this trial than of the first one. It was to be another chilling demonstration of the dictum of Roland Freisler, who was again on the bench, that "anyone who endangers the National Socialist way of life is guilty of High Treason and deserves to die."

Alexander Schmorell's name led the list of fourteen read out from the indictment as the trial opened, followed by Kurt Huber's and Wilhelm (Willi) Graf's. Two names not on the roster of defendants were repeatedly mentioned in the body of the indictment and they were never far from the consciousness of those involved in the proceedings: Hans and Sophie Scholl. Their personalities pervaded the trial from the start. "This trial," said Roland Freisler in his opening remarks, "stands in the closest relationship to the proceedings against the Scholls last February. They were the core of this treasonable movement." The prosecution seemed to regret that Hans and Sophie could not be tried, condemned, and executed over again.

When the texts of the leaflets were read out, murmurs of indignation and outrage became audible in the auditorium, and the trial had its first sensation. The lawyer representing Kurt Huber leaped to his feet, raised his arm in the Nazi salute, and shouted "*Heil Hitler!*" He then announced that he was disassociating himself from his client. "This is the first time I have heard the contents of these leaflets," he said. "As a German and a protector of the law of the German Reich I cannot tolerate such vilification of the *Führer.* I cannot

defend such a monstrous crime. I respectfully ask this court to be relieved of the obligation to defend my client.''

The speech was warmly received by Roland Freisler. "This court
thoroughly understands your position," he told the lawyer. "You
may lay down your brief.''

The lawyer bowed stiffly, turned on his heel, and having set the
tone for the rest of the trial, marched out of the courtroom to a smat-
tering of applause. Another lawyer in the courtroom, who had had
no opportunity to prepare a case for Professor Huber, was designated by Freisler to take over his defense. When the attorney protested that he could not possibly prepare himself in time, Freisler
waved the protest away. "I'll tell you anything you need to know
about the case, " he said.

Kurt Huber was visibly shaken. It was the second blow for him.
A friend of long standing, a respected historian on whom he was
counting as a character witness, had sent word that he was unable to
attend the trial, being "otherwise engaged out of town."

The preliminaries disposed of to Roland Freisler's satisfaction,
the court turned to the case of Alex Schmorell. In his interrogation
he had tried to explain his attitude to the war by describing how he
was emotionally affected by his birth in Russia, his Russian mother,
and his ties to that country. All this was dismissed by Freisler as
"twaddle." He was particularly outraged by Schmorell's statement,
made in open court, that he would shoot at no one, whether Russian
or German. Drumming on the bench with his fingers as he listened,
Roland Freisler could not contain himself and did not try. "Then
what did you do when you were at the front?" he bellowed at Alex.

"I took care of the wounded as a medical corpsman is expected to
do," Alex replied. He reminded the court that, as a recruit, he had
declined to take the oath of unquestioning loyalty to the person of
the *Führer* and did not feel himself bound by it. This set off another
of Freisler's choleric outbursts. He addressed the auditorium over
the head of the defendant standing before him.

"Look at this traitor!" he shouted. "He stabs the Fatherland in
the back at a time of great danger. And he's supposed to be a sergeant in the German army!"

With a snarl and a sweep of his scarlet arm, Roland Freisler dismissed Alex Schmorell from his presence. Alex turned away with a shrug and resumed his place among the other defendants, on a chair between two policemen. His day in court was over and no one there was in any doubt as to what the outcome would be.

For Willi Graf, when his turn came, the atmosphere was less sulphurous and there were fewer explosions from the bench. His open, level look and the quiet candor of his manner had a mollifying effect even on the prosecution. Of all the major defendants, it was hardest to think of Willi Graf as a candidate for death.

The indictment had linked him beyond denial to Hans Scholl and the Resistance Movement phase of the White Rose. His recruiting trips to the Rhineland had been traced almost step by step. The evidence was formidable. In his steady, unruffled way Willi had been able to fend off the Gestapo for days with carefully phrased answers that were not outright lies but that sometimes threw his interrogators off the scent nevertheless. Roland Freisler allowed a trace of respect to tinge his comments to Willi from the bench. "You had the Gestapo running in circles for a while, didn't you?" he said with what almost looked like a smile. "But in the end we were too smart for you, weren't we?" He made it sound like a sporting event in which Willi had come out second best after a good try.

This was not a note to which Willi Graf was likely to respond. His deepest concern was that he should not be thought of as having acted lightly or irresponsibly. He was not always certain that he had been right to act as he did. In times so troubled and confused, how could one ever be sure that the course one had taken was, without question, the right one? But what he had done was done for reasons that seemed to him serious and unsullied. He was willing to face the consequences but he wanted the motives that prompted him to be understood and respected.

He worried about what his father would think. "Tell him," he had asked his sister, "that it was not just a stunt of silly youngsters." In one of his last letters to her he wrote: "You know I didn't act frivolously but out of deep concern and in awareness of how serious the situation was." Roland Freisler's levity was painfully out of place in the case of Willi Graf.

There was a stir of sympathy for him in the crowded dock when he sat down again. His curiously clear eyes gave the impression of being turned inward and he seemed to isolate himself from his surroundings for the rest of the trial.

The clearest and boldest justification for the rebellion of the young Munich students came from the 51-year-old professor, Kurt Huber. For weeks, in his jail cell, he had been preparing his defense with the same scholarly care that went into his lectures. He wrote it all down, and the manuscript survived. He meant his speech to be a vindication not only of his own actions in opposing the National Socialist regime but also a defense of those accused with him. He made no denials or retractions. "What the indictment charges me with is true," he said. "And I retract nothing."

He trembled, and his head shook, as he took his place before the bench to make his statement, but not from fear. His tremors were caused by the physical affliction he had had to contend with, and overcome, all his life. He overcame it now. He stood upright and uncowed. Though his speech defect was noticeable when he began, he mastered both it and the trembling, as he did when lecturing to his students at the university. Here an additional ordeal was inflicted on him by Roland Freisler who interrupted him with jeering remarks and contemptuous asides. "You call yourself a professor," Freisler shouted at one point. "I don't see a professor before me, I see a *Lump* (a scoundrel)." During some of Kurt Huber's more forceful passages, the judge broke in with: "No political tirades here, if you please!" It was a triumph of character and mettle that the professor was able to express himself as eloquently as he did in that courtroom and in that atmosphere.

He traced his relationship with Hans Scholl from their first chance meeting at the home of Frau Dr. Mertens to the last Resistance Movement leaflet in which Kurt Huber appealed to university students to rise up against the Nazi tyranny. The corruption of German education while teachers and academicians stood by and did nothing was one of his most passionate concerns, he said. His statement ranged beyond his own sphere and touched on issues that involved all of society and civilization itself.

Of his own opposition to the established authority, he said:

"There is an ultimate limit to formal legality beyond which it be-comes invalid and immoral. That is when it becomes a cover for the cowardice that does not dare to stand up against the injustices of the state . . ." Standing up himself against the state, Kurt Huber said: *"I demand that freedom be given back to us Germans. We do not want to fritter away our short lives in chains, even if they are golden chains of prosperity and power."*

He made it clear that he had not acted as a revolutionary, a rebel. His whole intent, he said, was conservative in the true sense of fighting to retain ideals and values which were being destroyed or eroded. Throughout he had seen himself as a German patriot, an upholder of traditional imperatives and proprieties, never as a radi-cal. On this point he was firm and unequivocal: *"The return to clear moral fundamentals, to the rule of law, to the mutual trust of one person for another—that is not illegal but the opposite. It is the res-toration of legality."*

Kurt Huber pleaded with the court to weigh well the motives of the young people who were accused with him and to grant them what he called "creative justice" rather than mete out arbitrary pun-ishment. Consider, he urged, the spirit out of which they had act-ed—*" surely the most selfless and idealistic that can be imagined, it was a striving for no goal but absolute justice, decency, and verac-ity in the life of the state."*

Kurt Huber paused. His shoulders dropped. He was silent for a moment and when he resumed his voice was lower. As for himself, he said, a severe judgment had already been passed on him. He had been shorn of the rank and dignity of a university professor. His de-gree of Doctor of Philosophy, won *summa cum laude,* had been re-scinded. "And I leave behind me," he said, acknowledging the foregone verdict, "a broken wife and two grieving children, all without any means of support." He was reduced to petitioning the court for a stipend for his family that would correspond to his stand-ing as a German scholar and teacher.

The judges on the bench looked down at him unmoved. But his shoulders came back and his head went up as he concluded:

"But no trial for High Treason can ever rob me of my inner worth as scholar and teacher or as a man who unflinchingly professes—

that is what the title 'professor' means—his philosophical and politi-
cal convictions.

    "My actions and aims will be justified by the inexorable course of
history. On that I rely with rocklike confidence. I have acted as I had
to act, prompted by a voice that came from within . . ."

Kurt Huber limped, his right leg dragging, as he rejoined his
young comrades in the dock, but he moved with the special dignity
of a free man who, knowing his fate, has prepared himself to meet it
without cringing. There was a sober silence in the auditorium. Kurt
Huber had compelled attention that, for some, grew into respect as
he sat down, a *Schupo* of the security police towering on either side
of his trembling but indomitable form.

    To sustain the fiction ("farce," as one of the defense lawyers
called it) that the proceedings were legal and lawful, each of the accused was examined in turn and allowed to offer a defense. So it
was nearly 10 o'clock at night when the four judges, headed by
Freisler, retired to consider the verdicts.

    Though fourteen men and women were involved in the trial, all
interest and attention centered on the first three names in the indictment against whom the gravest offenses had been charged. No one,
of course, expected the "creative justice" Kurt Huber had pleaded
for. The course of the trial, and the outbursts of Roland Freisler, had
prepared everyone for the opening words of judgment when they
came: *"Alexander Schmorell, Kurt Huber, and Wilhelm Graf*
have, in time of war, produced leaflets urging sabotage of the arma-
ments industry and the overthrow of the National Socialist way of
life; they have also spread defeatist ideas and vilified the Führer *in*
the grossest manner; all of which aided and abetted the enemies of
the Reich and undermined the fighting capacity of our nation. They
are therefore condemned to death."

    The court asserted that these sentences, together with those im-
posed at the previous trial, would eradicate the "core group" of the
subversive White Rose operation. "Had such activity been punished otherwise than by death," the document announcing the sentence insisted, "it would have meant the start of a chain reaction of
the kind whose end once was 1918"—the dread year of Germany's
defeat in World War I. The document reserved its most furious de-

nunciation for Kurt Huber as a German educator who had betrayed his mission by failing to imbue his students with absolute faith in the *Führer* and by not molding them into iron-hearted warriors of the Third Reich. "Such a professor," the document said, "no longer belongs among us."

With all the sentences imposed, Roland Freisler left the bench in a swirl of scarlet, and the courtroom emptied. The fourteen convicted criminals were herded into the green police van again, this time for another trip to Stadelheim. As the van rolled through the now dark and deserted streets, the mood inside was queerly at odds with the situation of the occupants. "It was like a party," said Traute Lafrenz, who was there.

The long weeks in the detention cells had been depressing, the interrogations harrowing, the trial an ordeal. All that was behind them now. Tension broke and a kind of false catharsis took place. Spirits rose, unreasonably and without warrant. Faces that had been pale and set lighted up and, said Traute Lafrenz ,"We talked loudly and excitedly, despite the three death sentences. We told each other that condemned men were usually granted several months for appeals and so on, and by that time the war could be lost and over with." Maybe there wouldn't be any executions after all . . .

Professor Huber passed around photographs of his two children. Cigarets circulated freely and everyone smoked, taking long deep drags. Smoking in a police van was against regulations but the feeling was: What can they do to us now? The sentences of the three girls—Traute Lafrenz, Gisela Schertling, Katharina Schüddekopf— came to a year apiece, less than they had feared. Little Suse Hirzel's blonde Nordic prettiness had impressed Roland Freisler who called her "quite a decent girl." (Dark Sophie Scholl had been called "low" and "common.") Suse got only six months. Her brother Hans fared worse: five years.

Eugen Grimminger did not share in the general levity. He was crushed by the prospect of spending ten years in a Nazi penitentiary. Falk Harnack tried to buck him up. "Never mind," said Falk. "You'll never serve out the sentence. The war will be over long before then." It was a true forecast, but the war would not end before Harnack's wife Jennie, the full Jewess, perished in the Auschwitz extermination camp.

Alex Schmorell joined in the general conversation, musing over the defection of his friend Marie Luise to whom he attributed his arrest at the air-raid shelter. But, he said, he held no grudges and wanted no reprisals to be taken against her. In the midst of the lively chatter, little Katharina Schüddekopf suddenly felt ashamed of herself. Embarrassed, she looked at Willi Graf with the sentence of death upon him. "He sat there gazing straight ahead with those amazingly clear blue eyes," she remembered, "and he was smiling."

To everyone's astonishment, including his own, Falk Harnack had been given no sentence at all. He was acquitted, which was all the more strange since only eight weeks before his brother and sister-in-law had been strangled to death by the Gestapo in connection with the Red Orchestra affair and Falk's own activities had not been above suspicion. But, as it turned out, his acquittal was only a tactic. The Gestapo wanted to watch him after his release in the hope of linking him to his dead brother's organization. Falk Harnack later escaped execution himself only by going underground in Greece.

All animation died away when the doors of the green van opened in the courtyard of Stadelheim prison. There the fourteen were confronted by a police inspector with a list of their names and sentences in his hand. "The condemned will line up along the wall on the right," said the inspector. "The others to the left, where they will be sorted out according to length of sentence.

"Herr Harnack will report to the Gestapo to arrange for his release."

Before anyone could say a farewell to Willi Graf, or he to them, a prison guard hurried him through a door leading to the death cells. But Harnack had an opportunity to press Kurt Huber's hand and say a few quick words in parting. What he said was perhaps what Kurt Huber most wanted to hear and believe. "Remember," said Falk Harnack. "It was not in vain."

When they took Alex Schmorell away he called a last message over his shoulder to Harnack before disappearing through the door to the death cells. "Give my very best to Lilo!" he said. "Tell her I think of her often!"

The door clanged behind him.

* * *

For Alex Schmorell and Kurt Huber and Willi Graf there was no swift dispatch, no hysterical rush to sweep them instantly from the courtroom to oblivion, as with Hans and Sophie Scholl and Christoph Probst before them. Afterwards it would be said that the first three were fortunate, as if it were possible to think anyone fortunate who came under Johann Reichhart's knife in the bloom of youth, or ever. But the days and weeks and months of waiting that lay ahead for the second trio of the White Rose were indeed an ordeal that was spared the first.

Each of the second three came to terms in his own way, according to character and temperament, with the protracted terror of waiting helplessly and hopelessly for a terrible end. All three drew on the same spiritual resources to fortify themselves through the time that had to be endured until the day came that would bring release through extinction. They belonged to the great world of belief and there they found support and sustenance. For them God was refuge and strength, "a very present help in trouble"—a faith which is bulwark and rampart against tribulation for those able to accept it. That faith proved unfailingly true for the people of the White Rose even when put to the crucial, and excruciating, test of the death cell.

Their serenity in the face of what awaited them was further sustained by the surety that how they had acted, what they had done, was right. They had fought the good fight. What Robert Scholl said of his children when they were arrested could also be said of the three now waiting to follow Hans and Sophie to the headman's block. "If they have to die," Robert Scholl had said, "it will be like dying on the battlefield. But in a better cause."

What concerned Kurt Huber as his last days passed was that he might not be able to finish his book on Gottfried Wilhelm Leibniz. He worked away on it resolutely, hours on end. One of the Catholic chaplains, Father Ferdinand Brinkmann, used to marvel at his industry. One day a disturbing thought struck Father Brinkmann as he approached the narrow cell and saw Kurt Huber bent as usual over his little table—"his pen, that dangerous weapon, in his hand"—putting down his thoughts on the philosopher who argued that this was the best of all possible worlds. "There sat Kurt Huber, continuing the work he had chosen to do, even with certain death before his eyes," Ferdinand Brinkmann said. "It came to me with terrible clarity—this was a picture of the spiritual situation of Germany—the human spirit imprisoned and sentenced to death."

As the day of execution neared, Kurt Huber was still two chapters shy of finishing his book. He petitioned the People's Court to grant him the time to complete it, pointing out that this would in no way lessen the sentence that had been meted out to him. The petition was refused, but he kept working at his manuscript to the end.

A Munich lawyer named Siegfried Deisinger represented Alex Schmorell and though his function at the trial was hardly more than a charade, he came to feel a warmth and admiration for his client that went beyond the legal relationship. Deisinger visited Alex several times on the Stadelheim death row and left a detailed record of his observations and reactions. "Even in the last weeks of his life," the lawyer wrote, "Alex Schmorell never lost his self-possession or the confidence that what he had done was right. It was distressing to see this young man, so obviously gifted and full of promise, standing before me with so terrible a doom upon him; but where I was shaken, he was serene and even light-hearted."

This was the tone in which Alex himself wrote his final letters to his family. "Inwardly," he said in one of them, "I became more tranquil from day to day—yes, my mood is usually happier than it was before, when I was in freedom! How could such a thing come about? I will tell you: this 'misfortune' was necessary to put me on the right path, and so it was not a misfortune at all. . . . What did I know of faith, of true, deep faith, of the last and single truth, of God? Very little! But now I've reached a state where, even in my present situation, I feel calm and happy, come what may . . ."

The delay of the executions, which stretched to almost three months, was owing to Berlin's inertia in responding to the appeals of the three condemned men through their lawyers for pardon or leniency. Because Alex Schmorell and Willi Graf had been noncommissioned officers, their cases were passed up through the echelons of military justice to the very top, which at the last resort meant to the *Führer* himself. Toward the end of June came the decision: "I reject these appeals for leniency. A. Hitler."

Efforts through civilian channels on Kurt Huber's behalf were similarly fruitless and on learning there was no further hope of pardon or commutation he composed farewell poems to his daughter Birgit and his small son Wolfi.

His last letter to Clara thanked her for sweetening and enriching his life as no one else could have done. Before him in his cell, he said, were the Alpine roses she had sent him, the last gift he would receive from her. They were fading now, but they reminded him of the freedom of the mountains which he had loved so much. Now, he said, he was about to enter an even more glorious freedom and he would await her there.

A bottle of wine had been allowed him in his cell. "I drink a last, brave swallow of the noble port," he wrote. "I drink it in toast to you, my Clara, to the children, and to our beloved Fatherland."

The official order of execution, when it came, had only two names on it. Willi Graf's was absent. The date was July 13, 1943.

That afternoon Alex Schmorell's lawyer visited him in his cell to offer what comfort he could as the hour approached. Alex was not in need of any. "You probably wonder that I can be this calm," he said. "I can tell you that even if someone were to offer to take my place—say the prison guard here—I'd still choose to die. I am convinced that my life, short as it has been, should end now because I have already fulfilled my mission in the world. I don't know what there would remain for me to do if I were to be released . . ."

The execution order directed that Alexander Schmorell should be first, then Kurt Huber. The time was set for 1700 hours, or five o'clock, as it was for Sophie Scholl. But there was a delay. Three *SS* officers arrived at Stadelheim unannounced and produced Gestapo papers authorizing them to witness the execution. This was an unheard of imposition but the *SS* officers explained their mission. It was, they said, a matter of technical information: They wished to ascertain exactly how long it took for a man to strangle to death in a hanging and whether or not the length of time could be extended or shortened at will.

The *SS* men, smart and sinister in their well-cut black uniforms, were annoyed to learn that this was not to be a hanging but a beheading. In order that some professional benefit might nevertheless be derived from their visit, they delayed the execution further while they examined the guillotine and had its operation explained to them in detail. The prison officials, themselves accustomed to administering death, were shocked by this gross intrusion into proceedings which even the most heartless and debased were, by the common agreement of mankind, bound to respect. For Alex Schmorell's lawyer this was, again, a symbolic episode, another stark exposure of the spiritual mire into which Nazi Germany had sunk. "On the one side," it seemed to Siegfried Deisinger, "was idealism and the moral stature of a young man prepared to die for it. On the other side were those subhuman types with their obscene fixation on death and how to inflict it."

It needed the young man himself to restore dignity and some measure of decency to the occasion when the brutish interval was over. Alexander Schmorell, his young manhood intact, walked across the prison yard toward the unmarked building. He entered it with the same gallantry with which he had lived his life and which none of the abominations of a foul time had been able to destroy or sully.

Dignity, too, marked the passage across the prison yard of Kurt Huber, Doctor of Philosophy, scholar of the German folk song, university professor, teacher of youth, and freedom fighter in the ranks of youth, age 51. Dignity went with him despite the hindrance of a crippled leg and a trembling of the body which had never been the tremble of fear and was not now. "Manly and upright," were the words Ferdinand Brinkmann thought of as he watched Kurt Huber go.

Father Brinkmann saw him smile a little as, on the way to the last door he would ever enter, he momentarily lost one of his slippers. Kurt Huber's farewell to him echoed in the priest's mind: "*Auf Wiedersehen* on the other side!"

The unmarked building was visible from the window in the jail block where Father Brinkmann had stationed himself. Standing there, he heard the muffled thud that told him Kurt Huber had crossed the last threshold of all. From his window, Father Brinkmann made the sign of the cross toward the unmarked building.

"He's one of us," Hans Scholl had said when he first met Willi Graf but now Willi Graf was the last of them, the last of the six who had joined together under the symbol of the White Rose to call out the truth into the German night.

By nature the least rebellious of them all, Willi had entered the resistance not out of political passion or in support of any partisan dogma but simply because he could not reconcile himself to a system that was forcing him to live his life in violation of his deepest convictions. That he could not bring himself to do, and so in the savage dialectic of National Socialism, he had to die.

In the case of Willi Graf the system was taking its time. For seven months he was held in his death cell at Stadelheim while the Gestapo played a prolonged mongoose-and-cobra game with him. The Secret Police were determined to extract from him the last scrap and vestige of information that would expose the workings of the White Rose resistance once and for all. The Gestapo suspected that much more was involved in Willi Graf's missionary forays into the Rhineland than he had yet admitted. They did not intend to deliver him to Johann Reichhart until they had squeezed—crushed—him dry and empty, until he was fit only to be discarded.

They used a psychological torture that was alternately brutal and subtle, playing on what they knew of Willi Graf's character which, by now, was considerable. They tempted him by hinting of possible commutation of his death sentence if he should have the elementary good sense to cooperate with them by revealing the names of the many men and women who, they were sure, had been involved in the White Rose and were still at large. They varied the promises with snarling threats of ghastly new forms of physical torture and of reprisals against Willi's family if he failed to provide the answers they wanted. Here they came close to breaking him. The distress of his family was causing Willi far more anguish than his own situation. (*"Assuredly,"* he wrote them, *"my greatest sorrow and concern are for you; if I had only myself to think of, everything would be easier for me. . . ."*) In the end, neither the promises nor the threats moved Willi Graf to betray any of his secrets to the Gestapo. As the weeks and months of his solitary confinement mounted it was a solace and joy to him that not one new arrest was made in the Gestapo's investigation of the White Rose. There were people walking the streets of Germany, free of the clutch of the Secret Police, because Willi Graf had the loyalty and the strength of character to hold his tongue in Stadelheim.

Willi Graf's character had been formed and set long before the Secret State Police began to tamper with it, hoping to find lesions and vulnerabilities they could exploit. There were none. Not even the imminence of a singularly ugly and unmerited death could change or unsettle the basic Willi Graf. In his death cell he read the poems of Friedrich Hölderlin, which his sister Annaliese sent him, savoring their beauty and meaning as he might have done in his student's room in Munich when he was free. He continued to ponder, now more intently than ever, the ultimate questions which had absorbed him all his life. For Willi they had long since ceased to be questions and became certainties which the cataclysms of his time and the wanton unfairness of his own fate could not affect.

Where others groped or doubted or, worse, were indifferent, Willi Graf believed and for him belief was, just as the Scriptures promised, refuge and strength. He did not pretend to be able to unriddle the divine pattern behind the blindly chaotic events that had engulfed him and his people, but he was confident the pattern must be there. *". . . in every destiny, no matter how hard it may be,"* he wrote, *"there lies a distinct meaning, even though it may not be disclosed to us in this world. The more difficult the time we pass through, the closer we come to God."* Willi Graf could believe much. What he could not believe was that his anguish was without meaning and his life without purpose.

His end was mercifully swift when it came on the afternoon of October 12, 1943. With the heartless precision of Teutonic bureaucracy, it was officially recorded that only eleven seconds elapsed between the time "the above-named" was delivered into the hands of the executioner and the fall of the blade. "No untoward incidents occurred," said the routine document that was sent from Stadelheim to the Ministry of Justice in Berlin. The family was not notified. They learned of Willi's death only when a letter mailed to him was returned with "DECEASED" stamped across his name on the envelope.

From Stadelheim itself the definitive tribute to Willi Graf came, spoken by Father Brinkmann, who had spent many hours toward the end with the large, blond, slow-moving son of the Saarland whose pensive manner and quiet civility had won the affection of even the flinty guards on death row. "Willi Graf!" said Father Brinkmann afterwards. "He was like a candle. So straight. So upright. Consuming himself in a holy idealism . . ."

In his last letters, one of which was dictated only minutes before he died, Willi Graf made a request which meant so much to him that he repeated it over and over. To his parents, to his sisters, to his friends, he appealed that they hold him in their minds, that his memory be kept alive among them. *"Behaltet mich in guter Erinnerung"*—"Keep a good memory of me."

For Willi it was a personal request, private and touching. But the same appeal could properly be voiced on behalf of his comrades of the White Rose as well. They, all of them, individually and collectively—Hans and Sophie Scholl, Alexander Schmorell, Christoph Probst, Kurt Huber—are surely entitled to say to the world at large, and to posterity, what Willi Graf in his modesty said only to those who loved him. They are surely entitled to say:

"Remember us . . ."

Afterword

"What we did will make waves," said Sophie Scholl at her last meeting with her parents, just before she was taken away to the guillotine—*"Das wird Wellen schlagen."*

Like her brother Hans, like all her comrades of the White Rose, she was confident that the impact of what they had done would not end with their lives but would continue to be felt long after the blade of Stadelheim had done its work.

She was right.

Hans and Sophie and Christoph Probst were barely in their graves in the nearby Perlach Woods when a new version of their last leaflet, which the Gestapo thought had been suppressed, began to circulate with an added line in boldface type: DESPITE EVERYTHING, THEIR SPIRIT LIVES ON! The same saying appeared on the walls and pavements of Munich. Before the year of their death was out, war planes of the Royal Air Force were vastly and wonderfully extending the reach of their little hand-cranked duplicating machine by dropping over Germany millions of the same leaflets which they themselves had been able to circulate only in meager thousands. The Royal Air Force gave their last leaflet a new headline in strong, black letters which proclaimed: A GERMAN LEAFLET—MANIFESTO OF THE MU-

NICH STUDENTS. So after they died, the small tentative voice of the White Rose was amplified far beyond anything they could have dreamed of while they lived.

Through Sweden and Switzerland, the White Rose leaflets filtered into the free countries and there, too, the voice of a different Germany came to be heard. In the enslaved nations the leaflets, passing furtively and at risk from hand to hand, testified to the existence of an anti-Nazi underground inside Germany which most of the enslaved had not been aware of, and thus resistance abroad was heartened. The leaflets, or news of them, seeped into the KZs—the concentration camps: Dachau, Buchenwald, Auschwitz—where, again, they brought with them a whiff of encouragement and hope. "When we heard about what was happening in Munich," said one inmate of Auschwitz, "we embraced each other and applauded. There were, after all, still human beings in Germany!"

News of the White Rose reached the Soviet Union where a "Free Germany Committee" had been set up among captured officers and soldiers. On the "Free German Radio," which could be heard in the homeland, Hans and Sophie and their comrades were extravagantly eulogized as heroes of the freedom which, of course, did not exist in Russia itself. Poems in praise of the White Rose people were broadcast from Moscow—"*Lower the flags over the fresh graves of the freedom fighters!*" The Munich students were hailed with fanfares as the first to unfurl liberty's banner in Nazi Germany. From the United States, over the wartime channel called "The Voice of America," came the words of the exiled Thomas Mann who pictured Hans and Sophie and Probst and Professor Huber and the others as Germans who were redeeming the name of Germany before the world. "Gallant, glorious young people!" the Nobel laureate, who was the personification of German culture, called them.

Inside Germany there were underground reactions which ranged from private outrage at what had happened at Stadelheim to a fierce pride in the White Rose and what it represented. In Berlin a girl described in her diary how she smuggled the White Rose story into Switzerland and England by way of Sweden. "It can't hurt the Scholls and their friends now to spread the report of their illegal activities," she wrote. "But it is enormously important to let foreigners know there are decent people in Germany too—not only Jew-haters, Hitler Youth, and Gestapo jackals. Until now the world has known all too little of that."

A quarter of a century later, a journalist still remembered the tingle of surprise and shock she experienced when she first read a White Rose leaflet. "I will never forget the excitement," wrote Ursula von Kardoff on the twenty-fifth anniversary of the execution of the Scholls, "when a leaflet was pressed into my hand by somebody in the editorial room of the *Allgemeine Zeitung*. The leaflets were being circulated by White Rose followers in Hamburg. Something inflammatory, heartening—yes, magical!—emanated from these typewritten and hectographed lines. We copied them off and passed them on. A wave [Sophie's word!] of enthusiasm swept over us—we who risked so damned little in comparison."

The approval and admiration Ursula von Kardoff wrote of was far from universal among her fellow Germans at the time. On the evening of the day on which Hans and Sophie and Christoph Probst were executed, an assemblage of several thousand students in Munich roared its condemnation of the White Rose and everyone connected with it. The porter Jakob Schmid was loudly applauded when he appeared to take bows for his feat of capturing Hans and Sophie at the university. Shouts of *"Pfui!"* greeted every mention of their names. In a raging speech, the *Gau* student leader regretted that the executions had not taken place in front of the university. Next day the official account of the meeting reported, probably with truth, that "the Munich student body stands as before, and will continue to stand, solidly behind the *Führer* and his National Socialist movement." Not a professor or university official had protested the summary executions.

Back home in Ulm, where Hans and Sophie grew up, young people who knew them in their Hitler Youth period were saying: "How could anyone who once stood in our ranks do anything so inconceivable?" The repeated bellow of *"Ja!"* in response to Joseph Goebbels' "total war" speech in Berlin came closer to expressing the mood of the Germans in 1943 than the *"Nein!"* of the Munich students. But that the Munich students dared to say "No!" amid that thunder of herd affirmation to tyranny was, of course, their great and lasting glory. "If we believe absurdities," said the Indian philosopher Radhakrishnan, "we shall commit atrocities." The young people of the White Rose had, simply, refused to believe the Nazi absurdities that led to the Nazi atrocities. They were doomed by their own decency.

The persecution of the White Rose did not end with the six executions. There were more arrests and more trials in Hamburg and other German cities as well as Munich. When the Gestapo wiped out the Hamburg branch of the White Rose, Hans Leipelt was among those arrested. He had carried on his fierce vendetta against the Nazi regime by continuing to circulate White Rose leaflets and by collecting money for the support of the destitute Clara Huber and her children. (An official at Stadelheim presented Frau Huber with a bill for 3,000 marks for wear and tear on the guillotine in the execution of her husband!) Convicted of treason, Leipelt too was beheaded at Stadelheim. Seven others of the Hamburg group, including Leipelt's mother, perished in prisons and concentration camps.

The entire Scholl family was arrested by the Gestapo in the first instance in Nazi Germany of what came to be called *Sippenhaft*, a word that had not existed before. It meant arresting the kith and kin of dissidents and made mere blood relationship the basis of prosecution and punishment. This was a piece of legalized barbarism which even some members of the Gestapo, like Robert Mohr, found appalling. The Scholls, including the mother, were arrested at the breakfast table and given varying terms in jail, the heaviest term being meted out to Robert. He was sentenced to two years in a notoriously harsh prison but when air raids and military disasters combined to bring about the disintegration of German society, Robert Scholl was released before his sentence was up.

Werner Scholl was not arrested in the *Sippenhaft* because he was due to return to his unit on the Russian front, but fate did not spare him, either. He was later reported missing in action, and what happened to him is not known.

The advance of the Americans ended the imprisonment of the White Rose people who were still in jail and brought other repercussions in its wake, some of them ironic. Paul Giesler, the *Gauleiter*, committed suicide with his whole family at the approach of the

Americans. (An American bomb had already killed Roland Freisler during one of his treason trials in Berlin.) Robert Scholl became Lord Mayor of Ulm. Johann Reichhart, who had served the National Socialist regime so efficiently, continued to practice his specialty under the Allied Military Government, which availed itself of his expertise in the execution of the Nazi war criminals at Nuremberg. Ideology evidently means little to hangmen.

Schools, streets, squares, and foundations were named for the people of the White Rose. Both halves of divided Germany issued postage stamps in their honor; anniversary observances were held with suitable pomp and oratory; an opera titled *Die Weisse Rose* won a prolonged ovation when performed at the Dresden State Theatre. But there were also those who questioned the point and value of the White Rose dissidence, since it altered nothing in the course of events and did nothing to bring down the Hitler regime. The view was expressed that the Munich students were, after all, only impractical idealists with no organized cadres behind them and no clearly defined political objectives. This is the attitude, widespread in every society, which reduces all values to the level of the marketplace and makes the pragmatic payoff the sole gauge of all endeavor.

The most convincing testimony to the moral impact of the White Rose came, ironically, from the Nazis themselves. By the fury of their reaction they acknowledged that they feared the leaflets and saw them as a clear and present danger. The leaflets were bold and uncompromising expressions of the free human spirit. As such, they were an intolerable threat to the Nazi system and the concepts on which it was based and without which it could not survive.

The leaflets of the White Rose presented the case against German Fascism as powerfully as it had ever been done and they were the first to do so inside Germany. *"We will not be silent,"* said the fourth leaflet. *"We are your bad conscience. The White Rose will give you no rest."* Morally and historically, it is no small matter to make such a statement and then live up to it at the cost of life itself. In the vogue words of the time, the Scholls and their friends represented the "other" Germany, the land of poets and thinkers, in contrast to the Germany that was reverting to barbarism and trying to take the world with it. What they were and what they did would have been "other" in any society at any time. What they did transcended the easy division of good-German/bad-German and lifted them above the nationalism of time-bound events. Their actions made them enduring symbols of the struggle, universal and timeless, for the freedom of the human spirit wherever and whenever it is threatened.

In the journal that Friedrich Reck-Malleczewen was keeping during the Second World War—the journal that became known as *Diary of a Man in Despair*—there is an entry describing his emotions when word of the arrest and execution of Hans and Sophie Scholl reached him. "I never saw these two young people," wrote Herr Reck. "In my rural isolation I got only bits and pieces of the whole story of what they were doing, but the significance of what I heard was such that I could hardly believe it. The Scholls are the first in Germany to have had the courage to witness for the truth. The movement they have left at their death will go on . . .

"They died in all radiance of their courage and readiness for sacrifice, and thereby attained the pinnacle in lives well lived . . . We will all of us, some day, have to make a pilgrimage to their graves and stand before them, ashamed."

Now that, with the passage of time, the story can be told in full perspective, and not merely in the bits and pieces that Herr Reck and his contemporaries knew, this long-ago entry in a secret diary rings even more true than when it was written. It was a bow of respect, of homage, from a fellow German. Today his words can be taken as the definitive tribute to the people of the White Rose.

Index

311